AF477952

100 Questions

about

Women and Politics

100 Questions about Women and Politics

Manon Tremblay

Translated from the French by Käthe Roth

McGill-Queen's University Press

Montreal & Kingston • London • Chicago

First published in French as *100 questions sur les femmes et la politique*, edition revue et augmentée

© 2015 Manon Tremblay et Les Éditions du remue-ménage

English edition © McGill-Queen's University Press 2018

ISBN 978-0-7735-5502-0 (cloth)
ISBN 978-0-7735-5503-7 (paper)
ISBN 978-0-7735-5543-3 (ePDF)
ISBN 978-0-7735-5544-0 (ePUB)

Legal deposit third quarter 2018
Bibliothèque nationale du Québec

Printed in Canada on acid-free paper that is 100% ancient forest free
(100% post-consumer recycled), processed chlorine free

We acknowledge the financial support of the Government of Canada through the National Translation Program for Book Publishing, an initiative of the Roadmap for Canada's Official Languages 2013–2018: Education, Immigration, Communities, for our translation activities.

We acknowledge the support of the Canada Council for the Arts, which last year invested $153 million to bring the arts to Canadians throughout the country. Nous remercions le Conseil des arts du Canada de son soutien. L'an dernier, le Conseil a investi 153 millions de dollars pour mettre de l'art dans la vie des Canadiennes et des Canadiens de tout le pays.

Library and Archives Canada Cataloguing in Publication

Tremblay, Manon, 1964–
[100 questions sur les femmes et la politique. English]
100 questions about women and politics / Manon Tremblay ; translated from the French by Käthe Roth.

Translation of: 100 questions sur les femmes et la politique.
Includes bibliographical references and index.
Issued in print and electronic formats.
ISBN 978-0-7735-5502-0 (hardcover). – ISBN 978-0-7735-5503-7 (softcover).
ISBN 978-0-7735-5543-3 (ePDF). – ISBN 978-0-7735-5544-0 (ePUB)

1. Women – Political activity – Miscellanea. 2. Women politicians – Miscellanea. 3. Women – Political activity – Canada – Miscellanea. 4. Women – Political activity – Québec (Province) – Miscellanea. I. Roth, Käthe, translator II. Title. III. Title: One hundred questions about women and politics. IV. Title: 100 questions sur les femmes et la politique. English.

HQ1236.T7313 2018   320.082   C2018-902524-7
                                                      C2018-902525-5

Contents

Acknowledgments

A number of people helped me prepare this edition of *100 Questions on Women and Politics*, most of them by answering my questions or commenting on my text. I would like to thank the following people for their generous contributions and infinite patience: Sarah Andrews (New Democratic Party of Canada), Loleen Berdahl (University of Saskatchewan), Amanda Bittner (Memorial University), Gail Campbell (University of New Brunswick), Rosie Campbell (Birkbeck, University of London), Louise Carbert (Dalhousie University), Rachel Chagnon (Université du Québec à Montréal), Margaret Conrad (University of New Brunswick), Jennifer Curtin (University of Auckland), Joanna Everitt (University of New Brunswick), Marilyne Gauvreau (Université de Moncton), Elizabeth Goodyear-Grant (Queen's University), Jennifer Haire (University of Ottawa), Chantal Maillé (Concordia University), Thérèse Mailloux (Groupe Femmes, Politique et Démocratie), Pascale Navarro (journalist and TV commentator), Jocelyne Praud (University of Victoria), François Rocher (University of Ottawa), Shannon Sampert (University of Winnipeg), Marian Sawer (Australian National University), Marie-Thérèse Séguin (Université de Moncton), Réjane Sénac (Centre national de la recherche scientifique, Centre de recherches politiques de Sciences Po, Paris), and Melanee Thomas (University of Calgary). It goes without saying that I alone am responsible for any errors or omissions in this book.

Valérie Lapointe, doctoral student at the University of Ottawa, provided assistance with the adaptation and updating required for this English-language edition. I am grateful for her rapid responses to my many questions.

I have been working with Käthe Roth for a decade now. Her adaptation of my ideas is so elegant that sometimes I feel she knows better than I do what I'm thinking and want to say. She is thus a work colleague in a way, but above all she is a collaborator in the dissemination of my ideas in English. Thank you, Käthe.

My wholehearted thanks go to two colleagues who evaluated *100 Questions* and gave their opinions regarding its viability in English. They made very valuable proposals for adapting the book to an English-Canadian readership – proposals that obliged me to do research and discover things that I hadn't known about women in politics in the prairie provinces and Atlantic Canada.

Finally, I would like to thank the entire McGill-Queen's University Press staff, especially my editor, Jacqueline Mason. In all honesty, I hadn't thought this translation was possible, but Jacqueline's enthusiasm quickly changed my mind! Thank you, Jacqueline, for believing in this project. Ryan Van Huijstee has been a superb managing editor – efficient, straightforward, and patient. I would like to thank Judy Dunlop for her indexing of *100 Questions*; I admire her willingness to take on this Herculean task. Finally, I am grateful to my students who, over the years, have taken my "Les femmes et la politique" seminar at the University of Ottawa for their questions, input, and challenges. Without them, *100 Questions* would probably not have been written.

100 Questions

about

Women and Politics

Introduction

Is a book on women and electoral politics necessary when women are increasingly present in politics, including at the peak of state power as prime ministers, presidents, and mayors and when, in Canada – "because it is 2015" (as Prime Minister Justin Trudeau famously remarked) – the federal cabinet has full female–male parity?

These well-publicized success stories are the few trees that hide the forest. Worldwide, in 2016, fewer than one parliamentary seat in four and one ministerial position in five was occupied by a woman, and only some twenty countries were led by women. Girls and women are still less likely than boys and men to see politics as a career, and, it goes without saying, women who run for office are very likely to encounter more difficulties than are men. If they manage to enter the inner sanctum (the cabinet), the gender regime will catch up to them, confining them to the lower end of the executive hierarchy through assignment to "pink portfolios."

100 Questions on Women and Politics is based on a pedagogical approach that favours educational outreach. In this book, I aim to provide essential information – the minimum that one should know about women's participation in electoral politics in Canada and elsewhere in the world – in a simple, accessible style. This does not mean that I avoid theoretical debates and the concepts they convey or sidestep questions of justice and ethical dilemmas; it means that I deal with them as plainly as possible. The questions, most of which were asked by my students, are addressed in an order that fits with the particular ecology of a university course, but they do not have to be read in numerical order; rather, readers may browse to find the answers they seek. In this sense, *100 Questions* aims to provide a versatile, dynamic tool for courses on women's participation in electoral politics as well as a useful source for journalists and members of the general public who want to quickly wrap their minds around a question.

I have two additional goals with *100 Questions*. One is to supply factual information such as the year women acquired the right to vote in legislative elections in various countries, the year when a woman was elected to a national parliament or appointed to a cabinet for the first time, and explanations of electoral quotas and their various forms. The other objective is to encourage reflection on certain ideas associated with women's political participation such as questions of justice underlying pleas for increases in the number of women in politics, theoretical and conceptual considerations regarding the role of female politicians in representing female citizens, and the dilemma of electing nonfeminist women versus feminist men. As a consequence, the nature of the questions varies a great deal: some are about history, others about current events; some are theoretical, others more factual and empirical; some answers are brief, and others offer a more substantial discussion.

The participation of women in electoral politics in Canada and elsewhere in the world is the main topic of *100 Questions*. The idea of "women" refers to the gender regime and its outputs – women and men (see chapter 1). "Electoral politics" refers to a classic and institutional understanding of representative democracy: political parties, voters, electoral systems, elections, and legislative and executive institutions. This interpretation excludes extra-state mechanisms such as social movements, which, without a shadow of a doubt, also contribute to political representation. The limited definition of electoral politics in this book should not be interpreted as a negation of these extra-state mechanisms but as a consequence of the expertise that I have developed over time and, especially, a strategy of organizational and thematic efficiency – in other words, sticking to what I know.

This English-language edition of *100 questions sur les femmes et la politique* is not simply a translation of the French-language version published in 2015. The French-language version was aimed at an essentially Quebec readership, and as a consequence a number of questions were specific to Quebec. In this edition, some of those questions are replaced by others pertaining to Canada. New questions for the English-language version include, "Were there 'radical' suffragist struggles in Canada similar to those in the United States and Great Britain?" and "Which women have led a political party represented in the House of Commons or a provincial or territorial legislative assembly?"

This book has nine chapters. The first, which is about gender, is new to the English-language version. For some years now, gender has stood out as a category of analysis in the social sciences, particularly in political science. Essentially, gender offers explanations for, and interpretations of, numerous differences observed between women and men: differences in political opinions and behaviours, in respective representation within legislative and executive institutions, in political priorities once in power, in political career trajectories, and so on. For instance, if women and men differ in their political opinions and behaviours, it may be because they have been brought up with different socialization and social roles. If fewer women than men sit in legislative and executive institutions, it may be because women who aspire to run for office encounter more resistance than do their male counterparts. If the priorities of female and male politicians differ, it may be because they do not have the same understanding of their mandates of representation – a position influenced by socialization in childhood and adulthood. If the parliamentary career trajectories of women and men differ, it may be because women find themselves in ridings in which their electoral base is more fragile and their networks within their party are less deeply anchored. In short, all of these differences may be attributed to gender.

In chapters 2 to 8, I adopt an international perspective in order to make general observations and reveal major trends. These chapters cover, respectively, the rights to vote and to run for office, electoral behaviour, obstacles to the election of women, the proportion of women in parliaments, strategies to feminize parliaments, political representation, and participation in government. The final chapter, which includes twenty-five questions, revisits the themes addressed in the other chapters but with a focus on Canada.

Two types of responses are presented: those of a factual nature and opinions. The factual responses are objective, to the extent that they bear on facts that are not really open to discussion – in other words, there is consensus about them – for example, dates, names, and statistics. Opinion responses present more subjective content, in that I propound my own point of view. Other experts on women's participation in electoral politics might develop a completely different argument. For example, to the question "Do family responsibilities really pose an obstacle to women's involvement in politics?," I maintain that it is an overestimated difficulty. As another example, it is my view that Canada does not have to change its voting system to increase the number of women in the House of Commons (I do believe that the voting system should be changed, but for other reasons) – a view that many people vehemently oppose. Finally, the responses were written independently. They do not have to be read consecutively but may be consulted in random order. However, to provide deeper exploration of a subject, to enhance the material presented, and to favour the coherence of arguments, I have included cross-references from one question to another throughout the book. This approach may create an impression of repetition from one response to another.

In closing, once again I dedicate this book to everyone who is indignant about the monopoly on political life enjoyed by men (and, I must add, in particular men who are white, heterosexual, and with a middle-class sociodemographic profile). I have been thinking about women and electoral politics for three decades, and it seems clearer and clearer to me that women's underrepresentation in the institutions of representative democracy, aside from revealing the ignominy of the gender system, is an insult to simple egalitarian justice.

Manon Tremblay
February 2018

CHAPTER ONE

Studying Women's Participation in Electoral Politics

1 What is gender?

The disciplines of psychoanalysis and sexology in the United States in the 1960s and 1970s incubated the notion of "gender"; the feminist movement and the lesbian and gay movement brought the concept to maturity in the following decades by challenging gender roles (the roles within which women and men might be expected to operate). One idea that emerged from those early reflections is that of a coherent causal relationship between sex (postulated as a fact of "nature" dictated by the "organs of generation," to use Thomas Laqueur's quaint expression), and gender (a fact of "culture"); due to an incommensurable "truth" of the physical body, the female sex corresponds to "feminine" and the male sex to "masculine." By this reasoning, sex precedes gender, which confers upon it a sort of schematic for existing in society. Without entirely rejecting this reading, more recent research, conducted notably in queer studies, has added complexity.

Gender is both a process and a result with hegemonic scope. It is a result in that it gives rise to female and male genders (women and men) adapted to a given society. It is a process in that it is a system that produces, from birth (and even before) to death (and even after, as some caskets are made specifically for women and others for men), feminine women and masculine men as two opposed and hierarchical entities. The hegemonic scope of gender results from the fact that gender concepts are so pervasive that they become invisible, seeming to arise from common sense, from the order of things, even from nature. More specifically, according to Bereni et al. (2012), gender is 1) a social construct; 2) a relational process based on heterosexuality; 3) a power relationship; and 4) a component of other power relationships.

Gender is a social construct in that it is not innate: it is shaped by the society within which it is deployed and therefore is situated in time and space. Just as hands mould clay, socialization sculpts bodies and minds so that they will (re)produce the feminine and masculine, and it does this through various means, including family, school, work, religion, the media, and politics. On a practical level, a set of mechanisms combine to impose gender: culture (via popular music, movies, literature, visual art, and so on), emotions (women's irrationality versus men's rationality), physical manifestations (ways of standing, walking, sitting, dressing, doing one's hair), speech (timbre of the voice, word choice – some of which are deemed inappropriate for women), behaviour patterns (smoking a cigar is still seen as a male prerogative), academic and professional choices, drinking and eating, entertainment and sports, consumption habits, textiles (colours, motifs, textures), and more.

Gender is a relational process, in that "women/the feminine" and "men/the masculine" are related by virtue of the (alleged) first and foundational polarization: heterosexuality. Judith Butler has clearly shown how heterosexuality is at the heart of gender creation. She calls this process the heterosexual matrix, "that grid of cultural intelligibility through which bodies, genders, and desires are naturalized … a hegemonic discursive/epistemic model of gender intelligibility that assumes that for bodies to cohere and make sense there must be a stable sex expressed through a stable gender (masculine expresses male, feminine expresses female) that is oppositionally and hierarchically defined through the compulsory practice of heterosexuality" (Butler 1999, 194). Being a woman is to be attracted to a man, of course, but it is also to occupy the subordinate position in an eminently hierarchical relationship.

Gender is a power relationship in that, as Butler (1999) indicates, it is formed of hierarchical oppositions that draw their legitimacy from the original polarization of heterosexuality – which, in turn, is also consolidated by these oppositions. She is emotional and gentle, he is rational and strong: these human traits become complementary through heterosexuality. In a book with an evocative title, *Masculine Domination*, sociologist Pierre Bourdieu dissects a cosmology of antagonistic binomials involved in the making of genders: for men, they include outside, dry, top, above, right hand, hardness, strength; for women, they include inside, humid, bottom, below, left hand, soft, weakness (Bourdieu 2001, 10). Of course, polarizations are not problematic in themselves, but they become so when they are conveyed by inequalities. Anthropologist Françoise Héritier maintains that the feminine is constantly being devalued in comparison to the masculine, a dynamic that she pinpoints through the notion of "differential valence of the sexes." Emotion gets lower marks than reason, dependence than independence, letters than numbers, weakness than strength, fat than muscle, menstrual blood (negation of fecundity) than sperm (source of generation), and so on.

Finally, gender is a component of other power relationships in that it contributes to the network of tensions and inequalities that shape societies on the basis of age, social class, skin colour, religion, sexual preference,[1] or other factors. In this sense it falls within an intersectional approach to research. Intersectionality "describes the interaction between systems of oppression" (Weldon 2008, 193). Thus, gender is more than one system of oppression among others; as a transversal, and not vertical, principle of analysis, it passes through the other systems (though this does not necessarily mean that it precedes them, as the argument on parity would have it; see questions 51 and 52). An intersectional approach to research brings to light the plurality of power relationships that structure political society and, above all, their intertwined nature; from these relationships emerge unsuspected and complex forms of both social inequality – in other words, oppressions – and privilege. The claim that "women" are underrepresented in politics would lead one to believe that they are underrepresented monolithically and identically because of their sex/gender, which conceals inequalities among women resulting from intertwining oppressions linked to other inherent power relationships – for example social class, religion, skin colour, and sexual preference. Indeed, it is possible that the negative impact of sex/gender is attenuated for a white, socioprofessionally privileged woman identified with a dominant religion, or accentuated for a lesbian who has little education and is economically disadvantaged. In other words, intersectionality deconstructs the homogenizing myth of "women" to reveal inequalities compounded by various social-identity markers, of course, but also by resistances, alliances, and resignifications by dominated women.

---

1 In this book, I use the notion of "sexual preference" rather than that of "sexual orientation," as the latter term seems to me to be imbued with biologism, determinism, or fatalism, whereas the former term clearly involves choice – a choice that may even be political.

Gender forms a system (or regime) in the sense that it is built into an ideology with its attendant values, standards, and rules, and it involves actors who maintain (power) relationships in the context of institutions (the heterosexual and heteroparental family, the school, means of communication, and so on). However, gender is imposed on people not by state coercion and violence (there are no "gender police") but by consent and adherence to models advanced by civil-society institutions and conveyed by the state, such as the school system, the media, the family, the job market, the leisure market, the consumption system, governance, and leadership. In this, gender is hegemonic – that is, it constitutes a dominant power on the ideological and practical levels both within civil society and in the state.

In short, gender is the invisible, but very real, hand that creates socially comprehensible women and men through ideas and practices.

BIBLIOGRAPHY

Bereni, Laure, Sébastien Chauvin, Alexandre Jaunait, and Anne Revillard. 2012. *Introduction aux études sur le genre*, 2nd edition. Brussels: De Boeck. See, in particular, 23–33.

Bourdieu, Pierre. [1998] 2001. *Masculine Domination*, translated by Richard Nice. Stanford: Stanford University Press.

Butler, Judith. 1999. *Gender Trouble; Feminism and the Subversion of Identity*, 2nd edition. Abingdon: Routledge.

Héritier, Françoise. 1996. *Masculin/féminin: La pensée de la différence*. Paris: Odile Jacob.

Weldon, S. Laurel. 2008. "Intersectionality." In *Politics, Gender, and Concepts: Theory and Methodology*, edited by Gary Goertz and Amy G. Mazur, 193–218. Cambridge: Cambridge University Press.

2 How does gender as an idea contribute to research on women's participation in electoral politics?

The notion of gender is important when studying women's participation in electoral politics because it compensates for the insufficiencies of the notion of sex. This assertion requires an understanding of the different concepts of sex gap, gender gap, and sexuality gap.

The concept of sex gap fits within the methodological approach of naming and describing realities as experienced by women and men. For example, according to the data compiled by the Inter-Parliamentary Union, on 1 June 2016, 22.8 per cent of seats in the lower or single chambers of some 190 national parliaments around the world were filled by women; the proportion of men thus stood at 77.2 per cent: therefore, a chasm of more than 50 per cent separated women's representation and men's representation in the ranks of parliamentarians. Seen from a different angle, starting from the parity argument according to which one human being out of two is a woman, and therefore one parliamentary seat out of two should be occupied by a woman (see questions 51 and 52), women are underrepresented and men overrepresented in politics by 27.2 per cent each. Here's another example: according to Statistics Canada, in 2009, 26.9 per cent of women worked part time, as opposed to 11.9 per cent of men (Ferrao 2011, table 7). In short, the sex gap names and describes: 22.8 per cent of women against 77.2 per cent of men parliamentarians, and 26.9 per cent of women versus 11.9 per cent of men working part time.

The gender gap is explained in light of the gender regime (see question 1). If women represent less than one quarter of parliamentarians in the world, and men, therefore, represent three quarters, it may be because women encounter difficulties that men do not because men set the rules of the political game to comply with their homosocial capital (see question 20). For instance, is it possible that activist events held in the evening are more difficult for mothers than fathers of young children to attend because childcare is a role that still falls first and foremost to women (see question 24)? Is it possible that the candidate profile sought by political parties corresponds more to the socialization of men than of women (see question 20)? Might it be that the electorate is sexist toward female candidates (see question 14)? If one female worker in four – as opposed to one male worker in ten – works part time, might this be because women have family and domestic obligations shared little, if at all, by men due to gender roles? This may also explain why it is not socially acceptable for a man to work part time when his life partner has a full-time job, as this situation destabilizes the man/woman hierarchy inherent to the gender regime.

The sexuality gap, which refers to what is usually labelled "sexual orientation" (being lesbian, gay, or bisexual) and "gender identity" (transgender or transsexual people, also known as trans), is a variable used to both describe and explain social phenomena. For example, studies conducted in Iceland (Arnarsson et al., 2015) and Quebec (Montoro et al., 2015) show that rates of attempted and completed suicides are much higher among lesbian, gay, and bisexual (LGB) young people than among non-LGB populations. Both studies explain this gap as being due to LGB-phobic intimidation. That said, the study by Arnarsson et al. (2015) also reveals that although LGB adolescent girls are six times more likely than their heterosexual counterparts to say that they have attempted suicide, the proportion skyrockets to seventeen times more likely among LGB adolescent boys compared to straight adolescent boys. In both of these studies, the sexuality gap (LGB versus straight) and the sex gap (females versus males) are intertwined – a dynamic for which the gender gap offers explanations. Pedersen and Kristiansen (2008, 69), for instance, posit that "homosexuality is a lot more threatening and potentially in conflict with traditional male gender roles than we find to be the case for women," referring to the fact that traditional masculinity is defined to exclude perceived prejudicial activities that stigmatize gay lives (such as effeminate behaviour and unbridled sexuality).

To return to the initial question, there are at least three ways in which the concept of gender influences research into women's participation in electoral politics. Its first contribution is to "degeneralize" analyses and make them more sensitive to the specificities of women and men. For example, saying that Canada has had universal suffrage since 1867 is false for several reasons, one of which is that it was not until 1918 that women (and only some of them) attained this right (see question 77). Another example shows up in a recent study of the professionalization of municipal political personnel in Quebec: Mévellec and Tremblay (2016) observed that a large proportion of municipal councillors and mayors had parents who were engaged on social and political levels. This observation reveals the importance of childhood political socialization to an individual's adult political career path. However, this generalization conceals the fact that a higher proportion of women than men grew up in a socially and politically engaged family. If this detail is added to the observation, it may suggest that for women who decide to enter municipal politics, such an upbringing could compensate for the lack of existing female political models.

A second contribution is to denaturalize women and their life experiences to reveal the social and political content of the (power) relationships they maintain with men. Gender, as the result of power relationships, points the analytic focus directly at ideological and practical mechanisms that institute differences and hierarchies between women and men. For example, is it possible that women in cabinet positions find themselves at the bottom of the ministerial ladder managing "pink portfolios" (such as family, culture, and education) not because they are thought to excel in these areas due to "natural talents" or a "human touch" (see questions 72 and 73) but because these portfolios have less influence and power, and especially because they fit within the gender regime? Could it be that men are handed the "important" portfolios (finance, foreign affairs, defence, and others) because they are more powerful and therefore those portfolios are more appropriate for them under the gender system, thus reinforcing this system? Unfortunately, Justin Trudeau's parity cabinet does not completely escape the gender regime (see question 91).

A third contribution, which will not be examined in this book, is that of gender-based analysis. This comparison consists of examining public decisions in light of their presuppositions with regard to gender and their repercussions for women and men. For example, the federal government under Stephen Harper (2006–15) presumed that women had primary responsibility for children by issuing family allowance benefits to mothers even in cases in which the father was the guardian. The new Canada child benefit instituted by Justin Trudeau's government is paid to parents irrespective of sex/gender. Another example might be an assessment of street lighting through a focus on gender showing that inadequate luminosity may increase women's sense of insecurity and limit their mobility in public spaces when it is dark out. A woman might therefore choose not to take university courses at night or refuse a job with evening hours, thus limiting her job prospects and quality of life over the longer term. This being said, it is possible that men may also feel threatened by inadequate street lighting, especially if they belong to a sexual minority. The gender system reserves a position of being dominated for women and LGBT people – the former because of their sex, the latter their sexualities.

To sum up, gender as an idea contributes to the study of women's electoral participation by bringing women out of the shadows to which political science has confined them for too long.

BIBLIOGRAPHY

Arnarsson, Arsaell, Sigrun Sveinbjornsdottir, Einar B. Thorsteinsson, and Thoroddur Bjarnason. 2015. "Suicidal Risk and Sexual Orientation in Adolescence: A Population-Based Study in Iceland." *Scandinavian Journal of Public Health* 43 (5): 497–505.

Ferrao, Vincent. 2011. "Paid Work." In Statistics Canada, *Women in Canada: A Gender-based Statistical Report*, 6th edition. Ottawa: Statistics Canada (no. 89-503-X), accessed 3 August 2016, http://www.statcan.gc.ca/pub/89-503-x/2010001/article/11387/tbl/tbl007 -eng.htm.

Inter-Parliamentary Union. "Women in National Parliaments, World Classification," accessed 3 August 2016, http://www.ipu.org/wmn-e/classif.htm.

Mévellec, Anne and Manon Tremblay. 2016. *Genre et professionnalisation de la politique municipale; Un portrait des élues et élus du Québec*. Quebec City: Presses de l'Université du Québec.

Montoro, Richard, Brett Thombs, and Karine J. Igartua. 2015. "L'association des dimensions de l'orientation sexuelle, du harcèlement et du suicide: quelles minorités sexuelles sont les plus à risque?" *Santé mentale au Québec* 40 (3): 55–75.

Pedersen, Willy and Hans W. Kristiansen. 2008. "Homosexual Experience, Desire and Identity Among Young Adults." *Journal of Homosexuality* 54 (1–2): 68–102.

Vickers, Jill. 1997. *Reinventing Political Science*. Halifax: Fernwood Publishing.

– 2015. "Can We Change How Political Science Thinks? 'Gender Mainstreaming' in a Resistant Discipline. Presidential Address delivered to the Canadian Political Science Association, Ottawa, June 2, 2015." *Canadian Journal of Political Science* 48 (4): 747–70.

CHAPTER TWO

The Rights to Vote and to Run for Office

3 What was the suffragist movement?

The suffragist movement consisted of a series of mobilizations intended to gain women the right to vote in elections. Although it lasted different lengths of time in different countries (for example, it extended for more than a century in Switzerland; see question 7), in general the suffragist movement was active from the mid-nineteenth to the mid-twentieth century (see question 6). The first suffragist movements began around 1850 in Great Britain and the United States, where they grew quite large. American women demanded the right to vote in elections during the Seneca Falls Conference in 1848. In Great Britain, the first suffragist organization, the Sheffield Female Political Association, was formed in 1851. Not all countries have had a suffragist movement. For example, women and men had the right to vote in Finland as soon as that country gained independence, in 1906, and in Japan women were granted suffrage in two steps, in 1945 and 1947, under Allied occupation.

Most activists involved in suffragist movements were women, although men sometimes helped out (for example by sponsoring bills for the right to vote). A number of the women were well educated (at least, in comparison to their contemporaries), belonged to the urban middle class, and endorsed the ideals of liberal individualism. Nevertheless, less-well-off women also became involved (black women in the American and South African movements, for example).

Although the suffragist movement as a whole demanded women's right to vote, there was great diversity in terms of ideas and tactics. Struggles for women's suffrage encompassed what are today called egalitarian and differentialist factions: some activists demanded the right to vote in the name of sex/gender equality, whereas others did so in the name of the difference between women and men (see question 8). In addition, the movement included both reformist and radical activists. The former felt that working within the existing political system was the best path to gaining suffrage. Their tactics consisted, for example, of canvassing male politicians and handing them petitions. The radical activists, often called suffragettes, advocated more spectacular actions including disrupting parliament, demonstrating, and conducting hunger strikes; this trend was exemplified by Alice Paul and Lucy Burns's National Woman's Party in the United States and by Emmeline Pankhurst and Christabel Pankhurst's Women's Social and Political Union in Great Britain. History has recorded the extraordinary action of British suffragette Emily Davison, who died in 1913 after throwing herself before King George V's racehorse amid shouts of "The vote for women!" (see question 76 for qualification). Cracks within the movement also appeared between majority women and those of ethnic minorities, who were often relegated to the margin. The American movement is notable in this regard; the fact that black women obtained the vote at the same time as white women did raised much resistance within the white community.

The suffragist movement has taken its place within the broader narrative of the first wave of feminism. Early feminists were concerned with obtaining various civil rights (such as, for married women, the right to own property and to divorce), social rights (such as the right to education), economic rights (such as the right to be free of job and income discrimination), and political rights (such as the right to vote in elections). Many consider first-wave feminism to be synonymous with the suffragist movement, but this is a reductive vision; although suffrage was a prominent issue, it was nevertheless one among others. Second-wave feminism, which emerged in the mid-1960s, is often associated with the "women's liberation" movement. Again, this is a reductive vision: of course, the second wave was driven by women who claimed the right to autonomy, notably in terms of their bodies (a perspective closely associated with the right to voluntary termination of pregnancy through access to free and safe services), but it also included a faction concerned with obtaining equality in law – and in fact – between women and men (the transition from pay equality to pay equity is one example of this position).

A distinction should be made, however: there is a current within the study of women's history that challenges the relevance of thinking of the feminist movement in terms of "waves" and the corollary that the movement was dormant from the 1930s to 1960 as this ignores the continuity of women's mobilizations in their quest for equality and freedom.

Two wonderful films, Katja von Garnier's *Iron Jawed Angels* and Sarah Gavron's *Suffragette,* offer compelling images of the suffragist movement and the tensions that ran through it.

BIBLIOGRAPHY

Gavron, Sarah, director. 2015. *Suffragette.* Film on suffragist struggles in Great Britain.

Hannam, June, Mitzi Auchterlonie, and Katherine Holden. 2000. *International Encyclopedia of Women's Suffrage.* Santa Barbara: ABC-CLIO.

Von Garnier, Katja, director. 2004. *Iron Jawed Angels.* Film on suffragist struggles in the United States.

4 Did the rights to vote and to run for office in national legislative elections become accessible to women and men at the same time?

History has recorded epic suffragist struggles in the United States and Great Britain. However, as a general rule, women and men attained the rights to vote and to run for office at the same time and under the same conditions. This was the case in Australia, for example, when the Commonwealth of Australia was founded in 1901. It was also the case in Finland, where universal suffrage was instituted in 1906.

That the general trend was to grant the rights to vote and to run for office to women and men simultaneously is explained, for the most part, by the wave of decolonization from the 1950s to 1970: when they gained sovereignty, new nations accorded these rights to both sexes. It must also be said that several instruments of international law already in place, such as the Universal Declaration of Human Rights (1948), the Convention on the Political Rights of Women (1952), and the International Covenant on Civil and Political Rights (1966), very likely played an important role, although this remains to be proved (see question 41).

That being said, in some countries women obtained the rights to vote and to run for office in national legislative elections at different times and had to conduct separate struggles to achieve them. This was the case in, among other countries, Djibouti, Mexico, New Zealand, Norway, Turkey, and the United States. The time gap differs depending on the country: it was only two years in Canada (1918 for the right to vote and 1920 for the right to run for federal election) and the Netherlands (1917 for the right to run for office and 1919 for the right to vote), four years in Turkey (1930 and 1934), and eleven years in Myanmar (1935 and 1946). However, the gap was twenty-two years in El Salvador (1939 and 1961), twenty-six in New Zealand (1893 and 1919), and forty in Djibouti (1946 and 1986); in the United States, women could run for office in 1788 but did not have the right to vote until 1920 – a gap of 132 years! In fact, a woman (Jeannette Rankin from Montana) was elected to the US House of Representatives in 1917, three years before women were allowed to vote in federal elections.

Two details must be added to paint a more accurate picture of women's access to the rights to vote and to run for office. First, the legislation sometimes imposed conditions on women's right to vote (age, marital status, education, property ownership, or income) that were not applied to men. For example, in 1915, Iceland allowed women to vote in legislative elections on condition that they were over forty (the implication being that only women who were near or in menopause could participate in political life). In 1918, Great Britain also imposed an age limit: only women over thirty could vote (whereas men could vote at age twenty-one). Iceland, Finland, and Sweden at first reserved suffrage for single women and widows. The exclusion of married women was justified by the fact that they were represented by their husbands; granting them the vote, it was said, amounted either to a double vote if wife and husband shared the same political opinions or to the husband having his vote cancelled out by his "better half" (the inverse was never mentioned). In Portugal, women (but not men) could not vote unless they had finished high school or college.

Second, these conditions produced not only inequality between women and men but also divisions among women (for example, among women who were married, unmarried, and no longer married; between middle-class women and others; and among women of different ethnic groups). It is thus not surprising that women have had difficulty thinking of themselves as a politically significant group in terms of political representation (see questions 12 and 60).

BIBLIOGRAPHY

Rodriguez-Ruiz, Blanca, and Ruth Rubio-Marin. 2012. "Introduction: Transition to Modernity, the Conquest of Female Suffrage and Women's Citizenship." In *The Struggle for Female Suffrage in Europe: Voting to Become Citizens*, edited by Blanca Rodriguez-Ruiz and Ruth Rubio-Marin, 1–46. Leiden, The Netherlands: Brill.

Tremblay, Manon. 2005. "Introduction. Du droit d'élire et d'être élues au droit de représenter et d'être représentées: une lecture de la citoyenneté politique des femmes." In *Femmes et parlements: un regard international*, edited by Manon Tremblay, 21–54. Montreal: Remue-ménage.

5 In which countries did women first obtain the rights to vote and to run for national legislative office?

There are a number of examples of countries in which women once had the right to vote but then lost that right. In England under the Tudors and Stuarts, in the sixteenth and seventeenth centuries, women who owned property could vote for members of parliament – a right that they lost with the electoral reform of 1832. In Lower Canada (roughly, Quebec at the beginning of Confederation) female landowners could vote between 1791 and 1849, on the same footing as male landowners (see question 77). Women in Upper Canada, where Common Law prevailed (as opposed to Quebec's French-heritage civil law), did not have this right. In Connecticut and Massachusetts, women meeting certain property-ownership and residency requirements could vote. They were also able to vote in New Jersey between 1790 and 1807. Although the Isle of Man, the Pitcairn Islands, the territory of Wyoming (before it entered the American union), and New Zealand granted suffrage to women in 1838, 1866, 1869, and 1893, respectively, Australia was the first fully sovereign country in which women (though not Aboriginal women) and men were able to vote under the same conditions. Australia was not the only country to exclude indigenous women from suffrage; Canada, South Africa, and Zimbabwe also did. In Kenya, a British colony, European women could vote as of 1919, Asian women and men in 1923, but black women and men did not have this right until 1957. This gap between white and nonwhite women was essentially explained by two factors. The first was the colonialist mentality by which colonizers placed indigenous peoples under administrative supervision; the colonizers' mission was to master nature, and this implied that the state was to take charge of indigenous peoples' "well-being" and the "defence" of their interests. The second factor was racism under which doubt was raised that indigenous peoples had the "tools" (reasoning and discernment, culture, education, interest in public affairs, and so on) deemed essential to make enlightened decisions and assume responsibility for the obligations inherent to citizenship (or, at least, a certain colonialist comprehension of citizenship).

New Zealand was the first country in which indigenous (Maori) and nonindigenous (*pakeha* – non-Maori and therefore usually of Anglo-British descent) women obtained the right to vote in national legislative elections at the same time, although the country was overseen by the United Kingdom at the time. McLeay (2006) explains this progressive attitude by a number of factors. One is that Maori men, like their non-Maori counterparts, had had the right to vote since 1867; when suffrage was expanded to women in 1893, there simply was no question of excluding the Maori. Another factor, more persuasive, was that New Zealand was a new society, in which egalitarianism had a better chance than it did in the societies that the European women had left. This explanation is even more likely because women in another new country, neighbouring Australia, were the second (in 1902) to obtain the right to vote in national legislative elections.

Strictly speaking, the first country in which women were able to run for election to the national legislature was the United States. The 1788 constitution left the door open to women's eligibility, and Elizabeth Cady Stanton ran for office in 1866. Only in 1920, under the Nineteenth Amendment to the Constitution, however, were American women granted the right to vote in elections for Congress (several states already allowed them to vote for members of state legislatures, including Wyoming, which granted this right in 1869). This American "first" is explained in part by the inclusive wording of the Constitution, in which "person" was used (and the words "he," "male," and "man" did not appear), enabling women to vote unless they were specifically banned from doing so. However, the Fourteenth Amendment, adopted in 1868, introduced the word "male," causing women to lose the right they had held for seventy-eight years. A similar situation arose in Lower Canada (see question 77). In my view, Australia probably deserves the title of first country where women could run for national legislative election: although American women had the right by omission to run for office in 1788, the right was explicitly extended to Australian women in 1902.

Australia was also the first country in the Commonwealth in which women *simultaneously* obtained the rights to vote and to run for legislative office, in 1902, although it was not until the federal election of 1943 that a woman was voted into the Chamber of Representatives and another to the Senate. How can Australia's advance be explained? At the constitutional convention of 1897–98, which led to the creation of the Australian federation, the delegation from South Australia insisted that women from their state preserve the political rights that they had already acquired (namely, the rights to vote and to run for legislative election). The 1902 Franchise Act maintained these rights and extended them to all (except Aboriginal) women in the newly constituted federation.

BIBLIOGRAPHY

Gertzog, Irwin N. 1990. "Female Suffrage in New Jersey, 1790–1807." *Women & Politics* 10 (2): 47–58.

McCammon, Holly J., Karen E. Campbell, Ellen M. Granberg, and Christine Mowery. 2001. "How Movements Win: Gendered Opportunity Structures and U.S. Women's Suffrage Movements, 1866 to 1919." *American Sociological Review* 66 (1): 49–70.

McLeay, Elizabeth. 2006. "Climbing On: Rules, Values and Women's Representation in the New Zealand Parliament." In *Representing Women in Parliament: A Comparative Study*, edited by Marian Sawer, Manon Tremblay, and Linda Trimble, 67–82. Abingdon: Routledge.

Oldfield, Audrey. 1992. *Woman Suffrage in Australia: A Gift or a Struggle?* Cambridge: Cambridge University Press.

Sawer, Marian and Marian Simms. 1993. *A Woman's Place: Women and Politics in Australia*. St Leonards: Allen & Unwin.

6 What factors may have contributed to women's access to the rights to vote and to run for office?

As table 1 shows, the two world wars, the interwar period, and, especially, the period of decolonization from the 1950s to 1970s are significant milestones for understanding women's access to the right to vote and to run for office in legislative elections. A few countries, however, are outside this timeline, either because they were ahead of their time (such as Finland, where women were able to vote in 1906) or, on the contrary, due to their resistance to female suffrage (Swiss women had to wait until 1971 [see question 7], black women in South Africa until 1994, and Kuwaiti women until 2005).

Nevertheless, as a general rule, women were granted the right to vote as a form of acknowledgment for their contribution to the war effort (although this may have been more perception than fact). The suffragists won their cause in Canada and the United States after the First World War and in France after the Second World War. In Japan, the Allies made women's suffrage an intrinsic part of its occupation after the war, somewhat similar to how women's representation quotas (on candidates' lists, for example) are imposed on countries in the process of democratization (as in Afghanistan and Iraq) today. In a number of countries (mainly those in Africa), decolonization and the achievement of national sovereignty brought in their wake the right for women to vote in legislative elections. Finally, the creation of a new country (such as Israel) or a new constitutional order (as in South Africa) also favoured women's suffrage. By the end of the Second World War, women could vote and run for office in about half of the countries in the world.

Rodriguez-Ruiz and Rubio-Marin (2012) distinguish two general models to explain women's acquisition of the right to vote. The first model is characterized by a global conjuncture turned toward change: civil society was driven by broader social restructuring movements to which were grafted suffragist demands; there was no specific suffragist movement, as these demands were subsumed within other movements. In the view of Rodriguez-Ruiz and Rubio-Marin, Finland exemplifies this model, as do Denmark, Estonia, Ireland, Latvia, Lithuania, Luxemburg, the Netherlands, and Poland. The other model is based on the existence of a specific, relatively united suffragist movement that could count on the support of (male) progressive elites within parties and in legislative and governmental spaces. Examples of this model abound, as it represents the dominant trajectory of Western suffragism: Austria, Canada, France, Germany, Great Britain, Sweden, the United States, and others.

Beyond these macrosocietal approaches, a number of specific factors seem to have played significant roles in women's access to the rights to vote and to run for office. In fact, a number of forces generally combined to clear the way to women's suffrage. I will mention just a few of them here. One has to do with suffragist struggles themselves: women won the right to vote because they fought to obtain it, as in Great Britain and the United

Table 1

Women's access to the right to vote in national legislative elections measured against some key historical periods

Before the First World War	Australia (1902, 1962*), Finland (1906), New Zealand (1893), Norway (1913)
Around the time of the First World War (1914–20**)	Albania (1920), Austria (1918), Belarus (1919), Belgium (1919, 1948), Canada (1917, 1918, 1950, 1960), Czech Republic (1920), Denmark (1915), Estonia (1918), Georgia (1918, 1921), Germany (1918), Hungary (1918), Iceland (1915, 1920), Ireland (1918, 1928), Kyrgyzstan (1918), Latvia (1918), Lithuania (1918), Luxembourg (1919), the Netherlands (1919), Poland (1918), Russian Federation (1918), Slovakia (1920), Sweden (1919, 1921), Ukraine (1919), United Kingdom (1918, 1928), United States (1920)
Interwar period	Armenia (1921), Azerbaijan (1921), Bolivia (1938, 1952), Brazil (1932), Chile (1931, 1949), Cuba (1934), Ecuador (1929, 1967), Kazakhstan (1924, 1993), Maldives (1932), Mongolia (1924), Myanmar/Burma (1935), Philippines (1937), Portugal (1931, 1934, 1976), Romania (1929, 1946), Saint Lucia (1924), South Africa (1930 [whites], 1984 [mixed-blood and indigenous peoples], 1994 [blacks]), Spain (1931), Sri Lanka (1931), Tajikistan (1924), Thailand (1932), Turkey (1930), Turkmenistan (1927), Uruguay (1932), Uzbekistan (1938)

Table 1

Continued

Around the time of the Second World War (1939–47)	Argentina (1947), Bulgaria (1944), Cameroon (1946), Croatia (1945), Democratic People's Republic of Korea (1946), Djibouti (1946), Dominican Republic (1942), El Salvador (1939), former Yugoslav Republic of Macedonia (1946), France (1944), Guatemala (1946), Indonesia (1945), Italy (1945), Jamaica (1944), Japan (1945, 1947), Liberia (1946), Malta (1947), Mexico (1947), Pakistan (1947), Panama (1941, 1946), Senegal (1945), Singapore (1947), Slovenia (1945), Togo (1945), Trinidad and Tobago (1946), Venezuela (1946), Vietnam (1946), Yugoslavia (1946)
Decolonization period (1950s to 1970s)	Afghanistan (1963), Algeria (1962), Andorra (1970), Antigua and Barbuda (1951), Bahamas (1961, 1964), Barbados (1950), Belize (1954), Benin (1956), Bhutan (1953), Bosnia-Herzegovina (1949), Botswana (1965), Burkina Faso (1958), Burundi (1961), Cambodia (1955), Chad (1958), China (1949), Colombia (1954), Comoros (1956), Congo (1963), Costa Rica (1949), Côte d'Ivoire (1952), Cyprus (1960), Democratic Republic of the Congo (1967), Dominica (1951), Egypt (1956), Equatorial Guinea (1963), Eritrea (1955), Ethiopia (1955), Fiji (1963), Gabon (1956), Gambia (1960), Ghana (1954), Greece (1952), Grenada (1951), Guinea (1958), Guyana (1953), Haiti (1950), Honduras (1955), India (1950), Iran (1963), Israel (1948), Kenya (1963), Kiribati (1967), Lebanon (1952), Lesotho (1965), Libyan Arab Jamahiriya (1964), Madagascar (1959),

	Malawi (1961), Malaysia (1957), Mali (1956), Mauritania (1961), Mauritius (1956), Monaco (1962), Morocco (1963), Nauru (1968), Nepal (1951), Nicaragua (1955), Niger (1948), Nigeria (south, 1958), Papua-New Guinea (1964), Paraguay (1961), People's Democratic Republic of Lao (1958), People's Democratic Republic of Yemen (1967), Peru (1955), Republic of Korea (1948), Rwanda (1961), Saint Kitts and Nevis (1951), San Marino (1959), St Vincent and the Grenadines (1951), Seychelles (1948), Sierra Leone (1961), Somalia (1956), Sudan (1964), Suriname (1948), Swaziland (1968), Syrian Arab Republic (1949, 1953), Tonga (1960), Tunisia (1959), Tuvalu (1967), Uganda (1962), United Republic of Tanzania (1959), Yemen Arabic Republic (1970), Zambia (1962), Zimbabwe (1957)
Contemporary period (1970s to 2005)	Angola (1975), Bahrain (1973, 2001), Bangladesh (1972), Cape Verde (1975), Central African Republic (1986), Federated States of Micronesia (1979), Guinea Bissau (1977), Iraq (1980), Jordan (1974), Kuwait (2005), Liechtenstein (1984), Marshall Islands (1979), Mozambique (1975), Namibia (1989), Nigeria (north, 1978), Oman (2003), Palau (1979), Qatar (1999), Republic of Moldova (1978, 1993), Samoa (1990), Sao Tomé and Principe (1975), Switzerland (1971), Salomon Islands (1974), Vanuatu (1975, 1980)

* More than one year indicates that women obtained the right to vote in steps.
** The First World War lasted from 1914 to 1918, but the period under consideration was extended by two years to include countries in which women earned the right to vote as a form of recognition for their participation in the war effort. The same phenomenon was observed after the Second World War.
Source: Inter-Parliamentary Union, "Women's Suffrage," consulted 6 June 2016, http://www.ipu.org/wmn-e/suffrage.htm.

States. A second one is the prevalence of an egalitarian conception of social relations in general and of relations between women and men in particular. This factor explains, in part, the early adoption of female suffrage in Australia and New Zealand. On the other hand, for these two countries, we must add a third factor, intercountry contagion, from New Zealand (where women could vote in 1893) to Australia (where they gained suffrage in 1902). Quite often, and this is the fourth factor, political elites extended the right to vote to women for strategic reasons related to an election. For example, in Belgium, France, and Peru it was felt that the women's vote, presumed to be conservative, would counter communist advances. Religion is the fifth factor: in general, women obtained the right to vote earlier in Protestant-dominated countries than in Catholic-dominated countries. Canada exemplifies this scenario: in Quebec (in which the French language and Catholicism dominated), women obtained the right to vote in provincial elections in 1940; in the other provinces (English-speaking and Protestant), they gained suffrage between 1916 and 1925 (see question 77). A sixth factor concerns federalism: in Australia, women gained the right to vote in federal elections in order to limit electoral qualification differences between newly federated states in the Commonwealth. On the other hand, in the United States, in which each state establishes its own electoral rules, the suffragist struggle had to be conducted state by state, and lasted more than seven decades. A seventh factor is inevitability: at some point it was simply no longer possible to refuse women the right to vote. This factor played a role in Belgium, France, and Italy, and perhaps also in Quebec. However, Switzerland tenaciously resisted this factor (see question 7). A final factor is linked to concerns with modernization: granting women the right to vote showed advancement and modernity. Iran under the Shah is an example, and Saudi Arabia and the United Arab Emirates, in recent years, have evidenced some openness toward allowing women to vote. There are no legislative elections in Saudi Arabia, but in September 2011, King Abdullah announced that women would be able to vote and run in the 2015 municipal elections, and this did occur. Women are also members of the Majlis Ash-Shura (19.87 per cent as of October 2016), an advisory council with which the king consults in lieu of a legislative body. In the United Arab Emirates, indirect legislative elections are used to designate half (twenty) of the members of the federation's National Council; the other half are appointed by the governments of the different emirates. Women may be electors (they represent about 18 per cent of the very limited electorate of the Emirates, composed of some 6,700 citizens in 2006), elected, and appointed. In October 2016, 22.5 per cent (9 out of 40) of members of the National Council were women.

BIBLIOGRAPHY

Blom, Ida. 2012. "Structures and Agency: A Transnational Comparison of the Struggle for Women's Suffrage in the Nordic Countries During the Long 19th Century." *Scandinavian Journal of History* 37 (5): 600–20.

Inter-Parliamentary Union. "Women's Suffrage," accessed 6 June 2016, http://www.ipu.org/wmn-e/suffrage.htm.

Palm, Trineke. 2013. "Embedded in Social Cleavages: An Explanation of the Variation in Timing of Women's Suffrage." *Scandinavian Political Studies* 36 (1): 1–22.

Rodriguez-Ruiz, Blanca and Ruth Rubio-Marin. 2012. "Introduction: Transition to Modernity, the Conquest of Female Suffrage and Women's Citizenship." In *The Struggle for Female Suffrage in Europe: Voting to Become Citizens*, edited by Blanca Rodriguez-Ruiz and Ruth Rubio-Marin, 1–46. Leiden, The Netherlands: Brill.

Rubio-Marin, Ruth. 2014. "The Achievement of Female Suffrage in Europe: On Women's Citizenship." *International Journal of Constitutional Law* 12 (1): 12–34.

Towns, Ann E. 2010. *Women and States: Norms and Hierarchies in International Society.* New York: Cambridge University Press. See, in particular, 55–121.

Tremblay, Manon. 2005. "Introduction. Du droit d'élire et d'être élues au droit de représenter et d'être représentées: une lecture de la citoyenneté politique des femmes." In *Femmes et parlements: un regard international*, edited by Manon Tremblay, 21–54. Montreal: Remue-ménage.

7 What is the explanation for Switzerland's delay in granting women the right to vote in federal legislative elections?

Not until February 1971 did male Swiss citizens agree, by referendum, to grant female suffrage at the federal level. Swiss women thus voted for the first time in the federal legislative election in October 1971. The previous year, the National Council and the Council of States had pronounced themselves in favour of women's rights to vote and to run for office and had recommended acceptance to male voters. However, suffrage became truly universal only in 1990, in the sense that women and men could vote under the same conditions in all elections (even if other exclusions remain, such as those based on citizenship and residency). In fact, as of 1983, women could vote and run in all elections (federal, cantonal, and communal), except for those in the canton of Appenzell, where it was not until 1989 and 1990 that the *Landsgemeinde* (a direct-democracy system in which male citizens – and, finally, female citizens – meet once a year to resolve certain community problems, voting by raising hands) of Appenzell Rhodes-Extérieures and Appenzell Rhodes-Intérieures, respectively, granted these rights to women.

The fact that Swiss women gained the right to vote and to run for office at the federal level so late is surprising, especially because Switzerland is proud of its long tradition of democratic rule (although it should be recalled that democracy and women's participation in politics do not necessarily go together; see question 33). First and foremost, it is important to underline that Switzerland's delay cannot be attributed to the absence of a suffragist movement. Starting in 1868, explicitly in 1886–87, and up to 1971, Swiss women were actively demanding their rights to vote and to run for office in communal, cantonal, and federal elections.

But the extreme decentralization of the Swiss federal system, in which the twenty-six cantons have great administrative autonomy, acted as a brake on women's access to the rights to vote and to run for office at the federal level. Indeed, the extension of these rights to women required an amendment to the federal constitution that had to be voted in not only by a majority of the (exclusively male) electorate but also by a majority of the cantons. In other words, it was not the federal parliament (the National Council and the Council of State) but the cantons and their male electors who held the power to grant these rights to women, and the male electorate had historically adopted a conservative position on this issue. For example, in a referendum held in 1959 – when all the countries adjacent to Switzerland has already granted this right to their female citizens – 67 per cent voted no to women's suffrage. Therefore, it is no exaggeration to state that direct democracy impeded women's access to political citizenship in Switzerland (in the United States, direct-democracy mechanisms, such as referendums initiated by the population, have been used by the political and religious right to refuse rights to, or withdraw them from, sexual minorities – notably lesbians and gays, but also trans people). This restrictive effect is certainly not intrinsic to the institution of direct democracy; in this case, however, a male electorate pronounced itself in a conservative manner regarding women's political rights on the federal scene – a conservatism fully endorsed by the country's political class.

This conservatism also prevailed within Swiss legal elites. For instance, until 1990, before its ruling on female suffrage in the canton of Appenzell Rhodes-Intérieures, the federal court refused to interpret the word "Swiss" in the federal constitution in an inclusive way, as applying to both women and men. In effect, the federal constitution had stipulated the right of suffrage to "Swiss people" for more than twenty years, but the federal court preferred to hew to a restrictive interpretation of the word "people" as applying only to men. Finally, arguments put forward in other countries influenced the decision of the Swiss Federation to refuse women the right to vote and to run for election (see question 8).

To sum up, the struggle for female suffrage in Switzerland shows that the claim of democracy does not always include women. And, considering the large number of countries that, even today, use the label "democratic" despite the low feminization rate in their national parliaments, it must be admitted that this subterfuge continues.

BIBLIOGRAPHY

Ballmer-Cao, Thanh-Huyen. 1988. *Le conservatisme politique féminin en Suisse: mythe ou réalité?* Geneva: Georg Editeur.

– 2005. "Switzerland." In *Sharing Power: Women, Parliament, Democracy*, edited by Yvonne Galligan and Manon Tremblay, 159–70. Burlington: Ashgate.

Bendix, John. 1992. "Women's Suffrage and Political Culture: A Modern Swiss Case." *Women & Politics* 12 (3): 27–56.

Stämpfli, Regula. 1994. "Direct Democracy and Women's Suffrage: Antagonism in Switzerland." In *Women and Politics Worldwide*, edited by Barbara J. Nelson and Najma Chowdhury, 691–704. New Haven: Yale University Press.

Switzerland (Commission fédérale pour les questions féminines). 2009. "Le long chemin menant au droit de vote et d'éligibilité des femmes," accessed 6 June 2016, http://www.ekf.admin.ch/dokumentation/00444/00517/index.html?lang=fr (not available in English).

8 What arguments have been put forth in favour of and against female suffrage?

The arguments for and against women's right to vote may be organized around the notions of sex/gender equality and sex/gender difference. The first notion refers to a humanist position: women are human beings just like men, similarly invested with inalienable rights, and therefore they can and must take full part in society – it is only justice, pure and simple. Without denying that women and men belong fully and equally to humanity, the notion of sex/gender difference dwells, instead, on their specific attributes. This perspective promotes an essentialist vision of gender roles: women and men have distinct and specific roles in reproduction, and these roles frame their respective positions in society. For instance, because women give life, it is assumed that their natural position is to continue this role by taking care of and educating children. Similarly, because they give life, the assumption is that women see things differently from men: they are more altruistic and more humane, they seek harmony and avoid conflict, and so on. In short, according to the differentialist perspective, which in fact is closely associated with the gender regime (see question 1), women and men have distinct visions of the world – visions anchored in sexual (that is, procreative) roles – and these dictate gender roles.

The argument of sex/gender equality was often put forward to demand women's suffrage – in Australia, for example. It is also the argument that underlies the principle of "no taxation without representation": because they pay taxes, women, just like men, should have the right to vote. However, historically some women were able to vote not because they were equal to men but because they were property owners. We must therefore not exaggerate the importance of the sex/gender equality argument in the debates on women's suffrage; although today it is widely accepted that human beings are equal without regard for their sex/gender, their mental and physical capacities, the colour of their skin, their sexual preference, and other qualities, this conviction is relatively recent in history (and some still have not come around to this view). It was forcefully stated in a range of instruments of international law promulgated in the mid-twentieth century, such as the Universal Declaration of Human Rights (1948), the Convention on the Political Rights of Women (1952), and the International Covenant on Civil and Political Rights (1966) (see question 41). In short, it is important to avoid looking at the past through today's eyes and grant the principle of sex/gender equality a role that it did not necessarily play in the struggles for female suffrage.

On the other hand, it must be said that the differentialist vision was once popular. Interestingly, it was proposed both to refuse women the right to vote and to demand it. Proponents of the former argument maintained that since women and men are different (though not necessarily unequal), each is assigned specific roles and responsibilities: to men the affairs of government and to women those of the household. Permitting women to vote would be tantamount to breaking the natural order. There would be unfortunate consequences for both women (election fever would put their delicate natures and maternal qualities at risk) and family harmony (the family might fall prey to political conflicts if the woman decided not to vote the same way as her husband). At any rate, women did not need to vote, the argument went, as their interests, totally assimilated with the family's interests, were already represented by their husbands' vote. Men voted on behalf of their family.

Those making the latter argument, however, saw the sex/gender difference as a reason to grant women the right to vote. This point of view was justified through maternalism: because they are mothers, women are endowed with qualities and skills from which society might benefit, particularly in the areas of education, health, and welfare. Women must therefore participate in public governance to accomplish their mission of social restoration. For example, with their vote, women might press politicians to concern themselves with questions close to the female heart, such as alcoholism, public morality, infant mortality, urban hygiene, and violence. With an electorate composed of women and men, political governance would be more balanced and harmonious, less passionate and violent, more concerned with human beings and their environment. Female voters would make war less likely and would purge depraved political behaviours because of the values they gained from their experience as mothers. In short, women should have the vote, argued certain suffragists, because their feminine and maternal virtues would improve life in society.

BIBLIOGRAPHY

Bacchi, Carol Lee. 1983. *Liberation Deferred? The Ideas of the English-Canadian Suffragists 1877-1918*. Toronto: University of Toronto Press. See, in particular, 40–58, 104–16.

Binard, Florence. 2014. "'The Injustice of the Woman's Vote': Opposition to Female Suffrage after World War I." *Women's History Review* 23 (3): 381–400.

Cleverdon, Catherine L. [1950] 1974. *The Start of Liberation: The Woman Suffrage Movement in Canada*. Toronto: University of Toronto Press. See, in particular, 3–18.

Hannam, June, Mitzi Auchterlonie, and Katherine Holden. 2000. *International Encyclopedia of Women's Suffrage*. Santa Barbara: ABC-CLIO.

Rubio-Marin, Ruth. 2014. "The Achievement of Female Suffrage in Europe: On Women's Citizenship." *International Journal of Constitutional Law* 12 (1): 12–34.

Tremblay, Manon. 2010. *Quebec Women and Legislative Representation*, translated by Käthe Roth. Vancouver: UBC Press. See, in particular, 11–60.

9 Is there a link between the current proportion of female parliamentarians in a particular country and the year they obtained the right to vote?

There is little evidence of such a relationship. It is true that the Nordic countries, where women obtained the right to vote early (between 1906 and 1921), had a relatively high proportion of women parliamentarians in April 2016: between 37.4 per cent and 43.6 per cent. However, in a number of other countries, the rate of parliamentary feminization does not seem to be related to the year when women obtained the right to vote. For instance, in 1902 Australia became the first fully sovereign country in which women could vote in national legislative elections, whereas Switzerland finally assented to female suffrage almost seven decades later, in 1971 (see questions 5 and 7). Yet, as of April 2016, 26.7 per cent of those sitting in the lower house of the Australian parliament were women, whereas the Swiss lower house had a feminization rate of 32 per cent. Other cases also muddy the waters. In Belgium, women were granted suffrage in the late 1940s, and the House of Representatives had a feminization rate of 39.3 per cent in April 2016. This is much higher than in the British House of Commons (29.4 per cent women in April 2016), the Canadian House of Commons (26 per cent), and the United States House of Representatives (19.4 per cent), even though female suffrage was granted in Great Britain in 1928, Canada in 1918, and the United States in 1920.

Moreover, the results of studies based on observation of a large number of countries are contradictory. The gaps may be explained by the countries and indicators sampled, and by the models and procedures used for statistical analyses. For instance, some research indicates that the countries in which women gained the right to participate in national legislative elections early also show high rates of feminization of the national parliament. Other research, however, has not shown such a link. Canada offers an illustration of this: although Quebec women gained the rights to vote and to run for provincial election much later than did other women in other provinces, following the 2014 general election Quebec's National Assembly had a feminization rate of 27.2 per cent, slightly higher than the average in the House of Commons and the other eleven provincial and territorial legislatures, which was 24.9 per cent (see questions 77 and 89).

It is too simplistic, however, to explain the proportion of female parliamentarians through a single dataset – in this case, the year when women obtained the right to vote. The phenomenon is complex and cannot result from a single cause (see questions 18 and 19). In fact, it is more productive to envisage the feminization of parliaments as arising from a multitude of cultural, socioeconomic, and political forces, some more important than others, which, combined in a common environment, influence each other to create a dynamic unique to each political community.

BIBLIOGRAPHY

Kenworthy, Lane and Melissa Malami. 1999. "Gender Inequality in Political Representation: A Worldwide Comparative Analysis." *Social Forces* 78 (1): 235–68.

McAllister, Ian and Donley T. Studlar. 2002. "Electoral Systems and Women's Representation: A Long-Term Perspective." *Representation: The Journal of Representative Democracy* 39 (1): 3–14.

Paxton, Pamela. 1997. "Women in National Legislatures: A Cross-National Analysis." *Social Science Research* 26 (4): 442–64.

Paxton, Pamela, Melanie Hughes, and Jennifer L. Green. 2006. "The International Women's Movement and Women's Political Representation, 1893–2003." *American Sociological Review* 71 (6): 898–920.

Reynolds, Andrew. 1999. "Women in the Legislatures and Executives of the World: Knocking at the Highest Glass Ceiling." *World Politics* 51 (4) 547–72.

Tremblay, Manon. 2012. "Introduction." In *Women and Legislative Representation: Electoral Systems, Political Parties, and Sex Quotas*, revised and updated edition, edited by Manon Tremblay, 1–22. New York: Palgrave Macmillan.

CHAPTER THREE

Electoral Behaviour

10 What is the explanation for the gender gap?

The gender gap is an observed gap between women and men that is related to the gender regime (see questions 1 and 2). A number of explanations for the gender gap have been proposed. One refers to the socialization process and gender roles. Today, perhaps more than in the past, girls are exposed to hypersexualization, a particular socialization process that shapes girls to respond to the requirements of the private sphere and boys to become active in the public sphere. Gender roles confirm and reinforce this assignment of women to private life and men to public life: women are primarily responsible for the re/production of life (through maternity and mothering), whereas men are the main actors in economic and political life. Because of their association with private life, the logic goes, women address politics from this perspective. For example, women apparently view the welfare state more favourably than do men because it contributes to their quality of life on at least two levels: 1) women benefit more than men from redistribution policies promoted by the welfare state; 2) more women than men work in the public sector, which tends to expand under a welfare state. Furthermore, because they give and maintain life, women supposedly approach politics from the point of view of individuals, whereas men apparently adopt a more abstract and legalistic perspective (on this subject, see Gilligan 1982 and Tronto 1993, among others).

Another explanation is linked to the women's movement and the emergence of feminist consciousness. The women's movement has helped bring to light various mechanisms responsible for the social subordination of women. In general, the transformations that gender roles have undergone, especially since the 1970s – and the underlying discrimination brought to light – fostered feminist consciousness raising. The movement denounced, for example, the unfairness of roles prescribed by sex/gender, female–male income inequality and the feminization of poverty, violence against women, and women's exclusion from democratic institutions. Furthermore, it demanded adjustment mechanisms to encourage equality between women and men, as well as women's autonomy. It was only one step from feminist consciousness raising to a perspective that inspired women to take and act upon political positions. However, Thomas (2012) cautions that the influence of the women's movement on the gender gap may have been overestimated and that it may in fact be quite modest.

Today, the gender gap is recognized in politics as a basic structuring force. It is manifested on a number of levels, ranging from electoral preferences to public policy. For instance, in a number of Western countries, the female electorate leans further left than does the male electorate. However, an intersectional approach shows that things are not that simple: overall, young women lean further left than do young men, but older women lean further right than do men in their age group. When it comes to public policies, women are again often further left than men: they are less in favour of free private enterprise, military expenditures, and the death penalty, for example, and more in favour of public investment in education and healthcare, same-sex marriage, and more women in politics.

Thus, an intersectional approach (taking into account age, ethnic origin, level of education, civil status, income, urban or rural residency, and identification with a political party, for example) would add a wealth of detail to the general portrait. Indeed, Gidengil (2007) maintains that the gender-gap perspective involves a certain number of pitfalls, such as the risk of strengthening female and male stereotypes, generating unrealistic expectations, and, above all, promoting essentialism with regard to women's political behaviours. She therefore pleads for the adoption of a more nuanced and complex analysis of the gender gap that integrates other identity markers, such as class and ethnicity.

BIBLIOGRAPHY

Abendschon, Simone and Stephanie Steinmetz. 2014. "The Gender Gap in Voting Revisited: Women's Party Preferences in a European Context." *Social Politics* 21 (2): 315–44.

Gidengil, Elisabeth. 2007. "Beyond the Gender Gap: Presidential to the Canadian

Political Science Association, Saskatoon." *Canadian Journal of Political Science* 40 (4): 815–31.

Gidengil, Elisabeth, Janine Giles, and Melanee Thomas. 2008. "The Gender Gap in Self-Perceived Understanding of Politics in Canada and the United States." *Politics & Gender* 4 (4): 535–61.

Gilligan, Carol. 1982. *In a Different Voice.* Cambridge: Harvard University Press.

Lizotte, Mary-Kate and Andrew H. Sidman. 2009. "Explaining the Gender Gap in Political Knowledge." *Politics & Gender* 5 (2): 127–51.

Thomas, Melanee. 2012. "The Complexity Conundrum: Why Hasn't the Gender Gap in Subjective Political Competence Closed?" *Canadian Journal of Political Science* 45 (2): 337–58.

Tronto, Joan. 1993. *Moral Boundaries: A Political Argument for an Ethic of Care.* New York: Routledge.

11 Are the political orientations of women and men similar or different?

Many researchers have explored differences in women's and men's political orientations. Their findings have revealed that sex/gender constitutes a significant variable in understanding political orientation on certain subjects. In general, studies indicate that, all other things being equal, women tend to vote to the left and be interested in social questions; men tend to vote more to the right and be interested in economic and military questions. This cleavage is manifested in various ways. For instance, leaders on the right-hand side of the political spectrum find it more difficult to win over female than male voters. In the American presidential election of 1980, fewer women voted for the Republican candidate, Ronald Reagan, than for his Democratic counterpart, incumbent President Jimmy Carter. Eight years later, women turned out in greater numbers at the ballot box for the Democratic candidate, Bill Clinton, than did men. And then there was the thorny relationship between the female electorate and the 2016 Republican presidential candidate, Donald Trump – although it didn't keep him from winning the election. In Canada, since the 1990s, more women have voted for the New Democratic Party and more men for the (Progressive) Conservative Party. In the 2015 Canadian federal election, women's rejection of the Conservative Party led by Stephen Harper was clear, but their vote was split between the New Democratic Party and the Liberal Party, which they found very appealing under the leadership of Justin Trudeau.

This left–women versus right–men gender gap also exists at the level of public policy. Again, all other things being equal – that is, ignoring an intersectional approach sensitive to diverse identity-related markers and their effects on political opinions and behaviours – women are more in favour of a welfare state that redistributes the collective wealth to education, healthcare, ageing populations, and other issues. In other words, they would prefer the state to invest in improving healthcare, creating jobs, or reducing gaps between poor and rich. They have less confidence than do men in the virtues of private enterprise as an economic engine. Few of them support the death penalty and believe that severer punishment is an effective deterrent to crime. More than men, they support the rights of sexual minorities. Not surprisingly, they are more in favour of affirmative measures designed to accomplish true equality between the sexes/genders.

However, as the expression "all other things being equal" indicates, these are general trends. In other words, as an intersectional approach shows, those trends are true when other variables are not taken into account – such as age, education level, civil status, offspring, occupation, income, urban or rural place of residence, religion, and identification with feminism. For instance, older, married women who are mothers, have little education and a subordinate job, and are religious may be further to the right than highly educated young single men without children, with a professional job, and who are not religious. They may also lean further right than would their single, childless female counterparts who are well educated, professionals, and not religious. Women do not form a monolithic electoral bloc (see question 12). Identification or not with feminism may be the exception to this rule, however: young single women without children, with a high education level, professional, and not religious but who also are not feminists may be situated further to the right on the political spectrum than are their elders who are married and mothers, have a low level of education, work in a nonspecialized job, and are religious, but who are feminists. Feminist women even have political orientations closer to feminist men than to nonfeminist women.

To sum up, there is no definitive answer to the question of whether women and men have similar or different political orientations. It all depends on the themes and variables under consideration. What is certain is that we must guard against thinking of the political orientations of women and men as necessarily being polar opposites. Things are more complex than that.

BIBLIOGRAPHY

Conover, Pamela Johnston. 1988. "Feminists and the Gender Gap." *Journal of Politics* 50 (4): 985–1010.

Cook, Elizabeth Adell. 1989. "Measuring Feminist Consciousness." *Women & Politics* 9 (3): 71–88.

– 1993. "Feminist Consciousness and Candidate Preference Among American Women, 1972–1988." *Political Behavior* 15 (3): 227–46.

Cook, Elizabeth Adell, and Clyde Wilcox. 1991. "Feminism and the Gender Gap: A Second Look." *Journal of Politics* 53 (4): 1111–22.

12 Is there a "female vote"?

There has not been in the past, nor is there today, a "female vote" in the sense of women voting 1) in a bloc (or in the same way) or 2) voting for women. It would be a mistake to imagine that immediately after gaining the right to vote (see questions 3 to 7, 77, and 79), women formed a common front to vote in favour of the party or government coalition that had granted them suffrage, out of gratitude, or against the politicians who had opposed it, to take revenge.

In more recent times, women have not voted in a bloc simply because they do not form a homogeneous political entity. Indeed, there is no reason to think that women are a group defined by a single shared criterion; many more factors distance women from each other than bring them together. For instance, some women are poor and others are rich; some define themselves as heterosexuals and others as lesbian or bisexual; many are mothers and many do not have children; they belong both to the ethnocultural majority and to minorities; some women swing to the left politically and others to the right; and so on. Every woman's identity is shaped by many experiences, and these vary from one to another.

What is more, depending on the circumstances, a woman might define herself simply as a woman, or by her sexual preference, or on the basis of her socioprofessional status, residential environment, or ethnocultural community. Not only is identity complex but it changes over time, in space, and according to circumstance. This multiplicity of identity markers may even bolster the idea that women are opposed to each other. At first glance, is it believable that a well-off lesbian living in the city and a poor single mother living in the country share political interests that would lead them to vote in the same way? Young (1994) believes that it is possible to get beyond this impasse and think of women as a group without making them prisoners of their shared attributes. Indeed, women's identities form and change around fluid issues, objects, and situations in perpetual construction and reconstruction. It is a bit like people who form a group as they wait for a bus – a group that dissolves gradually as each person leaves for her or his destination.

The classic model of parliamentary representation adds to the difficulty of thinking of women in terms of a politically significant unit. Unlike sexual minorities or ethnocultural communities that are often geographically concentrated and may thus elect "their" representatives, women are spread throughout the territory, thus removing the possibility of representation based on location and place of residence.

That being said, a particular conjuncture may mobilize the women's movement, and female voters may then express a degree of unity. During the 1971 local elections in Norway, the women's movement mobilized to increase the number of women sitting on municipal councils (Means 1972). The Women's Alliance, a women's political party in Iceland (see question 55), mobilized the female vote in the parliamentary elections from 1983 to 1995 (Styrkársdóttir 1999, 2013). However, these examples arose from exceptional circumstances.

Furthermore, the notion of "female vote" may imply that certain female voters vote for candidates because they are women. This is not a general trend; however, certain female voters may vote this way – for example, those who call themselves feminists or wish to see more women in politics. Feminist voters' favouring of female candidates is not, however, an absolute. For instance, it is unlikely that a feminist voter will support a female candidate who professes opinions contrary to feminist ideas, strictly because she is a woman; it is much more likely that this voter will prefer a male candidate who supports these ideas. In fact, aside from sex/gender, there are other reasons that women may vote for women: the ideas that they promote, the political party for which they are running, or their visibility in the community.

Under certain circumstances, the fact that the candidate is a woman may attract the votes of certain female voters. Studies have shown that having a female candidate encourages some women to vote or, more broadly, to become politically engaged. In list proportional voting systems, the parties attempt to present sociodemographically diversified lists, precisely to please a variety of electoral clienteles, including women. A number of studies even indicate that being a woman may be an electoral asset (see question 16), especially in jurisdictions where politics is reputed to be corrupt.

Finally, the "female vote" – that is, the fact that certain female voters vote for women because of their sex/gender – is not as accentuated during legislative elections (to elect parliamentarians) as during executive elections (for example, for the French or American presidency). The results of studies are not, however, absolutely conclusive. Fortunately, the 2016 American presidential election and its repercussions will offer a rich laboratory for exploring this question in greater depth in coming years.

BIBLIOGRAPHY

Barnes, Tiffany D. and Stephanie M. Burchard. 2013. "'Engendering' Politics: The Impact of Descriptive Representation on Women's Political Engagement in Sub-Saharan Africa." *Comparative Political Studies* 46 (7): 767–90.

Esarey, Justin and Gina Chirillo. 2013. "'Fairer Sex' or Purity Myth? Corruption, Gender, and Institutional Context." *Politics & Gender* 9 (4): 361–89.

Goodyear-Grant, Elizabeth and Julie Croskill. 2011. "Gender Affinity Effects in Vote Choice in Westminster Systems: Assessing 'Flexible' Voters in Canada." *Politics & Gender* 7 (2): 223–50.

Means, Ingunn Norderval. 1972. "Women in Local Politics: The Norwegian Experience." *Canadian Journal of Political Science* 5 (3): 365–88.

Styrkársdóttir, Auður. 1999. "Women's Lists in Iceland – A Response to Political Lethargy." In *Equal Democracies? Gender and Politics in the Nordic Countries*, edited by Christina Bergqvist et al., 88–96. Oslo: Scandinavian University Press.

– 2013. "Iceland: Breaking Male Dominance by Extraordinary Means." In *Breaking Male Dominance in Old Democracies*, edited by Drude Dahlerup and Monique Leyenaar, 24–25. Oxford: Oxford University Press.

Young, Iris Marion. 1994. "Gender as Seriality: Thinking about Women as a Social Collective." *Signs* 19 (3): 713–38.

13 Do voters perceive female and male politicians differently?

A basic trend emerging from research results indicates that they do. Gender role models, the very ones that structure the socialization process, also inspire the electorate's perceptions of politicians. In other words, voters evaluate women and men in politics, including their character traits, behaviours, and skills, according to the stereotypes that shape the female and male genders. For example, it is expected that a male politician will be rational, ambitious, determined, and dynamic, even slightly aggressive; make objective and independent judgments; and know how and be able to have his decisions heard – and accepted. Although voters expect a female politician to have some of the traits and behaviours that they value in male decision makers (such as objectivity and rational judgment, determination, and the capacity to have decisions taken into account), they also admit that she may sometimes manifest typically female traits and behaviours: to not be totally objective in her decisions (to take a position), to be emotional (to be nervous, even to cry), to be humane in her decisions (to listen to others and understand them, to show compassion), to be calm, gentle, warm and smiling, conciliatory, and so on. Female politicians are also perceived as being more accessible to the population and more trustworthy, understanding, empathetic, and sensitive. They seem to be less inclined to engage in power struggles. They appear to be more pragmatic, concrete, and concerned with details and with the practical effects of their decisions on the population, less materialistic, and less disinterested than are men. In short, voters think that men have rational character traits and behaviours, and women have rational *and* emotional traits and behaviours (Pew Research Center 2015). The consequence is that female politicians often find themselves caught in the middle: they must bow to feminine stereotypes but also take on certain masculine traits and behaviours, depending on the circumstances.

Voters use gender role stereotypes to assess the skills of female and male politicians, particularly when little information is available about them. Thus, in general, men are perceived as more competent in economics, public works (construction and roadwork, for example), foreign and military affairs, and natural resource management, among others. Women are perceived as being more competent in education, healthcare, culture, community services, childcare, care for the aged and disabled, and so on. There are certainly overlapping areas, such as communications, the environment, justice, and tourism, in which voters see women and men coping equally well – though not necessarily under all circumstances (for example, a man may be perceived as being more competent to resolve a crisis that requires imposing force).

These stereotypes, in part modelled by the media (see question 27), affect voters' decision-making process (see questions 14 to 17). However, they are not impermeable, and other forces, such as the electoral situation, the questions on the election agenda, and identification with a political party, may intervene.

It is worth adding a word on the perception of lesbians in politics: are they perceived according to their sex/gender, their sexual preference, both, or do they fall prey to lesbophobic prejudices (see question 15)? At first glance, it seems that lesbians do not suffer from double discrimination – as women and as lesbians (Herrick and Thomas 1999). This may be, as Doan and Haider-Markel (2010: 86) maintain, because gender and sexual orientation intersect in such a way that "the masculine characteristics stereotypically associated with lesbians by heterosexual women interact to offset, and even compliment [*sic*], the gender stereotypes associated with female political candidates." As a consequence, openly lesbian candidates (who are often seen as masculine) may be perceived as being more competent in military matters than are openly gay candidates (often stereotyped as effeminate). The results of a recent study by Haider-Markel and Moore Bright (2014) lead to a similar observation: far from a disadvantage, being openly lesbian may help to bring in more resources to conduct an electoral campaign – whence the importance of conducting analyses that adopt an intersectional approach.

BIBLIOGRAPHY

Doan, Alesha E. and Donald P. Haider-Markel. 2010. "The Role of Intersectional Stereotypes on Evaluations of Gay and Lesbian Political Candidates." *Politics & Gender* 6 (1): 63–91.

Dolan, Kathleen A. 2004. *Voting for Women. How the Public Evaluates Women Candidates.* Boulder: Westview Press.

Haider-Markel, Donald P. and Chelsie Lynn Moore Bright. 2014. "Lesbian Candidates and Officeholders." In *Women and Elective Office: Past, Present, and Future*, edited by Sue Thomas and Clyde Wilcox, 3rd ed., 253–72. New York: Oxford University Press.

Hayes, Danny. 2011. "When Gender and Party Collide: Stereotyping in Candidate Trait Attribution." *Politics & Gender* 7 (2): 133–65.

Herrick, Rebekah and Sue Thomas. 1999. "The Effects of Sexual Orientation on Citizen Perceptions of Candidate Visibility." In *Gays and Lesbians in the Democratic Process*, edited by Ellen D.B. Riggle and Barry Tadlock, 170–91. New York: Columbia University Press.

Kahn, Kim Fridkin. 1996. *The Political Consequences of Being a Woman. How Stereotypes Influence the Conduct and Consequences of Political Campaigns*. New York: Columbia University Press.

Matland, Richard E. and Gune Murat Tezcur. 2011. "Women as Candidates: An Experimental Study in Turkey?" *Politics & Gender* 7 (3): 365–90.

Pew Research Center. 2015. "Women and Leadership: Public Says Women are Equally Qualified, but Barriers Persist," accessed 9 June 2016, http://www.pewsocialtrends.org/2015/01/14/women-and-leadership/.

14 Is the electorate sexist toward female candidates?

As a rule, the electorate does not discriminate against women who aspire to be politicians. Here again, not all voters are on the same page: just as there are female voters who vote for female candidates solely because they are women (see question 12), there are male voters who refuse to support female candidates because they feel that women have no place in politics. However, studies seem to show that both of these positions are marginal (though not distributed randomly in the population, as an intersectional reading of the electorate reveals) and may balance out in the end. It is also possible that sexism is expressed subtly rather than manifestly; for example, female candidates may be perceived as less competent because their presence in politics is the result of a quota system, whereas male candidates are perceived as competent as they are "naturally made" to be politicians – just as they are to be mechanics!

In an international study, Inglehart and Norris (2003) unearthed factors to explain why voters may support women. For instance, an egalitarian attitude toward gender roles is inseparable from support for female politicians. These attitudes are more likely to be manifested in postindustrial societies than in postcommunist and developing societies, as postindustrial societies are also the most developed socioeconomically and the most advanced socioculturally. Furthermore, younger people, particularly young women, tend to have more egalitarian attitudes. Culture – notably, egalitarian attitudes toward women–men relations – is important in this sense because it is more decisive than a proportional voting system in accounting for the relative number of women in parliaments (see question 19).

Yet, there is no cause-and-effect relationship between, on the one hand, a post-industrial society and egalitarian attitudes with regard to gender roles and, on the other hand, a high proportion of women parliamentarians. In this sense, the United States is a counterexample. Even though the US is highly developed socioeconomically and advanced with regard to attitudes toward gender roles according to the classification established by Inglehart and Norris (2003), American women must nevertheless overcome a number of prejudices inscribed in a narrow reading of gender roles before they can win elections.

In short, voters generally are not sexist toward female candidates, and these candidates benefit from egalitarian attitudes toward gender roles. Nevertheless, they cannot base their election solely on such predispositions.

BIBLIOGRAPHY

Brooks, Deborah Jordan. 2013. *He Runs, She Runs: Why Gender Stereotypes Do Not Harm Women Candidates*. Princeton: Princeton University Press.

Fulton, Sarah A. 2012. "Running Backwards and in High Heels: The Gendered Quality Gap and Incumbent Electoral Success." *Political Research Quarterly* 65 (2): 303–14.

Goodyear-Grant, Elizabeth. 2013. *Gendered News: Media Coverage and Electoral Politics in Canada*. Vancouver: UBC Press.

Inglehart, Ronald and Pippa Norris. 2003. *Rising Tide: Gender Equality and Cultural Change around the World*. Cambridge: Cambridge University Press. See, in particular, 127–46.

McDermott, Monika L. 2016. *Masculinity, Femininity, and American Political Behavior*. New York: Oxford University Press.

Valdini, Melody Ellis. 2013. "Electoral Institutions and the Manifestation of Bias: The Effect of the Personal Vote on the Representation of Women." *Politics & Gender* 9 (1): 76–92.

15 Is the electorate lesbophobic?

"Lesbophobia" is defined as hostility toward, or even hate for, lesbians. The question is, does the electorate refuse to vote for lesbians who have publicly stated their same-sex sexual preference? Answering this question is not easy, as there are as of yet very few studies on lesbian, gay, bisexual, and trans (LGBT) people in politics, and even fewer specifically on lesbians. To the paucity of knowledge is added the rarity of LGBT politicians. Of course, over the last few years lesbians and gays have assumed the highest government positions. On the international scene, Jóhanna Sigurðardóttir, prime minister of Iceland from 2009 to 2013, was the first head of government in the world to publicly reveal her nonheteronormative preference. A few years later, prime ministers Elio Di Rupo (Belgium, 2001–14), Xavier Bettel (Luxembourg, elected 2013), Leo Varadkar (Ireland, elected 2017) did the same thing. In Canada, the former premier of Ontario, Kathleen Wynne, and the premier of Prince Edward Island, Wade MacLauchlan, are open about their nonheteronormative sexuality (see question 99).

The results of the few works available on LGBT politicians suggest that their nonheteronormative preferences do not sound the knell for their political careers. First, their visibility has grown since the 1990s, although there are fewer lesbians than gays (just as there are fewer female than male heterosexual politicians). Their increased visibility no doubt has something to do with the interpretation of LGBT struggles in the light of human rights discourse ("LGBT rights are human rights").

Second, public opinion is less and less resistant to LGBT people running for office (Environics Institute 2012: 41; Gallup 2015; Haider-Markel 2010: 39–41). That said, in Canada and the United States, a number of surveys reveal that about one quarter of the electorate remains fiercely opposed to voting for LGBT candidates. Those voters would, in any case, be unlikely to vote for LGBT candidates as many of them support conservative parties (the Republican Party in the United States or the Conservative Party in Canada), and LGBT candidates usually run for progressive parties (the Democratic Party in the United States, the New Democratic and Liberal parties in Canada). In the United States, LGBT-phobic voters have the following profile: aside from their penchant for the Grand Old Party, they are typically male, white, have less education, are practising Christians (often "born again" and Evangelist), and rural dwellers. This may explain why in Canada, as Perrella and her colleagues (2012) have shown, less than 10 per cent of the LGBT electorate votes for the Conservative Party. However, things may change in coming years with the ideological "reframing" undertaken by the Conservative Party following its electoral defeat in 2015 and the departure of Stephen Harper – especially because the LGBTory, a group of LGBT people inside the Conservative Party, are now open about their preference and working to bring in LGBT voters who share conservative values.

Third, voters are no more hostile toward openly lesbian candidates than they are toward openly gay candidates. This is an important fact, as it seems to indicate that openly lesbian politicians do not face double discrimination – as both women and lesbians. In addition, women are less likely than men to assess openly lesbian candidates via negative stereotypes. This fact is also important because it feeds the idea of a "female vote" (see question 12) according to which female voters would be more sympathetic to openly lesbian politicians than would male voters. It is possible that this generally positive perception of lesbians and gays in politics has something to do with their overall positive media coverage – at least as long as they demonstrate their homonormative respectability (Lalancette and Tremblay, 2016).

Fourth, LGBT candidates in general, and lesbian candidates in particular, develop strategies to minimize the negative effects of the LGBT-phobic electorate in general and the lesbophobic electorate in particular. One strategy consists of running in ridings where there are few LGBT-phobic and lesbophobic voters or where voters are actually favourable to LGBT candidates, such as university districts. Another strategy for these candidates is to reveal their sexual preference only after they have won the election. Everitt and Camp (2014) note that LGBT people in Canadian politics have used these strategies. A third strategy consists of turning LGBT-phobic insults to advantage. Harvey Milk, the first openly gay elected official in California (Elaine Noble was the first openly lesbian or gay person elected to a state legislature, in Massachusetts, in 1974), liked to start his speeches by saying, "My name is Harvey Milk and I'm here to recruit you." He was thus flipping the LGBT-phobic insult that lesbians and gays had to recruit children because they could not reproduce in order to empower LGBT people.

Fifth, research shows that once elected, openly lesbian politicians represent LGBT people – that is, their political speech and actions defend and promote demands, needs, and interests associated with LGBT communities (such as adopting antidiscrimination laws for LGBT people; fighting intimidation, harassment, and violence; and acquiring equality rights). Representation of LGBT people also results in a transformation of attitudes among the public and the political class. For instance, in addition to acting as a model for young (and not-so-young) lesbians, an openly lesbian politician challenges the prejudices that circulate in the popular imagination, perhaps even leading her heterosexual colleagues to support legislative provisions in favour of LGBT people in general, and lesbians in particular.

In short, the answer to the question "Is the electorate lesbophobic?" is encouraging, according to the results of the few studies available on the subject: although a small portion of the electorate is certainly lesbophobic (and, more generally, LGBT-phobic), openly lesbian politicians develop strategies to forestall the negative effects of lesbophobia on their careers and on their mandate to represent LGBT communities in general, and lesbian communities in particular.

BIBLIOGRAPHY

Doan, Alesha E. and Donald P. Haider-Markel. 2010. "The Role of Intersectional Stereotypes on Evaluations of Political Candidates." *Politics & Gender* 6 (1): 63–91.

Environics Institute. 2012. *AmericasBarometer: The Public Speaks on Democracy and Governance Across the Americas. Canada 2012. Final Report*, accessed 8 August 2016, http://www.vanderbilt.edu/lapop/canada/Canada-2012-Report.pdf.

Everitt, Joanna and Michael Camp. 2014. "In Versus Out: LGBT Politicians in Canada." *Journal of Canadian Studies* 48 (1): 226–51.

Gallup. 2015. "Support for Nontraditional Candidates Varies by Religion," accessed 5 August 2016, http://www.gallup.com/poll/183791/support-nontraditional-candidates-varies-religion.aspx.

Haider-Markel, Donald P. 2010. *Out and Running: Gay and Lesbian Candidates, Elections, and Policy Representation*. Washington: Georgetown University Press.

Haider-Markel, Donald and Chelsie Lynn Moore Bright. 2014. "Lesbian Candidates and Officeholders." In *Women and Elective Office: Past, Present, and Future*, edited by Sue Thomas and Clyde Wilcox, 3rd ed., 253–72. New York: Oxford University Press.

Herrick, Rebekah. 2010. "The Legislative Effectiveness of Gay and Lesbian Legislators." *Journal of Women, Politics & Policy* 31 (3): 243–59.

Lalancette, Mireille and Manon Tremblay. 2016. "Media Framing of LGBT Politicians:

Is Sexual Mediation at Work?" Paper presented at the Canadian Political Science Association conference, workshop titled "LGBT People and Electoral Politics in Canada,"
    University of Calgary, 1 June.
LGBTory Canada, accessed 11 June 2016, http://www.lgbtory.ca/.
Litwin, Fred. 2015. *Conservative Confidential: Inside the Fabulous Blue Tent*. Toronto:
    NorthernBlues Books.
Perrella, Andrea M.L., Steven D. Brown, and Barry J. Kay. 2012. "Voting Behaviour
    among the Gay, Lesbian, Bisexual and Transgendered Electorate." *Canadian Journal
    of Political Science* 45 (1): 89–117.
Pierceson, Jason. 2016. *Sexual Minorities and Politics: An Introduction*. Lanham: Rowman and Littlefield.
Reynolds, Andrew. 2013. "Representation and Rights: The Impact of LGBT Legislators
    in Comparative Perspective." *American Political Science Review* 107 (2): 259–74.

16 Is it possible that being a woman is an advantage in an election?

Being a woman can be an advantage in an election (although it can also be
a millstone). Voters in the West have expressed cynicism about politics for
a number of years; some feel that parliaments do not represent the population and that the political class (composed mainly of men) is not held
accountable and is prone to splashy scandals. Because historically they have
been kept out of politics and have accessed the political arena quite recently,
women are sometimes perceived as being able to update governance and
the political class. This is even truer because certain character traits attributed to women by the electorate (such as honesty; see question 13) contribute to their being seen as saviours.

Certain circumstances and events seem to play in women's favour. In the
United States, the 1992 elections have often been called "the Year of the
Woman": in that year, the proportion of women running for office and
elected to Congress jumped. A number of possible explanations were proposed to explain these gains, including the Anita Hill–Clarence Thomas
controversy. In the early 1990s, President George H.W. Bush nominated
Clarence Thomas to sit on the Supreme Court of the United States. This
nomination caused a stir when Anita Hill, a law professor at the University

of Oklahoma, accused Thomas of having sexually harassed her when she was working for him a few years earlier. Hill had to explain her allegations to the Senate Judiciary Committee, composed only of men and from which women politicians were openly barred (see Conway, Steuernagel, and Ahern 1997). The spectacle of a woman facing this legislative committee investigating her sex life as if they were conducting an inquisition clearly brought to light not only the exclusion of women from the political scene but the misogynist culture in US politics, and it helped to mobilize the women's movement in a drive to increase the number of women in politics. The 2006 American election also saw some progress in the proportion of women in Congress, notably because pulling the American military out of Iraq was a major issue and voters saw women as being in favour of this plan. There is no doubt that the 2016 presidential election caused a shock with regard to women's participation in American politics, as Hillary Rodham Clinton embodied the hope of a (more) egalitarian United States for women and other minorities, and Donald Trump seemed to stand for a colonialist, sexist, and LGBT-phobic heritage. In short, the assets (and limitations) inherent to women's candidacies depend greatly on the circumstances and themes on the electoral agenda.

The circumstances and themes on the electoral agenda may also play against women. For instance, if an election campaign is dominated by economic, international relations, or security issues, certain segments of the electorate may believe that women candidates do not have the skills to manage those issues and vote for a man instead. Finally, sometimes women politicians deliberately exploit gender stereotypes. In the 2007 French presidential election, for example, Ségolène Royal (candidate for the Parti socialiste) made strategic use of her gender, and Marine Le Pen (candidate for the Front national in the first round) did the same in the 2012 French presidential election. Thomas and Lambert (2013) observe that quite a few parliamentarians in Canada have seen their parental status as an asset to their political career and therefore something to highlight through political marketing techniques.

BIBLIOGRAPHY

Brooks, Deborah Jordan. 2013. *He Runs, She Runs: Why Gender Stereotypes Do Not Harm Women Candidates*. Princeton: Princeton University Press.

Conway, M. Margaret, Gertrude A. Steuernagel, and David W. Ahern. 1997. *Women and Political Participation: Cultural Change in the Political Arena.* Washington: CQ Press. See, in particular, 106–7.

Holman, Mirya, Jennifer L. Merolla and Elizabeth J. Zechmeister. 2011. "Sex, Stereotypes, and Security: A Study of the Effects of Terrorist Threat on Assessments of Female Leadership." *Journal of Women, Politics & Policy* 32 (3): 173–92.

Sineau, Mariette. 2010. "Was Segolene Royal Defeated by the Women's Vote? The Gender Gap in the 2007 Presidential Election." *Modern & Contemporary France* 18 (4): 491–503.

17 Do women who are elected to office change their female electors' political orientations and behaviours?

It seems that they do. According to High-Pippert and Comer (1998), women represented by a woman are more interested in politics, become more involved in politics, and feel more skilled and effective. In this study, American women represented in Congress by a woman manifested more interest in politics than did those represented by a man. They were also more inclined to participate in political activities, to think that they had the skills to influence politics, and that they could do so effectively. Campbell and Wolbrecht (2006; see also Wolbrecht and Campbell 2007) obtained similar results in a study conducted in 1999 among adolescent girls attending 124 private and public schools in the United States: the more visibility female politicians had in the media, the more these teenagers wanted to be active in politics in the future. The results of a third study, this one conducted by Atkeson and Carrillo (2007), also showed that the presence of women politicians may change female voters' political orientations and behaviours: more-feminized legislative assemblies encourage the female population to develop a sense of trust in political governance. They also help to improve democracy, not only because representative institutions better reflect the diversity of the population (see questions 33, 34, and 40) but also because trust in the ruling class increases. In short, women in politics may have an empowering effect on girls and women.

The results of these studies buttress one of the arguments put forward to justify increasing the number of women in politics: they act as models (see question 40). By simply being active, female politicians send girls and women the message that politics is an accessible option for them. A sense of being skilful and effective in politics is a prerequisite to running for office and, eventually, getting elected (see question 28). In addition, the presence of women indicates that men do not hold a monopoly on political roles and functions. It is also possible that the influence exercised by female politicians on their female electors (and, more generally, on all women) varies when an intersectional approach is used. For example, will a white female politician exert the same influence over white female voters as over, for instance, Aboriginal or black voters? Such questions remain to be explored.

BIBLIOGRAPHY

Atkeson, Lonna Rae and Nancy Carrillo. 2007. "More Is Better: The Influence of Collective Female Descriptive Representation on External Efficacy." *Politics & Gender* 3 (1): 79–101.

Campbell, David E. and Christina Wolbrecht. 2006. "See Jane Run: Women Politicians as Role Models for Adolescents." *Journal of Politics* 68 (2): 233–47.

Fridkin, Kim L. and Patrick J. Kenney. 2014. "How the Gender of U.S. Senators Influences People's Understanding and Engagement in Politics." *Journal of Politics* 76 (4): 1017–31.

High-Pippert, Angela and John Comer. 1998. "Female Empowerment: The Influence of Women Representing Women." *Women & Politics* 19 (4): 53–66.

Wolbrecht, Christina and David E. Campbell. 2007. "Leading by Example: Female Members of Parliament as Political Role Models." *American Journal of Political Science* 51 (4): 921–39.

CHAPTER FOUR

Obstacles to the Election of Women

18 What steps does a woman seeking election have to take?

Every person, woman or man, who seeks election to parliament must pass through four stages: eligibility, recruitment, selection, and election. In other words, to sit in parliament, a person must have the right (or legal capacity) to do so, decide to run, be selected by a political party, and be chosen by voters to represent them. Eligibility and recruitment thus involve an individual's capacity and desire to run for office, whereas selection and election depend on the desire manifested by parties and the electorate to have that individual be elected. Gaining access to parliament may thus be thought of according to the economic model of supply (eligibility and recruitment) and demand (selection and election). This process does not take place in a vacuum but is inscribed within a broader narrative composed of socio-cultural (such as socialization and gender roles), economic (for example, employment structured by sex/gender), and political (the party and voting systems, for example) regimes. Figure 1 illustrates this process. Eligibility is the only stage that does not involve obstacles for women.

Eligibility is the legal capacity to run for office in an election. Usually, this capacity is subject to certain criteria, including citizenship and age; for example, a person who is not a British citizen or who is twelve years old may not run for office in the House of Commons of the United Kingdom of Great Britain and Northern Ireland. Other criteria may also apply, such as those regarding place of residency and birth. To run in European elections, a person must reside in the member state that she or he hopes to represent. To run for president of the United States, a person must have been born in that country. Eligibility is no longer a factor in limiting the presence of women in parliaments, as women may vote and run for office in national

Figure 1

The stages leading to election to parliament

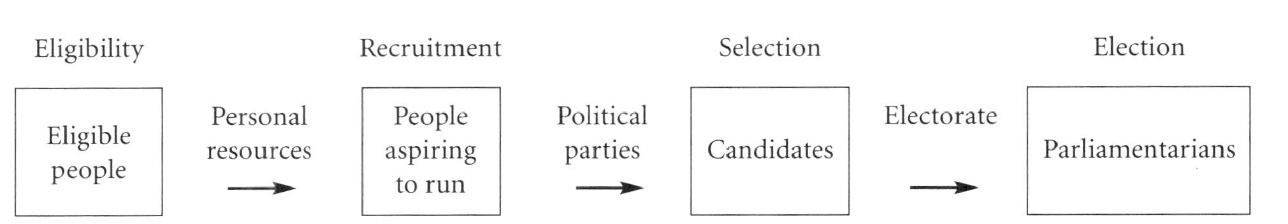

legislative elections in almost all countries (see question 6). Nevertheless, financial requirements linked to the deposit that candidates must pay (for example, in Turkish national elections, candidates must pay a nonrefundable deposit equivalent to US$30,000; in Armenia, candidates must deposit an amount equivalent to US$21,000, which is reimbursed if they are elected or obtain at least 4 per cent of the votes) may still play against disadvantaged women's eligibility in economic terms.

Recruitment "consists of identifying in the population as a whole the people who are interested in political activity and have the resources to take part in this activity; the idea is to form a pool of potential candidates likely to become engaged to various degrees in political governance" (Tremblay and Pelletier 1995: 13, our translation). Therefore, according to this reasoning, if women are not well represented in politics it is because too few of them have the resources needed, both material (money or access to a means of transportation, for example) and nonmaterial (such as education and profession, time, and networks, among other things, but also self-confidence, essential to political commitment; see question 28), to become candidates and make themselves known to political elites. It goes without saying that in an intersectional perspective, these resources are not distributed by chance among women but respond to certain regimes of oppression (such as social class or ethnicity). Achieving fairer representation by women in parliaments would thus be simply a question of time (for a critical perspective, see question 31) because socialization and gender roles are changing, more women are attending university and working in professions associated with a career in politics, and they may have greater access to alternative structures (such as day-care centres) to help them perform their domestic and maternal responsibilities. Until these changes occur, however, recruitment is a stage that poses real difficulties to women.

Selection consists of political parties choosing people who will run for them in an election. In other words, it is the demand expressed by the party elites for candidates. Recruitment and selection are closely linked. To use an analogy, recruitment corresponds to all the people who respond to a job offer, and selection refers to the list of people chosen for an interview (and election is equivalent to one person being hired). According to Norris and Lovenduski (1989), the selection process is not neutral; it is based on a set of values that define the ideal profile of a candidate. This profile varies from party to party – conservative and green parties, for instance, do not seek out the same types of candidates. Apparently, the parties that dominate the political chessboard favour candidates whose traits correspond more to masculine socialization and roles than to women's experiences (see questions 20, 21, and 23). Aside from these informal expectations, money (see question 25) and networks – along with the conditions and pace of turnover of political personnel – in conjunction with the voting system and parties' ideology (see questions 20 to 23), also pose difficulties to women wishing to be selected as candidates.

Sometimes it takes a great deal of money to capture a nomination, particularly if there is a real chance of winning the riding in the election. In general, women have more modest financial means than do men – although one cannot deduce that because women are generally less wealthy than men, they cannot be elected (see question 25). Networks also pose a problem, in that women may not have the relevant – and indispensable – support in civil society and within their political party to be selected as candidates. It is not that they are bereft of networks, but their relationships may be concentrated in cultural and sociocommunity circles, whereas support of a financial and political nature is a more significant asset when it comes to selection. It should be added that financial capacities and networks vary widely from woman to woman.

Turnover of political personnel – the conditions under which it occurs and the pace at which it happens – is also a source of difficulty for women, as parliamentarians who wish to keep their seats are generally selected by their party to run again. Because sitting parliamentarians are more likely to be men than women, the potential for a woman to be selected for the first time is reduced further. However, the impact of lack of turnover depends, in part, on the voting system: if a political party can select a number of candidates per riding rather than just one, in principle it will be more inclined to seek balance between sitting parliamentarians (a category into which many men fall) and new recruits (more likely to be women). The vast majority of researchers on women in politics agree that parties are more inclined to select women to run if they are among a number of candidates (rather than just one) running in a riding (see question 21). That said, a party's propensity to select female candidates also depends on its ideological positioning and the demands of its electoral base: traditionally, left-wing parties are more open to women than are right-wing parties, although this is not written in stone. In short, selection involves major obstacles, and women have fewer resources than do men to overcome them – although, once again, women tend to have widely varying resources.

Election is the procedure by which citizens who meet certain conditions designate, usually through a ballot, the people who will represent them in parliament. This last step in the path toward legislative power involves certain impediments to women in terms of turnover of parliamentarians (see question 26), media treatment of female candidates (see question 27), and voters' reaction to them (see questions 13 to 16). The voting system may be added to this list, although the greatest obstacles that it poses to women are manifested more indirectly, during the selection process (see questions 20 and 23). Nevertheless, voting systems vary in their requirements: as a rule, the proportion of valid votes needed for election (the representation threshold) is lower in proportional than majority voting systems. Female candidates may thus face more of an uphill battle in the latter systems, but the results of studies are not absolutely convincing in this regard. Further research would have to be conducted to attain conclusive results about the discriminatory effects on women of the representation thresholds of various voting systems.

In sum, the steps of recruitment, selection, and election pose obstacles to women who wish to be elected to a seat in parliament, and these difficulties flow from broader sociocultural, economic, and political factors (see question 19).

BIBLIOGRAPHY

"Candidate Selection: Parties and Legislatures in a New Era." 2016. Special issue, *Government & Opposition* 51(3): 351–528.

Carroll, Susan J. and Kira Sanbonmatsu. 2013. *More Women Can Run: Gender and Pathways to the State Legislatures*. New York: Oxford University Press.

Cheng, Christine and Margit Tavits. 2011. "Informal Influences in Selecting Female Political Candidates." *Political Research Quarterly* 64 (2): 460–71.

"Critical Perspectives on Gender and Politics: Gender and Political Recruitment." 2015. Special Issue, *Politics & Gender* 11 (4): 746–76.

Crowder-Meyer, Melody. 2013. "Gendered Recruitment Without Trying: How Local Party Recruiters Affect Women's Representation." *Politics & Gender* 9 (4): 390–413.

Fortin-Rittberger, Jessica and Berthold Rittberger. 2015. "Nominating Women for Europe: Exploring the Role of Political Parties' Recruitment Procedures for European Parliament Elections." *European Journal of Political Research* 54, 4: 767–83.

Hinojosa, Magda. 2009. "'Whatever the Party Asks of Me': Women's Political Representation in Chile's Union Democrata Independiente."*Politics & Gender* 5 (3): 377–407.

Inter-Parliamentary Union. 2016. "Turkey (Grand National Assembly of Turkey): Electoral System," accessed 26 February 2018, http://archive.ipu.org/parline-e/reports/2323 _B.htm.

– 2017. "Armenia (National Assembly): General Information about the Parliament," accessed 26 February 2018, http://archive.ipu.org/parline-e/reports/2013_A.htm.

Lühiste, Maarja and Meryl Kenny. 2016), "Pathways to Power: Women's Representation in the 2014 European Parliament Elections." *European Journal of Political Research*, 55, 3: 626–41.

Matland, Richard E. and Emilie Lilliefeldt. 2014. "The Effect of Preferential Voting on Women's Representation." In *Representation: The Case of Women*, edited by Maria C. Escobar-Lemmon and Michelle M. Taylor-Robinson, 79–102. New York: Oxford University Press.

Matland, Richard E. and Kathleen A. Montgomery. 2003. "Recruiting Women to National Legislatures: A General Framework with Applications to Post-Communist Democracies." In *Women's Access to Political Power in Post-Communist Europe*, edited by Richard E. Matland and Kathleen A. Montgomery, 19–42. Oxford: Oxford University Press.

Norris, Pippa and Joni Lovenduski. 1989. "Pathways to Parliament." *Talking Politics* 1 (3): 90–94.

Tremblay, Manon and Réjean Pelletier. 1995. *Que font-elles en politique?* Sainte-Foy: Les Presses de l'Université Laval.

19 Which factors have an impact on the proportion of women in parliaments?

A number of factors have an impact on the proportion of women in parliaments. These factors are cultural, socioeconomic, and political in nature, and they intersect with the steps of eligibility, recruitment, selection, and election described in question 18. For example, how gender roles (cultural factor) are conceived influences whether or not women will be granted the right to vote and to run for office (see question 8). The human development index (socioeconomic factor) gives some clues to the state of the supply (or recruitment) of and demand for (or selection of) female candidates. The voting system and the parties (political factors) affect women's capacity to be elected to parliament to the extent that the rules of the electoral game frame the parties' strategies for selecting their candidates (see questions 20 and 23). Even though they are separate factors, they intermingle and overlap to pave women's path to politics (Tremblay 2012).

Culture refers to the values, norms, beliefs, and attitudes that underpin a society and its institutions, and that shape its population's ways of living, speaking, and doing. Religion, education, and conceptions of gender roles are the main cultural factors used in studies about what determines the proportion of women in parliaments. In general, Protestantism as the dominant religion (as opposed to other religions), women's access to university studies, and an egalitarian conception of gender roles are the variables associated with women's access to parliament. What is more, research has shown that culture – in particular, an egalitarian conception of relationships between women and men – has more impact on the proportion of women in parliaments than does the voting system (including a list proportional voting system).

Socioeconomic factors include the conditions that make it possible to envisage a career in politics by affecting the supply of candidates (see question 18). One idea has it that there are few women in politics because they are underrepresented in the circles from which parties draw their potential candidates. Improvements to women's socioeconomic conditions should thus foster an increase in the proportion of women in parliament. The variables considered in this category include, among others, the type of society (agricultural, industrial, or postindustrial), the human development index, the fertility rate, the proportion of women in the labour force, the woman–man income ratio, per capita gross domestic product, public expenditures in education and health, and urbanization rate. Studies have shown that the proportion of women in parliaments is positively influenced by factors such as their labour-force participation (notably in specialized jobs), a high human development index, a postindustrial society, and a developed welfare state. However, the impact of socioeconomic factors on the proportion of women in parliament seems to be less important than are the impacts of cultural and political factors.

Two political factors concern the demand (selection and election) for candidates (see question 18): women's political rights and the profile of the political regime. The first, referring to women's political citizenship, has been measured mainly by the year when women were granted the right to vote in national legislative elections. It is not clear, however, that there is a link between this gain and the proportion of women in parliaments (see question 9).

A number of variables have been used to explore the impact of the political regime on the proportion of women parliamentarians, including state structure (unitary or federal), structure of the parliament (single or bicameral, number of seats, and maximum duration of a legislative session, for example), legislative careers (including turnover of parliamentarians), the party system (the number of parties presenting candidates, the number of parties represented in the parliament, the ideology of the parties forming the government, the process of selecting candidates, and so on), and the electoral system itself (the voting system, the number of seats per riding, the nature of the lists – closed or open – and other factors).

For instance, a low rate of turnover of parliamentarians has long been identified as an obstacle to women's access to legislative assemblies (see questions 18 and 26). A parliament in which a number of parties are represented would offer female candidates more chance of being elected than would a parliament in which two parties hold the majority of seats. Political parties situated to the left and in the centre of the ideological spectrum offer women better prospects for election than do right-wing parties, particularly if they form the government. Obviously, quotas have the capacity to feminize parliaments, but they must have certain characteristics in order to do so (see questions 43 and 44). Finally, the voting system is a very important determinant of the feminization rate of parliaments: majority voting systems discourage the election of women, whereas proportional voting systems favour them (see questions 20 to 23).

BIBLIOGRAPHY

Elder, Laurel. 2012. "The Partisan Gap Among Women State Legislators." *Journal of Women, Politics & Policy* 33 (1): 65–85.

Joshi, Devin K. and Kara Kingma. 2013. "The Uneven Representation of Women in Asian Parliaments: Explaining Variation Across the Region." *African and Asian Studies* 12 (4): 352–72.

Paxton, Pamela, Melanie Hughes, and Matthew A. Painter II. 2010. "Growth in Women's
    Political Representation: A Longitudinal Exploration of Democracy, Electoral System
    and Gender Quotas." *European Journal of Political Research* 49 (1): 25–52.
Ruedin, Didier. 2012. "The Representation of Women in National Parliaments: A Cross-
    National Comparison." *European Sociological Review* 28 (1): 96–109.
Tremblay, Manon. 2012. "Introduction." In *Women and Legislative Representation: Elec-
    toral Systems, Political Parties, and Sex Quotas,* revised and updated edition, edited
    by Manon Tremblay 1–22. New York: Palgrave Macmillan.

20 Why are majority voting systems less likely to contribute to the election of women?

Majority voting systems, it is said, discourage the election of women to parliaments more than do proportional voting systems due not so much to
the system, as such, but to how candidates are selected and how many seats
are in a riding. In most cases, majority voting systems are single constituency – that is, each riding is represented by a single person. This means
that each political party designates a single candidate per riding and not
several, as it would in a proportional voting system. In majority voting systems, the person who wishes to run for a political party in a given riding is
judged as an individual and not as a member of a larger team. Because only
one person per riding and per political party may be designated, there is
great pressure to select a candidate perceived as the most likely to win. Not
everyone has equal value in this game, however, as an informal model apparently frames the process of selecting a candidate – a model that, according to Norris and Lovenduski (1989), is a better fit for men's experiences
than for women's. For instance, all things being equal, the candidate selected
will have a high degree of education and a high-level job; will be heterosexual, married, and have children; will have been active and in positions
of responsibility in the party for a long time; and so on. This profile does
vary by political party, however; a left-wing party would likely build a different candidate profile than would a right-wing party. The rules of the political game thus do not deliberately discriminate against women on the
basis of their sex/gender. Rather, they may offer an opportunity for indirect
(or systemic) discrimination linked to the fact that women are less likely
to correspond to the "winning" candidate profile.

What is more, a good number of the people who participate in the selection of candidates are male, which poses another obstacle to women. One theory related to the consequences of not belonging to a dominant group offers some dimensions for understanding why (male) political elites would be less likely to choose a woman as a candidate (and, it must be said, especially a woman who is not from the "majority" – not white, not wealthy, not heterosexual, and so on), rather than a man. According to this theory, the members of an organization evaluate people who do not belong to their group through the prism of stereotypes: these outsiders are perceived through unilaterally attributed, generalized characteristics that overlook personal qualities. For example, one stereotype has it that women are too timid to perform in politics. So, when a woman seeks a party's nomination in a riding, and most of the people who select candidates are men, she will be evaluated on the basis not of her intrinsic personal skills but of stereotypes linked to her sex/gender (or the colour of her skin, her ethnic origin, or other characteristics); to use the above example, they will see her as too shy to step up, confront the electorate, and win. Bjarnegård (2013) reinforces this model with the notion of "homosocial capital": people who resemble each other assemble and form networks that constitute essential capital for accessing societal power. Yet, whereas men's homosocial capital is strong enough that they can win political power without enlisting the support of women, the opposite is not true; women must "heterosocialize" their capital by investing in male networks. Simply put, whereas men have networks that enable them to capture political power without women, women cannot count solely on other women; they must form alliances with men.

Candidate-selection committees are not the only entities involved. Although the electorate generally does not discriminate against women running for election, certain voters, both female and male, do (see questions 12 to 16). Majority voting systems are usually based on a "personal vote" – that is, the voter makes a choice based on the candidate's attributes, such as her or his personal traits, skills, accomplishments, and reputation. Therefore, if a female voter is hostile to the idea of women in politics, she may not vote for a female candidate running for the party that she usually supports. On the other hand, when the electorate votes for a closed list composed of women and men, the personal vote is less important as voters make their choice not on the basis of single candidates but on a list (a sort of package deal). However, the personal vote may be significant in a proportional vote when the list is open – when the electorate is voting not for a list as a whole but for one or several candidates on a list (and this might favour women; see question 21).

To sum up, majority voting systems, in themselves, do not hinder the election of women; rather, the obstacle is thrown up by the conjuncture of a predominant informal model for a winning candidate whose traits resemble men's profiles and experiences and the obligation imposed on each political party to retain only one candidate per riding. In this sense, the goodwill of the parties is an essential condition for increasing the proportion of female parliamentarians (see questions 23, 45, and 54).

BIBLIOGRAPHY

Bjarnegård, Elin. 2013. *Gender, Informal Institutions and Political Recruitment: Explaining Male Dominance in Parliamentary Representation*. Basingstoke and New York: Palgrave Macmillan): 1–51.

Cheng, Christine and Margit Tavits. 2011. "Informal Influences in Selecting Female Political Candidates." *Political Research Quarterly* 64 (2): 460–71.

Hayward, Margaret. 2014. "The Influence of Party Leaders on Women's Representation in Parliament, 1935–1975: The Case of New Zealand." *Journal of Commonwealth and Comparative Politics* 52 (2): 254–70.

Norris, Pippa and Joni Lovenduski. 1989. "Pathways to Parliament." *Talking Politics* 1 (3): 90–4.

Valdini, Melody Ellis. 2013. "Electoral Institutions and the Manifestation of Bias: The Effect of the Personal Vote on the Representation of Women." *Politics & Gender* 9 (1): 76–92.

21 Why are proportional voting systems more likely to favour the election of women?

In studies on factors that affect the proportion of women in parliaments, there is a fundamental idea that party-list proportional representation (except for the single transferable vote used in Malta and the Republic of Ireland) is likely to favour the election of women. This is not borne out by fact, however. Here, too, we should remember that the impact of voting systems also depends on how they are structured; the sociocultural, economic, and political environments in which they are deployed; and the entities that manipulate them – the political parties (see questions 20 and 23).

One general characteristic of list voting systems that should help make them more favourable to the election of women than majority voting systems is the way they are set up to function: whereas the latter are limited to a single candidate per party and per riding and the person selected is judged on her or his own merits and not as a member of a larger team (see question 20), the former involve a number of candidates per party and per riding. In this scenario, it would be a bit embarrassing for a political party – and, moreover, it would not be a good electoral strategy – to offer voters a team composed solely of men.

According to Matland (2003, 2005), several conditions must be met in order for list proportional voting systems to boost women's access to parliaments. First, the legislative assembly must have a relatively high number of seats: the fewer seats to fill, the stiffer will be the competition to fill them – a context that disadvantages women. This criterion must, however, be considered carefully. In May 2016, the parliament of Rwanda, with only eighty seats, had a feminization rate of 63.8 per cent. Following the 2003 election, the sixty seats in the National Assembly for Wales were filled by an equal number of women and men. However, since then the number of women has continually declined, perhaps because over time these seats became more sought after. In contrast, in May 2016, the lower chambers of some of the largest legislative assemblies in the world had less than 20 per cent women: Indonesia (555 seats, 17.1 per cent), Turkey (550 seats, 14.9 per cent), India (543 seats, 12 per cent), Brazil (513 seats, 9.9 per cent), the Democratic Republic of the Congo (492 seats, 8.9 per cent), Japan (475 seats, 9.5 per cent), the Russian Federation (450 seats, 13.6 per cent), the United States (434 seats [one seat was vacant at the time] 19.4 per cent), and Myanmar (433 seats, 9.9 per cent).

Second, the parties have to be able to hope that several of their candidates will be elected per riding. In list voting systems, each electoral district (or riding) is represented by a number of parliamentarians. In Brazil, for example, the number of representatives per district varies between eight and seventy; in Finland, between six and thirty-three (except for the single-constituency riding of the province of Åland); and in Japan, between six and twenty-nine for the eleven multiple-constituency ridings. Studies show a strong correlation between the number of seats to be filled in an electoral district and the number of candidates that a political party elects: the more seats a party wins in a district, the more women may hope to accede to parliament. The reason is that the number of seats to fill forces the parties to descend low enough on their candidate lists to where women are often found. According to Rule and Norris (1992), seven seats is the number beyond which the tide would turn in favour of women.

A third condition identified by Matland concerns a high representation level. The representation threshold refers to the minimal proportion of votes, on a national scale or in a smaller electoral zone (such as a region or riding), necessary for a party (or a candidate) to win a seat in parliament. This proportion is usually around 4 or 5 per cent, but it may be lower (it is 0.67 per cent in the Netherlands and 3.25 per cent in Israel) or higher (it is occasionally 7 per cent of the total votes in Russia and 10 per cent of all valid votes on the national scale in Turkey). The lower the threshold, the more proportional the representation will be – that is, the smaller will be the gap between the proportion of votes obtained by a party and the proportion of seats that it occupies in the parliament. However, too low a threshold has the effect of multiplying the number of parties in parliament, and thus of dividing up legislative representation, fostering what some have called "governmental instability." Set at a relatively high level, the representation threshold increases the number of votes lost (that is, votes that do not contribute directly to designation of representation) and also limits the number of parties among which the seats in parliament will be distributed. Each party thus obtains more seats and may attribute more of them to women, whether voluntarily (with a concern for balancing representation) or not (because it must descend lower in its list, where women are often found).

Finally, Matland suggests that closed lists are more favourable to women than are open lists. Lists are "closed" when voters cannot change the order of the candidates established by the parties. They are "open" when the voters can change the order and even specify their preferences for one or another candidate on the list (we then speak of a "preferential" or "personal" vote; see question 20). Closed lists would be better for women because they would allow the women's movement to pressure parties to place female candidates on their lists in positions where they may hope to be elected. The absence of women on a list, or their relegation to the bottom, makes it look like the party is closed to women, which could be expensive electorally. The idea that closed lists are more favourable to women is increasingly in question, however; not only has Matland (2006) qualified his position, but recent research (Kunovich 2012, Matland and Lilliefeldt 2014, Valdini 2012) shows that open lists may give women a better chance.

To this must be added a final criterion: contagion, the process through which political parties adopt measures introduced by their electoral adversaries. For instance, a traditional party might see a strategic obligation to promote women's candidacies if one of its competitors, usually smaller and farther to the left on the political spectrum, offers voters a wide range of female candidates. However, contagion affects the voting system less than it does the political parties as a key mechanism affecting the proportion of women in parliaments (see question 23).

That said, proportional votes do not necessarily generate more-feminized parliaments. Moreover, the results of recent research give the lie to what had been taken for granted in studies on women in politics (Fortin-Rittberger and Rittberger 2014, Moser and Scheiner 2012, Roberts et al. 2013, Rosen 2013, Salmond 2006, Schmidt 2009). This is so because – at the risk of repeating myself – a voting system is not a closed system: its effects on the proportion of women in parliament are conditioned by a wide range of broader sociocultural, economic, and political factors (see question 19). The interjection of these factors explains why proportional voting systems "make" parliaments sometimes with a high proportion of women and sometimes with a more conservative proportion. And so, these variations put the lie to the "proportional voting system = more-feminized parliament" equation.

BIBLIOGRAPHY

Fortin-Rittberger, Jessica and Berthold Rittberger. 2014. "Do Electoral Rules Matter? Explaining National Differences in Women's Representation in the European Parliament." *European Union Politics*, 15 (4): 496–520.

Kunovich, Sheri. 2012. "Unexpected Winners: The Significance of an Open-List System on Women's Representation in Poland." *Politics & Gender* 8 (2): 153–77.

Matland, Richard. 2003. "Women's Representation in Post-Communist Europe." In *Women's Access to Political Power in Post-Communist Europe*, edited by Richard E. Matland and Kathleen A. Montgomery, 321–42. New York: Oxford University Press.

– 2005. "Enhancing Women's Political Participation: Legislative Recruitment and Electoral Systems." In *Women in Parliament: Beyond Numbers*, revised edition, edited by Julie Ballington and Azza Karam, 93–111. Stockholm: International IDEA.

– 2006. "Electoral Quotas: Frequency and Effectiveness." In *Women, Quotas and Politics*, edited by Drude Dahlerup, 275–92. London: Routledge.

Matland, Richard E. and Emilie Lilliefeldt. 2014. "The Effect of Preferential Voting on Women's Representation." In *Representation: The Case of Women*, edited by Maria C. Escobar-Lemmon and Michelle M. Taylor-Robinson, 79–102. New York: Oxford University Press.

Moser, Robert G. and Ethan Scheiner. 2012. *Electoral Systems and Political Context: How the Effects of Rules Vary Across New and Established Democracies*. Cambridge: Cambridge University Press. See, in particular, 208–35.

Roberts, Andrew, Jason Seawright, and Jennifer Cyr. 2013. "Do Electoral Laws Affect Women's Representation?" *Comparative Political Studies* 46 (12): 1555–81.

Rosen, Jennifer. 2013. "The Effects of Political Institutions on Women's Political Representation: A Comparative Analysis of 168 Countries from 1992 to 2010." *Political Research Quarterly* 66 (2): 306–21.

Rule, Wilma and Pippa Norris. 1992. "Anglo and Minority Women's Underrepresentation in Congress: Is the Electoral System the Culprit?" In *United States Electoral Systems: Their Impact on Women and Minorities*, edited by Wilma Rule and Joseph F. Zimmerman, 41–54. New York: Praeger.

Salmond, Rob. 2006. "Proportional Representation and Female Parliamentarians." *Legislative Studies Quarterly* 31 (2): 175–204.

Schmidt, Gregory D. 2009. "The Election of Women in List PR Systems: Testing the Conventional Wisdom." *Electoral Studies* 28 (2): 190–203.

Urbatsch, Robert. 2016. "Gendered Electoral Systems in the French *Sénat*." *West European Politics*, 39, 4: 859–69.

Valdini, Melody Ellis. 2012. "A Deterrent to Diversity: The Conditional Effect of Electoral Rules on the Nomination of Women Candidates." *Electoral Studies* 31 (4): 740–49.

22 What is the impact of mixed voting systems on the feminization of parliaments?

Although, from a conceptual and structural point of view, mixed voting systems are situated halfway between majority and proportional systems (an attempt, as the title of the book by Matthew Soberg Shugart and Martin P. Wattenberg would have it, to make "the best of both worlds"), the performance of mixed voting systems is similar to that of proportional voting systems with regard to feminization of parliaments. In fact, a quick analysis of proportions of women in parliament of eighty-five countries that, in 2016, were considered free according to Freedom House reveals that the thirty parliaments elected under a majority voting system had an average of 14.3 per cent women, whereas the forty-five parliaments elected under a proportional voting system and the ten elected under a mixed system showed average feminization percentages of 27.5 and 24.4 per cent, respectively. In other words, the countries in which the population designated its representatives through a majority vote had about half the proportion of women in the national parliament as did those in which the population expressed its will through a mixed vote or, especially, a proportional vote.

Mixed voting systems, very popular since the 1990s, consist of a hybrid formula under which some members of a parliament are elected through a majority vote and others through a proportional vote. This kind of blended system is intended to fulfil two objectives: first, to create assemblies that better reflect the electorate's sociodemographic profile and range of preferences (proportional list votes perform better in this field); second, to create governments that are effective (a trait often related to stability and therefore to majority governments). Among the countries with a mixed voting system are Bolivia, Germany, Hungary, Japan, Lesotho, Mexico, New Zealand, Ukraine, and Venezuela.

Mixed systems make it possible to observe the effects of different voting systems in a single political environment. Because studies tend to demonstrate that list proportional votes contribute more to the election of women than do majority vote systems, it is logical to think that more women are elected under the proportional section than the majority section of mixed votes. However, there are numerous examples of the reverse occurring – among others, in Scotland in the elections of 1999, 2003, 2007, and 2011 (in the Scottish National Party); in Hungary in the 1995 and 1999 elections; in Lesotho in the 2002 election; in Wales in the 1999, 2003, and 2011 elections (for all parties except the Plaid Cymru); and in Russia in the 1995 and 1999 elections. In New Zealand, in the 2002 election, a small gap (2 per cent) separated the proportion of female riding representatives from their list counterparts: 27.5 per cent and 29.4 per cent, respectively, and following the 2011 election an equal number of women were elected under the majority and proportional components.

Several factors may explain why the proportional component of mixed systems does not automatically give rise to higher proportions of women parliamentarians than does the majority component. First, social change is a complex process that cannot be triggered by the application of some kind of magic potion. Second, voting systems do not evolve in a vacuum; their effects on the feminization of parliaments are conditioned by other sociocultural, economic, and political factors (see question 19). Finally, because they share a political environment, the majority and proportional components of a mixed vote are not independent of each other but, instead, influence each other. According to Ferrara, Herron, and Nishikawa (2005), there is "contamination" when the electorate's choices, the political parties' strategies, and the behaviours of candidates and parliamentarians in one component (for example, the majority vote) are affected by the rules of the game that prevail in the other component (for example, the proportional vote). For instance, a voter may decide to vote for a female candidate in the majority vote with the goal of avoiding the stigmatization that sitting in parliament essentially due to the proportional component would cause to women. A party may designate female candidates in good ridings in the majority vote because it reserves the best positions on its lists for other social minorities. A female candidate may be elected in both the majority and the proportional component, and decline the latter mandate because it is associated with the representation of minorities.

In sum, assessments of how mixed voting systems perform with regard to the election of women tend to oversimplify, similar to how list proportional votes are seen as the cure-all for the low rate of feminization of parliaments.

BIBLIOGRAPHY

Ferrara, Federico, Erik S. Herron, and Misa Nishikawa. 2005. *Mixed Electoral Systems: Contamination and Its Consequences.* New York: Palgrave Macmillan. See, in particular, 8–9.

Fortin-Rittberger, Jessica and Christina Eder. 2013. "Towards a Gender-Equal Bundestag? The Impact of Electoral Rules on Women's Representation." *West European Politics* 36 (5): 969–85.

Freedom House. "Freedom in the World 2016, FIW 2016 data," accessed 12 June 2016, https://freedomhouse.org/report/freedom-world/freedom-world-2016.

Shin, Ki-young. 2014. "Women's Sustainable Representation and the Spillover Effect of

Electoral Gender Quotas in South Korea." *International Political Science Review* 35 (1): 80–92.

Shugart, Matthew Soberg and Martin P. Wattenberg, eds. 2001. *Mixed-Member Electoral Systems: The Best of Both Worlds?* New York: Oxford University Press.

Tremblay, Manon, ed. 2012. *Women and Legislative Representation: Electoral Systems, Political Parties, and Sex Quotas*, revised and updated edition. New York: Palgrave Macmillan. See, in particular, 183–237.

23 How do political parties interfere with voting systems to exert influence on the proportion of women in parliaments?

The impact of voting systems on the proportion of women in parliaments depends, at least in part, on political parties, which play an essential role in the selection of candidates (see questions 18 and 20). In fact, parties adapt their candidate-selection strategy to the voting system used in the respective election. This occurs particularly in countries in which several voting systems are used, such as France, which uses majority, single-constituency, two-turn votes for legislative elections and proportional votes for European and municipal elections.

When a party can designate only one person per district, it will seek a median candidate – one who is perceived as most likely to win the favour of the greatest number of voters. On the other hand, when a political party is able to designate several candidates per electoral district, it will present a team that is balanced – diversified – in terms of demographics and ideas: women and men who will reach across other divisions, such as a range of ages, various religions, rural and urban environments, sexual minorities, and so on. By balancing its list of candidates a party will also respond best to various pressures within its own ranks, whether they come from the "women's," "youth," "green," or other factions. What is more, if the lists are closed and do not allow for a preferential or personal vote (see question 20), the parties enjoy absolute control over the composition of the parliament, whereas if they are open and allow for a preferential or personal vote, the electorate has a greater say (with less input from the parties) in who will represent it.

The voting system thus stands as an intermediary variable between legislative representation by women and political parties. It establishes the rules of the game under which seats in parliament are distributed among the various political parties, but first, the political parties designate the candidates – and thus, indirectly, who will sit in those seats. However, the parties do not select their candidates by chance; they do so in response to the expectations of their electoral base, certainly, but also in light of parameters established by the voting system (for example, one or more candidates per district) and, above all, according to how they gauge their chances of success in light of that system.

Whether the voting system is majority or proportional, the goodwill of political parties seems to be key to increasing the feminization of parliaments. Indeed, more than the system itself, this goodwill is essential to having more women sit in parliaments. And it must be real and sincere. France offers an example in which the parties' lack of goodwill proved more decisive for the proportion of female representatives than was a closed-list proportional voting system. In 1986, the legislative elections took place under a list proportional vote: 5.9 per cent of new representatives in the National Assembly were women, a slight increase of 0.6 per cent over the preceding legislative elections in 1981, held under a majority vote. For the following elections, in 1988, France returned to a two-round single-constituency majority system; the result was 5.7 per cent women sitting in the assembly. Thus, not only was representation of women in the French National Assembly in the 1980s relatively stable despite changes made to the voting system but adoption of the list proportional system in the 1986 election did not result in an increased proportion of women in the lower chamber. The main reason for this was that women were not in eligible positions on the lists submitted to the electorate by the parties. Another reason was the absence of women's mobilizations in the electoral field, which is a fundamental element for increasing the feminization of political institutions (see questions 42, 46, and 55). The 1986 defeat no doubt helped to mobilize women a few years later during the debates on parity (see questions 50 to 54).

A final detail should be noted with regard to political parties' influence on the number of female parliamentarians: in the vast majority of countries, the parties select the candidates for elections, but this role may sometimes be secondary. For example, the primary system in the United States may severely curb the parties' influence regarding the selection of candidates. In Ireland, the parties exert upstream control on the composition of the parliament: candidates must obtain accreditation from the parties, but the electorate's preferential votes for each candidate, and not the parties' rankings, determine who will sit in parliament. Yet, despite the diminished role of the American and Irish parties in the selection of their respective countries' candidates, parliaments in the United States and Ireland are not very feminized. We thus cannot conclude that the absence of women in parliaments is the responsibility of the political parties alone.

BIBLIOGRAPHY

Caul Kittilson, Miki. 2006. *Challenging Parties, Changing Parliaments: Women and Elected Office in Contemporary Western Europe.* Columbus: Ohio State University Press.

Lovenduski, Joni and Pippa Norris, eds. 1993. *Gender and Party Politics.* London: Sage.

Matland, Richard E. and Emilie Lilliefeldt. 2014. "The Effect of Preferential Voting on Women's Representation." In *Representation: The Case of Women*, edited by Maria C. Escobar-Lemmon and Michelle M. Taylor-Robinson, 79–102. New York: Oxford University Press.

Matland, Richard E. and Kathleen A. Montgomery. 2003. "Recruiting Women to National Legislatures: A General Framework with Applications to Post-Communist Democracies." In *Women's Access to Political Power in Post-Communist Europe*, edited by Richard E. Matland and Kathleen A. Montgomery, 19–42. Oxford: Oxford University Press.

McGing, Claire. 2013. "The Single Transferable Vote and Women's Representation in Ireland." *Irish Political Studies* 28 (2): 322–40.

Norris, Pippa, R.J. Carty, Lynda Erickson, Joni Lovenduski, and Marian Simms. 1990. "Party Selectorates in Australia, Britain and Canada: Prolegomena for Research in the 1990s." *Journal of Commonwealth & Comparative Politics* 28 (2): 219–45.

24 Do family responsibilities really pose an obstacle to women's involvement in politics?

It is my opinion that family responsibilities are advanced almost automatically to explain the underrepresentation of women in politics, and it may be that family obligations pose obstacles to the political ambitions of some women. Examples include those who have young children at home and wish to stay with them; those who are heads of single-parent families or whose life partner does not participate actively in parental responsibilities; those who do not have the means to pay for alternative housekeeping, caregiving, and child-care services; and those who simply wish to take an active role in their children's education and spend the most time possible with them.

On the other hand, the family argument cannot explain why more women without children or who have been freed of their family responsibilities do not enter the political arena. In a study conducted in the early 1990s among twenty-four female and twenty-four male members of the National Assembly of Quebec and the Quebec caucus of the House of Commons of Canada, Tremblay and Pelletier (1995) found that although the majority of female members (fourteen of twenty-four) stated they had no family constraints, ten of them had children (although in eight cases the children were at least twelve years old). The presence in politics of these mothers makes it clear that family does not systematically bar women from having political aspirations. In addition, Stalsburg (2010) has observed that not having a child may cause female candidates – though not male ones – to be seen in a negative light (the implication being that they are closeted lesbians, an accusation made of the former prime minister of New Zealand, Helen Clark). This is a reminder that many people still find it impossible to think of women independently of children. In other words, under the gender regime (see question 1), is a woman without children "really" a woman?

It is not my intention here to deny the constraints that family may place on some women's political ambitions, but to add nuance to the hegemonic scope of that argument, which is advanced as if it were an absolute fact, an incontestable truth. The idea that women with children are elected to political office and that, furthermore, more women without offspring (because they do not have any or because their children are independent) are not elected (Tremblay 2013, 210), or even that female politicians without children may eventually have a political cost to pay, forces us to take a second look at the strength of the "family" argument as an explanation for the low proportion of women in politics. In other words, is it possible that "family" is discursively constituted as an obstacle to the election of women, a difficulty made to look bigger than it really is?

BIBLIOGRAPHY

Stalsburg, Brittany L. 2010. "Voting for Mom: The Political Consequences of Being a Parent for Male and Female Candidates." *Politics & Gender* 6 (3): 373–404.

Thomas, Melanee and Amanda Bittner, eds. 2017. *Mothers and Others: The Impact of Parenthood on Politics*. Vancouver: UBC Press.

Tremblay, Manon. "Hitting a Glass Ceiling? Women's Presence in the Assemblée nationale du Québec." In *Stalled: The Representation of Women in Canadian Governments*, edited by Linda Trimble, Jane Arscott, and Manon Tremblay, 192–213. Vancouver: UBC Press.

Tremblay, Manon and Rejean Pelletier. 1995. *Que font-elles en politique?* Sainte-Foy: Les Presses de l'Universite Laval. See, in particular, 17–18, 76–82.

25 Does money pose a real obstacle to the election of women?

For a very long time, the cost of campaigning was considered a significant obstacle to the election of women. However, a number of recent studies have challenged the relevance of this factor in explaining the low proportion of female politicians: female candidates today have election coffers as full as those of male candidates and they spend as much on their campaigns. Funding sources for women and men differ, however, at least in the United States: women fill their war chests with a multitude of small donations, whereas men receive fewer, larger donations. In the United States, foundations devoted to funding the election campaigns of female candidates have greatly contributed to reducing the obstacle that money might pose to them.

One of those foundations is EMILY's List (EMILY for Early Money Is Like Yeast), which gives support, mainly financial, to progressive, pro-choice female candidates. In 2004, it was the largest political fundraising foundation in the United States, ahead of even the powerful National Rifle Association (Paxton and Hughes 2007). There are also the WISH (Women in the House and Senate) List, which supports Republican pro-choice female candidates, and the Susan B. Anthony List, which supports Republican antichoice female candidates. Openly lesbian candidates in the United States may also count on the Gay and Lesbian Victory Fund. Senator Tammy Baldwin remarked, "It made a huge difference for me. It made it possible for me to keep a fundraising edge against my opponents, which gave me credibility as a candidate at a time when people were skeptical that an out lesbian could win" (https://www.victoryfund.org/get-involved/run-office). EMILY's Lists have been created outside the United States – for example, in Australia and Great Britain.

It is important to put into context the effect of money on women's access to political institutions. Of course, money is needed to gain political power. To get elected councillor in a municipality may not be very expensive, whereas getting elected to the United States Senate requires a good deal of money. The competitiveness of a political position determines, in part, the amount of money needed to win it. Moreover, the rules regarding electoral financing vary a great deal, and where a public program for financial assistance to candidates exists (as in Canada and a number of its provinces, where, under certain conditions, some candidates' election expenses are reimbursed by the public treasury) it is likely that money represents less of a barrier. Finally, politics is elitist, and women who make the leap into the political arena generally belong to a professional, economic, or cultural elite – or more than one of these. In this, they do not differ from their male colleagues. Seen differently, it is important to recognize, through the focus of an intersectional approach, that access to money for an election campaign is not equal from woman to woman: for women of modest means and those from minorities (ethnic, religious, or sexual, for example), money may pose challenges that women who are well-off and women of the majority do not have to face.

In short, although, in general, the financial resources available to women are more modest than those for men – and if it is reasonable to deduce that money represents a bigger obstacle to their political ambitions than to those of men – women who run for office are generally not disadvantaged economically and money may not be as great a barrier for them as was once a presumed.

BIBLIOGRAPHY

Burrell, Barbara. 2013. "Political Parties and Women's Organizations: Bringing Women into the Electoral Arena." In *Gender and Elections: Shaping the Future of American Politics*, edited by Susan J. Carroll and Richard L. Fox, 211–40. New York: Cambridge University Press.

EMILY's List, accessed 13 June 2016, http://www.emilyslist.org/.

Gay and Lesbian Victory Fund, accessed 8 October 2016, https://www.victoryfund. org/get-involved/run-office.

Malcolm, Ellen R. with Craig Unger. 2016. *When Women Win: Emily's List and the Rise of Women in American Politics.* Boston: Houghton Mifflin Harcourt.

Paxton, Pamela and Melanie M. Hughes. 2007. *Women, Politics, and Power. A Global Perspective.* Los Angeles: Pine Forge Press. See, in particular, 123, 282–83.

Susan B. Anthony List, accessed 13 June 2016, http://www.sba-list.org/.

WISH List (The), accessed 13 June 2016, http://www.gopchoice.org/wish-list/.

Young, Lisa. 2006. "Women's Representation in the Canadian House of Commons." In *Representing Women in Parliament: A Comparative Study*, edited by Marian Sawer, Manon Tremblay, and Linda Trimble, 47–66. Abingdon: Routledge.

26 Would limiting the number of consecutive mandates (term limits) favour the feminization of legislative assemblies?

Not necessarily. Certainly, studies have shown that the low turnover rate in parliaments constitutes one of the major barriers to their feminization (see question 18). In a context in which the number of seats to fill is limited, people who do not vacate them block access to new recruits. Indeed, as a rule, political parties are very happy when their parliamentarians express the desire to run for reelection; these candidates usually are more likely to be elected than are new recruits because they often have better field organization, are better known to the public, and can mobilize a larger network of human resources – in short, they have greater homosocial and political capital (see question 20). Furthermore, women and men are not distributed randomly between sitting parliamentarians and new recruits: in May 2016, 77 per cent of people sitting in parliaments throughout the world were men. One might therefore think that term limits would have the effect of encouraging the access of new actors to legislative arenas – in other words, that such a measure would help to feminize parliaments by forcing men to retire.

And yet, studies conducted in US states that have term limits do not show that these states' legislative assemblies have a significantly higher feminization rate. One reason advanced to explain this rather surprising result is that women are also affected by term limits – like men, they must leave

political life at the mandated time, and they are not necessarily being replaced by other women. Furthermore, men are not necessarily replaced by
women; in fact, their seats are usually filled by men. Finally, imposing parliamentary term limits has consequences that many see as undesirable –
for example, that of impeding the professionalization of the political class.

BIBLIOGRAPHY

Carey, John M., Richard G. Niemi, Lynda W. Powell, and Gary F. Moncrief. 2006. "The
    Effects of Term Limits on State Legislatures: A New Survey of the 50 States." *Legislative
    Studies Quarterly* 31 (1): 105–34.

Kunioka, Todd and Stanley Malcolm Caress. 2012. *Term Limits and Their Consequences:
    The Aftermath of Legislative Reform*. Albany: State University of New York Press. See,
    in particular, 46–69.

Schwindt-Bayer, Leslie A. 2005. "The Incumbency Disadvantage and Women's Election
    to Legislative Office." *Electoral Studies* 24 (2): 227–44.

Vaughan, Heather J. 2011. *Term Limits and Tokenism: Increasing Female Representation
    in State Legislatures*. Washington, DC: Georgetown University, Faculty of the Graduate
    School of Arts and Sciences, accessed 13 June 2016, https://repository.library.george
    town.edu/bitstream/handle/10822/553945/vaughanHeather.pdf?sequence=1.

27 Are the media sexist?

A large number of studies show that the media treat women and men in
politics not only differently but often according to stereotypes that are
detrimental to women. Many women politicians have testified to this. That
the media present women and men in politics differently is not, in itself,
surprising: the media participate in the broader economy of the gender
regime and respond to the electorate's expectations of what female and
male politicians should look like (see questions 1 and 13). As a rule, a female
politician is expected to be feminine and a male politician to be masculine,
a rule to which the few trans people who have recently become involved in
politics are also subjected. Anyone who thinks that she or he can avoid the
gender regime steamroller will quickly be brought back into line. What is
troubling about the media treatment of female politicians are the stereotypes and often negative values associated with the female gender – in this
case, a stereotyped female gender that usually is also "white."

Even though female politicians are public figures, the media tend to associate them with the private sphere (the family) – a focus that associates their political interests with those supporting their traditional family roles. By "privatizing" women in this way, such a media framing may give rise to questions with regard to their competencies in general. For instance, the media associate women with well-defined social questions (culture, education and childhood, health, community services, and so on) with which they are often expected to deal in the private domestic sphere. This may trigger doubt: do women who are entrusted with traditionally male responsibilities really have the competency to assume them? The media also depict women as being more aware of their feelings, more humane (because it is assumed that they are involved with giving and maintaining life on a daily basis), and more concerned with the effects of their decisions on people's lives. Those who endorse such a reading of women's role in politics may wonder, for instance, whether women are capable of taking on foreign or military affairs. Female politicians are also suspected by the media of representing the interests of women rather than of "the person on the street" (no doubt an unfounded suspicion; see questions 12, 60, and 63) – of being biased and having a particular point of view rather than embracing a global and "neutral" position on public affairs. They are presented as particularly likely to practise politics on a consensual rather than conflictual basis, perhaps because they must often settle family disputes. This perspective may feed the stereotype according to which women lack the nerve to sustain the power relationships that politics often requires. Conversely, if women adopt an aggressive style, they risk seeming too masculine and thus transgressing the rules of the gender regime.

From a more quantitative point of view, the media devote less space and time to female politicians than to their male colleagues. In covering female politicians, the media also exaggerate the importance of appearance – clothing, makeup, hairstyle, and so on – to the detriment of ideas and accomplishments. In the end, the treatment of female politicians by the media reinforces a stereotyped reading of women, casting doubt on their competencies and credibility, even challenging their legitimacy as politicians.

Four details must be added to this general portrait. First, stereotyping is not always negative for women. Indeed, it may play in their favour if the circumstances and themes on the political agenda fall within the perceived bailiwick of the female gender. For instance, women may benefit if a struggle against corruption is on the agenda, as they are seen as less corrupt than men. If the election campaign is oriented toward education, health, or ageing of the population, female politicians may attract more voters (see question 16). Second, recent research has shown that although the media present women politicians today in a less caricatured way than in the past, there is still some sexism. But, more subtly, the perspectives through which the news is organized hew more to male than female socialization by emphasizing hegemonic masculinity. The media often use sports and military lingo – traditionally associated with men (at least when it comes to professional sports such as boxing and extreme sports) or even with hyper-virility – to describe and analyze politics. On the other hand – and as a third point – research reveals that, from a quantitative point of view, women and men are starting to be treated more equally. Indeed, both women and men politicians are tending to use a more androgynous style, in which female and male traits intermingle. The position of secretary of state in the United States, for which the responsibilities are eminently "masculine," has recently been occupied mainly by women (Madeleine Albright from 1997 to 2001, Condoleezza Rice from 2005 to 2009, and Hillary Rodham Clinton from 2009 to 2013), whose gender generated no trouble, to paraphrase Judith Butler (perhaps by melding the feminine and masculine genders). And finally, women (and men) in politics may make strategic use of their sex/gender through political marketing techniques; in this respect, women politicians cannot be thought of simply as victims of media sexism, as they employ it to their own ends.

BIBLIOGRAPHY

Goodyear-Grant, Elizabeth. 2013. *Gendered News: Media Coverage and Electoral Politics in Canada*. Vancouver: UBC Press.

Kahn, Kim Fridkin. 1996. *The Political Consequences of Being a Woman: How Stereotypes Influence the Conduct and Consequences of Political Campaigns*. New York: Columbia University Press.

Miller, Melissa K. and Jeffrey S. Peake. 2013. "Press Effects, Public Opinion, and Gender: Coverage of Sarah Palin's Vice-Presidential Campaign." *International Journal of Press/Politics* 18 (4): 482–507.

Ritchie, Jessica. 2013. "Creating a Monster: Online Media Constructions of Hillary Clinton During the Democratic Primary Campaign, 2007–8." *Feminist Media Studies* 13 (1): 102–19.

Trimble, Linda. 2018. *Ms. Prime Minister: Gender, Media, and Leadership.* Toronto: University of Toronto Press.

Trimble, Linda, Daisy Raphael, Shannon Sampert, Angelia Wagner, and Bailey Gerrits. 2015. "Politicizing Bodies: Hegemonic Masculinity, Heteronormativity, and Racism in News Representations of Canadian Political Party Leadership Candidates." *Women's Studies in Communication* 38 (3): 314–30.

28 Are women responsible for how few of them are in politics?

Yes and no. Yes, in the sense that to be elected women must first make the decision to run for office. Every individual, woman or man, who wishes to assume a mandate of political representation must satisfy certain eligibility criteria, be selected by a political party, and be elected by the people. But these individuals must also self-designate (or self-recruit; see question 18) – that is, they must decide to make the leap into the political arena. Several recent studies (Carroll and Sanbonmatsu 2013, Lawless 2012, Lawless and Fox 2010) show that women are less likely than men to believe that they have the skills to enter politics, and that they are more reluctant to run for office (Kanthak and Woon 2015). In addition, they are less often encouraged to launch a political career. As a consequence, in my view, women bear a share of the responsibility for their low numbers in politics: as long as there are few women expressing a desire to run for office, pressure on the parties will be insufficient to force their doors open. Only when women push the parties into a corner will those parties have no choice but to consider women competitive candidates and invite them in. An increase in the number of women offering to be candidates for political parties is the prerequisite to the feminization of political life, as Maurice Duverger emphasized back in 1955.

Nevertheless, women are not responsible for their low numbers in politics in the sense that factors of a social nature curb their ambitions; these factors act unequally depending on the systems of oppression (those of social class, race or ethnic origin, and sexuality, among others) involved. For example, if, in general, voters regard female candidates neither positively nor negatively (see question 14), many people – and perhaps more than we believe – still hold prejudices supported by the gender regime regarding women's participation in politics: women are either too emotional or not aggressive enough, or their primary role is private and maternal rather than public and political, or they are not assertive enough to impose power relations, or men are simply more suited to politics. It is very possible that voters who subscribe to these sexist prejudices will never vote for a female candidate. Gender roles also explain why some women do not enter politics. Family responsibilities are often put forward as a reason, although the hegemonic scope of the argument, making the family the definitive explanation for women's low presence in politics, must be nuanced (see question 24). "Homosocial" capital (with all it means in terms of resources such as networks and money) is another aspect of the explanation for the low number of female politicians (see question 20). These social factors explain, in part, why few women offer to run as candidates on the political market.

That said, it seems important to explore possible reasons why few women are tempted by the adventure of politics, especially reasons of a symbolic order inherent to the gender regime. For instance, could it be that because of its culture, rules, and practices, politics is both a mechanism and a space of hegemonic performance of masculinity (a little like the military or sports), such that women are less likely than men to see themselves as full participants in it? This is quite possible.

BIBLIOGRAPHY

Carroll, Susan J. and Kira Sanbonmatsu. 2013. *More Women Can Run: Gender and Pathways to the State Legislatures.* New York: Oxford University Press. See, in particular, 42–62.

Connell, Raewyn W. and James W. Messerschmidt. 2005. "Hegemonic Masculinity: Rethinking the Concept." *Gender & Society* 19 (6): 829–59.

Duverger, Maurice, 1955. *The Political Role of Women.* Paris: UNESCO. See, in particular, 87.

Kanthak, Kristin and Jonathan Woon. 2015. "Women Don't Run? Election Aversion and Candidate Entry." *American Journal of Political Science* 59 (3): 595–612.

Lawless, Jennifer L. 2012. *Becoming a Candidate. Political Ambition and the Decision to Run for Office.* New York: Cambridge University Press.

Lawless, Jennifer L. and Richard L. Fox. 2010. *It Still Takes a Candidate: Why Women Don't Run for Office,* revised edition. New York: Cambridge University Press. See, in particular, 112–35.

CHAPTER FIVE

The Proportion of Women in Parliaments

29 What is the proportion of women in national parliaments around the world?

According to Reynolds (1999), the twenty-six democratic states in the West immediately following the Second World War had an average of 3 per cent women among their parliamentarians. By 1955, this proportion had grown to 7.5 per cent (on the basis of sixty-one democratic countries); it rose to 8.1 per cent in 1965 (ninety-four countries), 10.9 per cent in 1975 (115 countries), 12 per cent in 1985 (136 countries), and 11.6 per cent in 1995 (176 countries). Since 1997, the Inter-Parliamentary Union has systematically compiled data on the proportion of women in national parliaments. This is an extraordinary and reliable tool for researching women's legislative representation, notably because it clearly exposes the underrepresentation of women (or the overrepresentation of men) in parliaments.

Table 2 lists the feminization rate (or proportion of women) in the lower or single chambers of some 190 national parliaments around the world, providing a general glimpse at women's global presence in legislatures in the mid-2010s. For instance, in June 2016 only two countries (Rwanda and Bolivia) had at least as many women as men in their parliaments (although Cuba's parliament, with a feminization rate of 48.9 per cent, was not far behind). Thirty-two countries had reached a critical mass (at least one-third; see question 39) of women, but not parity (see questions 50 to 54). The vast majority, 118, had a feminization rate of between 10 and 33.2 per cent. In fact, as of June 2016 more than half (101/191, or 52.9 per cent) had less than 20 per cent women in the lower or single chambers of their national parliaments. Although it might seem incredible, seven countries offered the sad spectacle of parliaments composed solely of men: Haiti, Palau, Qatar, Tonga, Vanuatu,

Table 2

Feminization rates of national parliaments (lower or single chambers)
of 191 countries, June 2016

Feminization rate	*Number of countries*
50 per cent or more	2 (1.0 per cent)
33.3 per cent to 49.9 per cent	32 (16.7 per cent)
25 per cent to 33.2 per cent	33 (17.3 per cent)
10 per cent to 24.9 per cent	85 (44.5 per cent)
0.1 per cent to 9.9 per cent	32 (16.8 per cent)
0.0 per cent	7 (3.7 per cent)

Source: Inter-Parliamentary Union, "Women in National Parliaments, World Classification," accessed 6 July 2016, http://www.ipu.org/wmn-e/classif.htm.

Yemen, and the Federated States of Micronesia – the last having never elected a woman to its national legislature. And the world has never seen a parliament composed solely of women.

The feminization rate of national parliaments may also be appreciated in light of other criteria, such as the democratic ideal (see questions 33 and 34), voting systems (see questions 20 to 22), and geographic region. There are, in fact, major differences in feminization rates from region to region. In June 2016, the average feminization rate in the parliaments of the five Nordic countries stood at 41.1 per cent (on the leading position of the Nordic countries, see question 37), the Americas stood at 27.7 per cent, Europe (excluding the Nordic countries) at 24.3 per cent, sub-Saharan Africa at 23.1 per cent, Asia at 19.2 per cent, the Arab states at 18.4 per cent, and the Pacific region at 13.5 per cent.

To sum up, considering that women constitute a bit more than half the population, and, therefore, of the electorate, the term that best describes the current proportion of women in politics is underrepresentation. In the short term, this situation will not change drastically, but parity is on the horizon over the medium term.

BIBLIOGRAPHY

Inter-Parliamentary Union. "Women in National Parliaments, World Classification,"
     accessed 6 July 2016, http://www.ipu.org/wmn-e/classif.htm.
Reynolds, Andrew. 1999. "Women in the Legislatures and Executives of the World:
     Knocking at the Highest Glass Ceiling." *World Politics* 51 (4): 547–72.

30 How have feminization rates in national parliaments changed?

In addition to supplying information on current proportions of women
in national parliaments, the Inter-Parliamentary Union website offers historical data that give an idea of the fairly glacial rate of advancement in
women's access to parliamentary representation. For instance, a consultation of the IPU's archives reveals constant, though modest, overall growth
in the feminization rate of lower or single chambers of national parliaments (see table 3). In January 1997, 12 per cent of members of lower or
single chambers of parliaments were women. Twenty years later, in January
2016, this rate had progressed by only 10 per cent, to 22.8 per cent – an average annual growth rate of 3.5 per cent. A linear projection shows that if this
growth rate is maintained constantly in coming years, and all other things
being equal (that is, if nothing comes along to impede or accelerate women's
access to parliaments), equal representation between women and men will
become a reality in the lower or single chambers of national parliaments
only in 2039.

In the French edition of this book, published in 2015, this table showed
the average annual growth rate for the period from 1997 to 2014, which was
3.7 per cent, whereas for the period from 1997 to 2016 it is 3.5 per cent. At
the latter rate, female–male parity in national parliaments is delayed by two
years, from 2037 to 2039; more generally, this change shows that, in fact, *all
things are never equal*, and the annual growth rate may slow or accelerate
under the effect of one force or another. This rate was only 0.9 per cent
from 2014 to 2015 but doubled from 2015 to 2016, although it remained well
below the 1997–2016 average of 3.5 per cent. It is true that a two-year delay
would be insignificant given how long women have been waiting to gain
an equitable position in parliaments.

Table 3

Rates of annual growth in the proportion of women in the lower or single chambers of national parliaments, 1997–2016, and growth projections until parity is reached.

Year	Per cent of women	Annual growth rate (per cent)
January 1997	12.0	–
January 1998	12.2	1.7
January 1999	13.3	9.0
January 2000	13.5	1.5
January 2001	14.1	4.4
February 2002	14.5	2.8
January 2003	14.9	2.8
January 2004	15.2	2.0
January 2005	15.9	4.7
January 2006	16.5	3.8
January 2007	17.1	3.6
January 2008	18.0	5.3
January 2009	18.5	2.8
January 2010	19.0	2.7
January 2011	19.3	1.6
January 2012	19.9	3.1
January 2013	20.7	4.0
January 2014	22.2	7.3
January 2015	22.4	0.9
January 2016	22.8	1.8
Average 1997–2016	17.1	3.5

Growth projections until parity is reached

	Per cent of women	Annual growth rate (per cent)
2016	22.8	3.5
2020	26.2	3.5
2025	31.1	3.5
2030	36.9	3.5
2035	43.8	3.5
2039	50.3	3.5

Source: Inter-Parliamentary Union, "Women in National Parliaments, World Classification," accessed 6 July 2016, http://www.ipu.org/wmn-e/classif.htm.

Because linear projection is unlikely to realistically convey the future evolution of women's presence in parliaments, models have been developed to take into account the complexity and diversity of possible scenarios. Paxton and Hughes (2007) have come up with five patterns for the trajectories of women's advances in parliaments: "flat," "increasing," "big jump," "small gains," and "plateau." Trimble, Tremblay, and Arscott (2013) performed the same exercise for Canada.

In countries with a "flat" pattern, the proportion of women in parliament is relatively stable over time; it neither increases nor decreases significantly but maintains a constant level, varying between 2–3 per cent and 20 per cent, with an average of 10 per cent. This model fits many countries in Africa (such as Egypt, Ghana, and Nigeria), Asia (India, Japan, North Korea, South Korea, Sri Lanka, and Thailand, for example), and the Arab world (Iran, Kuwait, the United Arab Emirates, and Yemen).

The "increasing" pattern describes countries in which the proportion of women in a national parliament rises slowly but steadily. This model, which applies to the West and some countries in other regions (see below), has two components: the time when the proportion of women begins to grow in parliaments and the proportion that they may eventually occupy in those parliaments. Until 1975, these parliaments were relatively unfeminized, but starting in the mid-1970s, under the influence of the second wave of the women's movement and various instruments of international law (including the Convention on the Elimination of All Forms of Discrimination Against Women, adopted in 1979; see question 41), the number of women officeholders began to rise at a sustained pace that was likely to continue over time. Many of the first countries to engage in this process have the most female parliamentarians today: the Nordic countries and other European countries (Austria, France, Germany, Iceland, the Netherlands, and Switzerland), Africa (Mozambique, Senegal, Tanzania, and Uganda, for example), and the Americas (the Bahamas, Bolivia, and Mexico, among others).

In the "big jumps" pattern, the proportion of female parliamentarians progresses quickly over a very short time period, in many cases due to the implementation of quota measures for women in politics (see questions 43 and 44). Rwanda and Bolivia offer striking examples of this model. Following the 2003 election in Rwanda, the proportion of women in the Chamber of Deputies jumped from 25.7 per cent to 48.8 per cent.

In Bolivia, thanks to an extremely strict electoral quota (see question 44), the 2014 election saw the proportion of women in the lower chamber of the national parliament explode from 25.4 per cent to 53.1 per cent. Other countries also fit this model, including Argentina, Australia, Belgium, Bosnia-Herzegovina, Botswana, Costa Rica, Croatia, Ecuador, Great Britain, Iraq, Laos, Pakistan, South Africa, Spain, and Turkmenistan.

In the "small gains" pattern, the proportion of women in parliaments progresses at a ridiculously slow pace, a little like a car with a stuck brake. Unlike the "flat" pattern, "small gains" shows some progress, but it is extremely halting. Among Western industrialized countries, Canada, Ireland, and the United States are exemplary of this model. Azerbaijan, Brazil, Burkina Faso, Chile, Colombia, Malta, Syria, and Uruguay are among the Eastern and Southern countries in which women's representation in the national parliament is progressing in the "small gains" pattern.

Finally, the "plateau" pattern is the only one that takes account of the fact that, contrary to popular belief, the presence of women in parliaments may decline (see question 31). This model shows trajectories in which the proportion of female legislators increases, then stabilizes, and ultimately regresses. Most countries falling into this model once had communist governments (such as Albania, Bulgaria, Cambodia, Czechoslovakia, Hungary, Mongolia, Poland, Rumania, and the Soviet Union) or are authoritarian left-wing regimes (such as Guinea-Bissau). Through quotas, the feminization level of the institutions that stood in as parliaments was kept artificially high, and it fell as these countries were democratized. This is another piece of evidence that there is no link between democracy and the presence of women in politics (see questions 33, 34, and 40).

BIBLIOGRAPHY

Inter-Parliamentary Union. "Women in National Parliaments, World Classification," accessed 6 July 2016, http://www.ipu.org/wmn-e/classif.htm.

Paxton, Pamela and Melanie M. Hughes. 2007. *Women, Politics, and Power: A Global Perspective*. Los Angeles: Pine Forge Press. See, in particular, 67–79.

Trimble, Linda, Manon Tremblay, and Jane Arscott. 2013. "Conclusion: A Few More Women." In *Stalled: The Representation of Women in Canadian Governments*, edited by Linda Trimble, Jane Arscott, and Manon Tremblay, 290–314. Vancouver: UBC Press.

31 Is it possible that over time women will come to occupy half of the seats in parliaments?

In my view, there is no guarantee that, even with time and patience, women will come to occupy half of the seats in parliaments – despite hopes raised by the projection made in question 30. The reason is that there is no law called "natural increase in the number of women parliamentarians." The idea that women will eventually comprise half of all parliamentarians is widespread but not well founded. Of course, according to the projections in table 3, one parliamentarian in two will be a woman around 2039. This projection is based on the assumption that the future will reflect the past – that variables regulating women's past progress in politics not only will be the same in the future but will also behave the same way. But reality and assumptions don't always match.

Setbacks may occur. For instance, the archives of the Inter-Parliamentary Union's statistical data show regressions (to various degrees) in the proportion of women in parliaments in recent years, in, for example, Argentina (40 per cent in 2008 and 35.8 per cent in 2015), Belgium (39.3 per cent in 2010 and 38 per cent in 2013), Colombia (11.8 per cent in 1998 and 8.4 per cent in 2007), Haiti (4.2 per cent in 2010 and 0 per cent in 2015), Iceland (42.9 per cent in 2009 and 39.7 per cent in 2013), Japan (11.3 per cent in 2009 and 8.1 per cent in 2012), Kuwait (6.3 per cent in 2012 and 1.5 per cent in 2013), Mongolia (7.9 per cent in 1996 and 6.6 per cent in 2007), Norway (39.4 per cent in 1997 and 36.1 per cent in 2008), Thailand (15.8 per cent in 2011 and 6.1 per cent in 2014), Vanuatu (3.8 per cent in 2004 and 0 per cent in 2016), and Vietnam (27.3 per cent in 2004 and 25.8 per cent in 2007). The National Assembly of Chad had 16.4 per cent women in 1995 but only 5.2 per cent in early 2011. Of course, for the vast majority of countries, the basic trend is one of increasing feminization of the national parliament. Nevertheless, the few declines observed, though not dramatic, not only give the lie to the idea that each election leads to an increase in the presence of women in parliaments but feeds the belief that a glass ceiling still blocks the advancement of women in politics (see question 39).

A number of factors may explain these setbacks. For example, a change to the rules of the political game may lead to a lower proportion of women in parliament. In 1989, the fall of the Berlin Wall shook up political trends in nearby countries. In several (such as the Czech Republic, Hungary,

Poland, Romania, Russia, and Ukraine), this transformation resulted in a drop in feminization rates in the parliaments instituted by the new political order inspired by the "free and democratic world," notably because quotas that had ensured women political representation under communism were withdrawn. It seems that although democratization may favour feminization of parliaments (Paxton, Hughes, and Painter II 2010), nothing guarantees it.

Changes to electoral rules may also affect feminization rates. For example, for the 1997 UK general election the British Labour Party instituted a policy of positive action for women (see question 49). However, this measure was seen as contrary to the principle of equality and the party subsequently abandoned it, so there was no measure to stimulate demand for (or selection of) female candidates for the 2001 election. The proportion of female members of the House of Commons fell slightly in that election, from 18.4 per cent to 17.9 per cent, despite the Labour Party's electoral success. Most analysts blame this decline on the fact that the policy was dropped.

A final factor is that in general, right-wing parties are less open to female candidates than are left-wing parties. The electoral success of a right-wing party may therefore result in a slower rise, stagnation, or even a drop in the proportion of women in parliament. This happened in Ontario in 1995, when Mike Harris's Conservative Party won the election and the proportion of female assembly members dropped from 21.5 per cent to 14.6 per cent. Similarly, the proportion of women in the National Assembly dropped by 5.6 per cent following the victory of the Liberal Party of Quebec, a party to the right of its predecessor, the Parti Québécois, in the 2014 election. This factor also explains the lower proportion of women in the Hungarian parliament following the 1998 elections, when the socialist-liberal coalition was replaced by a conservative coalition.

BIBLIOGRAPHY

Childs, Sarah. 2004. *New Labour's Women MPs: Women Representing Women*. London: Routledge. See, in particular, 204–11.

Inter-Parliamentary Union. "Women in National Parliaments, World Classification," accessed 6 July 2016, http://www.ipu.org/wmn-e/classif.htm.

Paxton, Pamela, Melanie Hughes, and Matthew A. Painter II. 2010. "Growth in Women's

Political Representation: A Longitudinal Exploration of Democracy, Electoral System and Gender Quotas." *European Journal of Political Research* 49 (1): 25–52.

Rueschemeyer, Marilyn and Sharon L. Wolchik, eds. 2009. *Women in Power in Post-Communist Parliaments*. Bloomington: Indiana University Press.

32 Are there more women in parliaments today because parliament as an institution is losing power?

Answering this question in the affirmative would be cynical. Whereas the greater presence of women in parliaments is an observable fact, the idea that "parliament as an institution is losing power" is totally subjective. Certainly, globalization has reconfigured the decision-making power of parliaments and governments, but they retain their capacity to make decisions within their respective borders. Furthermore, it is hard to believe that the power of parliaments and governments to decide for their community has always been autonomous – that it has always been sheltered from the influence of international forces. And if parliaments have so little power, why do independently wealthy men (such as Paul Martin in Canada and Pierre-Karl Péladeau in Quebec) – even billionaires (such as Silvio Berlusconi in Italy and Donald Trump in the United States) – move heaven and earth to get elected?

The increased proportion of women in the lower or single chambers of national parliaments since the turn of the century (from an average of 13.7 per cent in 2000 to 22.8 per cent in June 2016) is also observable in other spaces of power. For instance, women are swelling the ranks of professions traditionally associated with a career in politics, such as law and medicine. There are more female senior civil servants and diplomats and more women in the business world (although their progress in this sector is more modest). Christine Lagarde, executive director of the International Monetary Fund since 2011, is one of the most powerful people in the world. During the 1990s – and, more particularly, in the wake of the Fourth World Conference on Women, held in 1995 in Beijing – the question of women in parliaments was placed on the international agenda and conveyed in mobilizations by the women's movement for the adoption of electoral quotas. In 2016, quotas, in various forms, were being used in 125 countries (see questions 43 to 46).

In my view, the idea that there are more women in parliaments because parliaments are losing power conveys a perspective of victimization. If there are more women in parliaments today, it is thanks mainly to mobilizations by the women's movement in the field of electoral politics. It is thanks also to states and political parties that have adopted quotas for women in politics, often under pressure from women's movements but also for reasons related to electoralism. Nevertheless, these quota measures have frequently led to remarkable results (see questions 43 to 46). As well, I believe that if there are more female parliamentarians today, it is because there are now more women who possess the skills and assets needed to perform well in politics – a change that the parties do not seem to have absorbed and that may explain why women's underrepresentation in politics endures.

In short, the greater presence of women in parliaments is not an effect of presumed loss of decision-making power of the legislative institution. Rather, women themselves must be seen as the main force behind their greater presence in parliaments.

33 Is there a link between democracy and the proportion of women in parliaments?

There is no statistical link. If we use the Freedom House Gastil Index (frequently employed in political science studies to discern the extent of democracy in a given state) to categorize countries as nondemocratic, partially democratic, or democratic, in 2016 the fifty nondemocratic and fifty-six partially democratic countries had, respectively, an average of 19.9 per cent and 18.7 per cent women within the lower or single chamber of their national parliaments, as opposed to 22.5 per cent in the eighty-five democratic countries. Here are a few examples illustrating that democracy does not necessarily involve high proportions of women in parliaments: in June 2016, the United States House of Representatives had a feminization rate of 19.4 per cent; the British House of Commons, 29.4 per cent; the Canadian House of Commons, 26 per cent; and the French National Assembly 26.2 per cent. On the other hand, the feminization rates in the lower or single chamber of the parliaments of Rwanda, Uganda, and Zimbabwe were 63.8 per cent, 33.5 per cent, and 31.5 per cent, respectively. In fact, as Paxton, Hughes, and Painter II (2010) note, the influence of democracy on the proportion of female parliamentarians is better appreciated over the long term than at a specific point in time. In other words, although the state of democracy in a country at a given moment is not related to the feminization rate of the national parliament, democratization (democracy as a process deployed over the long term) is. Today, the proportion of women in a national parliament is posed as one criterion, among others, for assessing the state of a country's democracy – even if a low presence of female parliamentarians is not enough to conclude that a country is not democratic.

Although the link between democracy and feminization of parliaments is seen as increasingly important, it finds little backing in theoretical, historical, or practical references. According to Freedom House, in 1989 there were forty-one electoral democracies in the world; this number grew to forty-six in 1990, fifty in 1991, fifty-three in 1992, fifty-seven in 1993, sixty in 1994, and eighty-nine in 2013. This rise in numbers makes it possible to posit the paradigm that parliaments of new democracies must reflect the diversity of the populations that they represent. In turn, this reading makes it possible to push the imperative of women's representation and make their presence in good numbers in elective bodies a measure of the quality of democratic life. It is a paradigm that is promoted by international organizations (such as the United Nations) and regional ones (such as the South African Development Community) and is implicitly stated in a number of major instruments of international law, such as the Beijing Platform for Action (1995), the Universal Declaration on Democracy (1997), and the African Charter on Human and Peoples' Rights (2003) (see question 41). This explains why quotas for women in politics spread like wildfire during the 1990s and 2000s. It must also, no doubt, be seen as part of the reason for the adoption of quotas in Afghanistan and Iraq, in which the presence of women in political institutions is an intrinsic aspect of constitutional and electoral reengineering (and may also be a new form of Western colonialism and imperialism imposed on the rest of the world).

And yet, from a theoretical, historical, and practical point of view, democracy and women seem to have a distant relationship. In ancient Greece, known as the cradle of democracy, a citizen was a free man born to Athenian parents. In fact, democracy was founded on the exclusion of women. Theoreticians of the social contract and sovereignty of the people – among others, Hobbes (1588–1679), Grotius (1583–1645), Locke (1632–1704), Madison (1751–1836), Pufendorf (1632–1694), and, of course,

Rousseau (1712–1778) – either, at best, ignored women or, at worst, declared that they should be confined to the private and familial sphere. Of course, there were some – Condorcet, Olympe de Gouges, John Stuart Mill, and Mary Wollstonecraft – who gave women some consideration, but their works (except for Mill's) remained essentially on the margin of democracy theories. What is more, the great revolutions that opened the path to representative democracy – the Glorious Revolution of 1688, the American Revolution of 1775–83, and the French Revolution of 1789 – were not effective at bringing women into governments. In fact, in France, the abstract "individual" underlying republican universalism explicitly shut women out of political citizenship (see questions 50 to 53). Finally, although Nordic countries, recognized for the quality of their democratic governance, tend to confirm the existence of a connection between democracy and a high proportion of women parliamentarians (see question 37), Rwanda, a country not well known for its democratic values, and that had a parliament that was, as of June 2016, the most feminized in the world (see questions 29 and 36), tends to disprove such a connection. A number of authors have shown that parliaments in more democratic countries are not more feminized than those in less democratic countries (see questions 33 and 34).

BIBLIOGRAPHY

Freedom House. "Freedom in the World 2016, FIW 2016 data," accessed 9 July 2016 https://freedomhouse.org/report/freedom-world/freedom-world-2016.

Inter-Parliamentary Union. "Women in National Parliaments, World Classification," accessed 6 July 2016, http://www.ipu.org/wmn-e/classif.htm.

Pateman, Carole. 1988. *The Sexual Contract*. Cambridge: Polity.

Paxton, Pamela, Melanie Hughes, and Matthew A. Painter II. 2010. "Growth in Women's Political Representation: A Longitudinal Exploration of Democracy, Electoral System and Gender Quotas." *European Journal of Political Research* 49 (1): 25–52.

34 Does a low proportion of female parliamentarians mean a democratic deficit?

In my view, the answer to this question depends on your conception of democracy. A common definition of democracy is that given by Abraham

Lincoln, in 1863, when he was president of the United States: "Government of the people, by the people, and for the people." In practice, this form of democracy, direct democracy, is not possible today (except in Switzerland, perhaps, in the *Landsgemeinde*, for some questions, but this form of democracy did not serve Swiss women's suffrage well; see question 7). That is why we speak of "representative" democracy; through a procedure called "elections," the people (more precisely, voters) designate a limited number of people who, on their behalf, will make decisions essential to governance of the political community. This way of doing things raises a number of questions, including the one of representativeness; are the people designated in this way representative of the people as a whole? Once again, everything depends on the conception of representation – descriptive or substantive (see question 60).

According to a descriptive conception of representation, the low proportion of women in politics does imply a democratic deficit, because of the gap between their proportion in the population (a bit more than 50 per cent) and their proportion in political institutions (in June 2016, they represented 22.8 per cent of members sitting in lower or single chambers of some 190 national parliaments; see question 29). If this democratic deficit did not exist, women would be expected to occupy about half of the decision-making positions. This reading of women's political representation has been very popular since the mid-1990s; it is promoted by a number of international and regional organizations and is found in major instruments of international law, such as the Beijing Platform for Action (1995), the Treaty of Amsterdam (1997), and the Paris Declaration (1999) (see question 41).

In a substantive conception of representation, the low proportion of women in politics cannot be interpreted in terms of democratic deficit. According to this reading, the identity markers (such as sociodemographic traits, sexual preference, cultural and ethnic group membership, and so on) of elected representatives do not play a role in their political mandate; these officeholders form an abstract, disembodied group that acts in the best interests of the nation, which is also seen as an abstract, disembodied whole. This detachment from identities enables the body formed of elected people to represent the interests and opinions of the population. In short, since identity markers do not interfere with representation activities, the low presence of women in politics cannot be seen as a democratic deficit.

However, some argue that the reduced presence of women in the institutions of representative democracy means that public policies do not take adequate account of the interests and opinions of the female population, which, as a consequence, suffers a democratic deficit. This argument calls upon a descriptive conception of representation, which postulates that only women can represent women or, at least, that they are better at doing so than men are. A number of studies show that female politicians are more sensitive than their male colleagues to portfolios that are of primary concern to women's living conditions (such as childcare and violence against women; see questions 60 and 63). However, I believe that nothing supports the idea that a low number of female politicians results in public policies that ignore women. If that were the case, it would be difficult to explain how women had obtained the rights to vote and to run for office in legislative assemblies composed exclusively of men, or how parliaments constituted mainly of men adopt quota measures designed to favour the election of women, or pass legislation to fight against violence against women, or vote in favour of women's right to terminate undesired pregnancies.

To conclude, as we will see in question 60, representation is also constructed through discourse, formatting, and marketing. A low proportion of female parliamentarians will be seen as a democratic deficit if it is modelled as such by sociopolitical actors and if a significant audience sees this reading as legitimate.

BIBLIOGRAPHY

Urbinati, Nadia. 2012. "Why *Parité* Is a Better Goal than Quotas." *International Journal of Constitutional Law* 10 (2): 465–76.

35 Do economically developed countries have more-feminized parliaments than do developing countries?

There is no direct link between a country's level of socioeconomic development and the proportion of women sitting in its parliament (see question 19). This is shown clearly in the rankings established by the Inter-Parliamentary Union: with 63.8 per cent women parliamentarians in mid-2016, Rwanda, a country whose economy is dominated by agriculture and whose estimated gross domestic product per capita in 2015 was US$1,800, has the most feminized national parliament in the world (see questions 29 and 36). In June 2016, the economically disadvantaged countries of Mozambique (39.6 per cent female parliamentarians, the 15th-most feminized lower or unique chamber), Uganda (33.5 per cent; 31st rank in the Union's ranking), Zimbabwe (31.5 per cent; 38th rank), and Cameroon (31.1 per cent; 41st rank) were ahead of wealthy countries such as Austria (30.6 per cent; 44th rank), the United Kingdom (29.4 per cent; 48th rank), Australia (26.7 per cent; 56th rank), France (26.2 per cent; 60th rank), Canada (26 per cent; 62nd rank), Monaco (20.8 per cent; 81st rank), and the United States (19.4 per cent; 96th rank). However, one must not draw the opposite conclusion – that all economically disadvantaged countries are ahead of all wealthy countries: with respective proportions of 43.6 per cent (fifth rank), 41.5 per cent (10th rank), 41.3 per cent (11th rank), and 39.6 per cent (15th rank, tied with Mozambique) of women parliamentarians in June 2016, Sweden, Finland, Iceland, and Norway, respectively, have also been high in the rankings with regard to the presence of women in national parliaments for a number of decades.

It must be said that Nordic countries stand out for their leadership (see question 37). It must also be said that Afghanistan, Burundi, Rwanda, Uganda, and, since May 2013, Zimbabwe have constitutions that set out quotas for women (see question 44), and that the dominant party in Mozambique, the Front for the Liberation of Mozambique, has a quota of 40 per cent women for the composition of its electoral lists, in which female candidates must also be listed "fairly" – that is, in eligible positions. On the other hand, in "old democracies," quotas are often perceived as contrary to the liberal ideal in which merit should ensure the selection of the "best people" to assume mandates of political representation (see question 47).

BIBLIOGRAPHY

Inter-Parliamentary Union. "Women in National Parliaments, World Classification," accessed 6 July 2016, http://www.ipu.org/wmn-e/classif.htm.

Quota Database, accessed 9 July 2016, http://www.quotaproject.org/en/index.cfm.

36 Why does Rwanda have the most-feminized parliament in the world?

A policy of seats reserved for women is one reason that women occupied almost two-thirds of the seats in the Rwanda Chamber of Deputies following the September 2013 election. Another reason is that the Rwanda Patriotic Front previously instituted policies regarding equality of women and men. A final reason is the social capital built up by women after the 1994 genocide, notably their mobilizations as part of the peace process.

In Rwanda, of the eighty seats in the parliament's lower chamber, twenty-four (or 30 per cent) are reserved for women. This quota is enshrined in Rwanda's constitution; it is formal, obligatory, coercive, and permanent (see question 44). Section 9(4) of the Constitution of the Republic of Rwanda, adopted by referendum on 26 May 2003, obliges the Rwandan state to conform to the principle of "equality of all Rwandans and between women and men reflected by ensuring that women are granted at least thirty per cent of posts in decision making organs." Three other articles in the constitution combine to favour equality of the sexes/genders in terms of political representation. Article 11 forbids discrimination based on sex/gender. Article 54 states, "Political organizations must constantly reflect the unity of the people of Rwanda and gender equality and complementarity, whether in the recruitment of members, putting in place organs of leadership and in their operations and activities." Finally, article 77 provides, "The list [of candidates submitted by the parties to the electorate] shall be compiled in full respect of the principle of national unity … and the principle of gender equality in matters relating to elective offices." Those sitting in seats reserved for women are elected not directly by the population, but indirectly, "by a joint assembly composed of members of the respective District, Municipality, Town or Kigali City Councils and members of the Executive Committees of women's organizations at the Province, Kigali City, District, Municipalities, Towns and Sector levels" (article 76, par. 2 of the Constitution of the Republic of Rwanda). This means that women play a prominent role in designating their female representatives in parliament.

According to Longman (2006), three factors led to Rwanda writing into its constitution an electoral policy for women: a plea by international organizations for it to include women in political institutions (see question 41), strong mobilization by the Rwandan women's movement on the question of legislative representation, and devastation of the male population by the genocide and the ensuing imprisonments, which reduced competition for the seats in parliament. To these factors must be added the fact that the population, shocked by the abhorrent treatment of women during the genocide, was open to measures designed to improve their lot in the postgenocide period. Furthermore, according to Paxton and Hughes (2007), the transitional government instituted following the genocide saw the inclusion of women in decision-making structures as contributing to political stability. It is also possible that the authoritarian president of Rwanda, Paul Kagame, was deploying a strategy to keep control of parliament while rebuilding his brand on the international scene.

Aside from the twenty-four seats reserved for women, twenty-seven of the remaining fifty-six seats were won by female candidates in the 2013 election. How can such a success be explained? A first factor concerns the positions taken and policies passed by the Rwandan Patriotic Front (RPF) with regard to equality between women and men, and notably a policy of equality with regard to the selection of candidates during primaries and their inclusion on the RPF lists (Munyaneza 2013). A second factor concerns women's mobilizations as part of the peace process following the genocide and the social capital that they drew from it. According to Anderson and Swiss (2014), the societal fractures engendered by the genocide led women to organize politically and invest more decisively in the public sphere. At the same time, according to Burnet (2011), Rwandan women solidified their social capital through better access to education, an improved capacity to express themselves and be heard in public, and a greater say in family matters.

BIBLIOGRAPHY

Anderson, Miriam J. and Liam Swiss. 2014. "Peace Accords and the Adoption of Electoral Quotas for Women in the Developing World, 1990–2006." *Politics & Gender* 10 (1): 33–61.

Burnet, Jennie E. 2011. "Women Have Found Respect: Gender Quotas, Symbolic Representation, and Female Empowerment in Rwanda." *Politics & Gender* 7 (3): 303–34.

– 2012. "Women's Empowerment and Cultural Change in Rwanda." In *The Impact of Gender Quotas*, edited by Susan Franceschet, Mona Lena Krook, and Jennifer M. Piscopo, 190–207. New York: Oxford University Press.

Longman, Timothy. 2006. "Rwanda: Achieving Equality or Serving an Authoritarian

State?" In *Women in African Parliaments*, edited by Gretchen Bauer and Hannah E. Britton, 133–50. Boulder: Lynne Rienner Publishers.

Munyaneza, James. 2013, September 19. "Rwanda: Women Take 64 Per cent Seats in Parliament." *AllAfrica*, accessed 9 July 2016, http://allafrica.com/stories/201309190110.html.

Paxton, Pamela, and Melanie M. Hughes. 2007. *Women, Politics, and Power: A Global Perspective*. Los Angeles: Pine Forge Press. See, in particular, 173–6.

Quota Database. "Rwanda," accessed 9 July 2016, http://www.quotaproject.org/country/rwanda.

World Intellectual Property Organization. "Constitution of the Republic of Rwanda," accessed 9 July 2016, http://www.wipo.int/edocs/lexdocs/laws/en/rw/rw033en.pdf.

37 Why were the Nordic countries ahead of the field?

First, it must be specified that despite the rather reductive idea of the "Nordic countries," Denmark, Finland, Iceland, Norway, and Sweden do not form a homogeneous political and societal group – as the suffragist struggles, marked with many national specificities, quickly make obvious (Blom 2012). Nevertheless, these countries do share a history of being ahead of the field with regard to women's political rights, as a number of firsts occurred in one or another of them. In Finland, not only did a woman sit in the national parliament for the first time in 1907 but nineteen seats were occupied by women – 10 per cent of the seats. It was also in Finland that a female president (Tarja Kaarina Halonen, who held the position from 2000 to 2012) had the first two female ministers in her cabinet (Anneli Jäätteenmäki in 2003 and Mari Kiviniemi in 2010–11; see question 68). Women took on ministerial functions for the first time in the noncommunist world in Denmark in 1924 and then Finland in 1926 (see question 71). In 1980, Iceland was the first country in which a woman (Vigdís Finnbogadóttir) became president in a direct general election (she served until 1996). The following year, in 1981, Gro Harlem Brundtland became prime minister of Norway, a position that she led for a decade (see question 68). In 1986, Sweden became the first country to form a parity government. Finally, between February 2009 and May 2013, in Iceland, Jóhanna Sigurðardóttir was the first open lesbian to join the small circle of leaders of national governments.

Sociocultural and political factors help to explain the advance of the Nordic countries. For instance, because Scandinavian societies became secularized relatively early, women had a greater space within which to manage their private and public roles autonomously. The Nordic countries are also known for values of social democracy and consociationalism (which fosters the sharing of power among different sociocultural groups), to the detriment of liberalism. The result is that the representation of groups (such as political representation for women) is perceived as self-evident and has inspired women's political action since the late nineteenth century. The ideology of equality (between sexes/genders of course but also among classes, for example), also well accepted, went hand in hand with the emergence and institution of welfare states that were for many years (and still are occasionally) the envy of a number of countries. It must be added that in the 1960s, women entered the education and labour markets en masse, which had an effect on their socialization and politicization. Feminist movements were also powerful agents for women's political socialization. Moreover, unlike in countries in which feminist movements avoided electoral politics (such as France and Great Britain), in the Nordic countries they decided to work with and within established political parties (notably the social-democratic parties). This strategy enabled women to infiltrate the parties and gain enough power in them to put the feminization rate in parliaments on the agenda. The parties being the gateway to political power, this strategy also enabled women to put pressure on parliament to promote their demands.

The Nordic countries have political (including electoral) institutions favourable to the election of women (see question 21) (although the goodwill of the political parties is a decisive element in a voting system's effect on the feminization of parliaments; see questions 23, 45, and 54). For instance, all use a list proportional voting system and plurinominal electoral districts to elect members to national parliament. In Finland, the electoral lists are open – the electorate votes not for a list compiled by a political party but directly for the candidates on the list (see question 21). Caul Kittilson (2006) maintains that this option fosters the election of women for two reasons: first, female candidates are thus able to avoid the some parties' annoying tendency of putting women at the bottom of the list, thus limiting their chances of being elected; second, on some occasions, female candidates are able to benefit from the mobilization of female voters on their behalf. That said, Matland and Lilliefeldt (2014) are more cautious about the benefits of open lists to the election of female candidates. It also seems that women form a powerful electoral bloc in Nordic countries (notably due to the legitimacy enjoyed by the representation of groups), in the sense that if a party is reluctant to respond to their demands for representation, they can either turn to a different political party or set up (or threaten to) a women's political party (or a feminist party; see question 55).

To conclude, I would like to emphasize that the strong feminization of Nordic parliaments has little to do with quotas. First, where such measures do exist, they were adopted when women already constituted at least one-quarter of parliamentarians. Second, none of the five Nordic countries has obligatory and coercive legal quotas; only party quotas, voluntary measures, and incentives have been adopted (see question 44). Third, Finland has never had quotas and yet, in June 2016, its parliament contained 41.5 per cent women. In Denmark, the few parties that had quotas have now abandoned them. In short, although quotas are powerful tools for feminizing parliaments, the real desire of political parties to open their doors to women is the vehicle most likely to achieve this objective (see questions 23, 45, and 54).

BIBLIOGRAPHY

Bergqvist, Christina. 2011. "The Nordic Countries." In *Women in Executive Power: A Global Overview*, edited by Gretchen Bauer and Manon Tremblay, 157–70. London and New York: Routledge.

Blom, Ida. 2012. "Structures and Agency: A Transnational Comparison of the Struggle for Women's Suffrage in the Nordic Countries During the Long 19th Century." *Scandinavian Journal of History* 37 (5): 600–20.

Caul Kittilson, Miki. 2006. *Challenging Parties, Changing Parliaments: Women and Elected Office in Contemporary Western Europe*. Columbus: Ohio State University Press. See, in particular, 103–17, 129–36.

Freidenvall, Lenita, Drude Dahlerup, and Hege Skjeie. 2006. "The Nordic Countries. An Incremental Model." In *Women, Quotas and Politics*, edited by Drude Dahlerup, 55–82. London: Routledge.

Matland, Richard E. and Emilie Lilliefeldt. 2014. "The Effect of Preferential Voting on Women's Representation." In *Representation: The Case of Women*, edited by Maria C.

Escobar-Lemmon and Michelle M. Taylor-Robinson, 79–102. New York: Oxford University Press.

Raaum, Nina C. 1999. "Women in Parliamentary Politics: Historical Lines of Development." In *Equal Democracies? Gender and Politics in the Nordic Countries*, edited by Christina Bergqvist et al., 27–47. Oslo: Scandinavian University Press.

Sjogren, Asa Karlsson. 2012. "Women's Voices in Swedish Towns and Cities at the Turn of the Twentieth Century: Municipal Franchise, Polling, Eligibility and Strategies for Universal Suffrage." *Women's History Review* 21 (3): 379–98.

Tremblay, Manon. 2016. "Les femmes et la représentation parlementaire." In *Social-démocratie 2.1. Le Québec comparé aux pays scandinaves*, 2nd edition, revised and expanded, edited by Stéphane Paquin with Pier-Luc Lévesque and Jean-Patrick Brady, 385–414. Montreal: Presses de l'Université de Montréal.

38 Where and when was a woman elected to a national parliament for the first time?

Finland has the honour of being the first country in which a woman was elected to a national parliament, the Eduskunta. In 1907, just one year after the country gained independence and established universal suffrage for women and men, women (nineteen of them) were elected to the Eduskunta. This amounted to 10 per cent of the seats – and there was no women's movement specifically devoted to promoting their political representation. It took several more decades for that same 10 per cent threshold to be reached in the other Nordic countries: in 1953 in Sweden, 1966 in Denmark, 1973 in Norway, and 1983 in Iceland. According to Paxton and Hughes (2007), less than 30 per cent of countries elected a woman to parliament in the election immediately following the acquisition of female suffrage.

Why did Finland have such a head start? There are a number of reasons, including a tradition of political mobilization among both women and men, supported by the desire for national independence from imperial Russia, and the establishment of democracy through universal suffrage. Conferring the right to vote on all adults on an equal basis, the 1906 electoral reform was part of an undertaking to define and consolidate national unity, which had been put at risk by an unstable sociopolitical context. Nevertheless, this mobilization helped to politicize women and encourage them to be involved in politics. In addition, their high rates of participation in political parties and in the job market must also be taken into account to explain Finland's advance on the rest of the world.

BIBLIOGRAPHY

Paxton, Pamela and Melanie M. Hughes. 2007. *Women, Politics, and Power: A Global Perspective*. Los Angeles: Pine Forge Press. See, in particular, 64–8.

Raaum, Nina C. 1999. "Women in Parliamentary Politics; Historical Lines of Development." In *Equal Democracies? Gender and Politics in the Nordic Countries*, edited by Christina Bergqvist et al., 27–47. Oslo: Scandinavian University Press.

Tremblay, Manon. 2016. "Les femmes et la représentation parlementaire." In *Social-démocratie 2.1. Le Québec comparé aux pays scandinaves*, 2nd edition, revised and expanded, edited by Stéphane Paquin with Pier-Luc Lévesque and Jean-Patrick Brady, 385–414. Montreal: Presses de l'Université de Montréal.

39　What are "critical mass," the "contagion effect," the "glass ceiling," and "glass walls"?

Essentially, these are tools for analyzing the descriptive representation of women in politics (see question 60). The notion of critical mass is inspired by nuclear physics; it refers to the quantity of material necessary to trigger a chain reaction leading to a new and irreversible state. These days, scientists often use it to describe the environmental point of no return. Applied to women's political participation, "critical mass" conveys the idea that when a minority group (in this case, women) reaches a certain proportion within an organization (such as parliament) it is in a better position to defend and promote its interests. This proportion is generally set between 15 and 30 per cent, although the United Nations uses the upper limit of this range, 30 per cent, as its parameter (United Nations Development Programme 1995: 108–9).

As a theory, critical mass originated with the research by Rosabeth Moss Kanter (1977) on women within large commercial organizations in the United States. Kanter posited that the relative proportion of women and men in an organization influences their opinions, roles, and behaviours. She identified four types of groups according to the ratio of women to men. A uniform group is one in which all members are similar (for example, there are only men); the culture in which the organization exists is also homogeneous. The skewed group is one in which the majority–minority ratio is around eighty-five to fifteen – that is, one category of individuals dominates. Like the uniform group, the dominant category in the skewed group controls the organizational culture, imposing its values, standards, and models of behaviour. In this type of organization, not only do women become symbols of their category but they are also perceived according to two forms of polarization, in which both the points of convergence among them and the points of divergence between them and men are exaggerated. When the ratio is around thirty-five to sixty-five, the group is tilted, characterized by a mixed culture; the numerically dominant category is no longer able to completely control the organizational culture and must deal with the values, standards, and behavioural models of the minority category. In other words, the minority party represents a sufficiently large weight within the organization to challenge the cultural parameters of the majority party and force it to pay attention. The last group, the balanced group, corresponds to parity. Here, in principle, no group is able to impose its views on the other or on the organization as a whole.

Critical mass links descriptive and substantive representation (see question 60). It is based on the idea that the numerical weight of one category within an organization (descriptive representation) will enable it to exert influence on the organization's orientations and decisions (substantive representation). In other words, a greater number of women in parliament results in an agenda on which there are questions that concern women and their life experiences; public policies that are more sensitive to their needs, demands, and interests; and a political style that is more in sync with women's socialization.

The contagion effect is somewhat similar to critical mass, in that it also suggests a chain reaction. It describes "a process by which one party in a multiparty system stimulates other parties to adopt their policies or strategies" (Matland and Studlar 1996: 708). An example of a contagion effect would be when a large political party copies a smaller rival party by adopting a similar measure with regard to political representation of women (a quota, for example) in a context in which it is presumed that an electoral gender gap exists (see questions, 2, 10 to 17).

The results of empirical research conducted to date in a number of countries do not, however, supply convincing proof that critical mass and the contagion effect exist. Indeed, although observations made by a number of authors support these ideas, more and more studies are throwing doubt on the idea that a greater number of female politicians produces governance that is more sympathetic to women (see the section "Critical Perspectives on Gender and Politics: Do Women Represent Women? Rethinking the 'Critical Mass' Debate," *Politics & Gender* 2, no. 4 [2006], and, more recently, Chaney 2012; Childs and Krook 2008, 2009; Holli 2012; MacDonald and O'Brien 2011).

There are a number of reasons for the weak resonance of the notion of critical mass. First, it presumes that women form a politically significant group in terms of parliamentary representation, an assumption that generates many theoretical issues (see questions 12, 60, and 63). It also suggests that women constitute a homogeneous group, a premise that is not well defended (see question 12). Second, the notion of critical mass leads one to believe that female politicians not only are aware of their identity as "women," but that they give priority to this identity marker to the detriment of others (such as belonging to a political party, for example), a hierarchy that remains to be demonstrated. Third, in the social universe numbers are not magical; a large proportion does not automatically translate into equivalent influence, as can be seen in the contrasting situations of women and the business class. Fourth, and as a corollary, other factors besides demographic weight intervene to shape power, for better or worse, within an organization. For instance, female cabinet members have a level of influence that female backbenchers can only envy. Thus, a few women with real decision-making power within government are no doubt better armed to represent women than are a larger number without such power, even in a parliament that is balanced as to sex/gender. Furthermore, research has shown that belonging to a left-wing party and identification with feminism are much more closely linked to substantive representation of women than is simply the proportion of female parliamentarians (see questions 60 and 63). The notion of critical mass would therefore gain credibility if it took account of the party affiliation of elected women. In effect, is it realistic to believe that parliamentarians from different political orientations would unite to represent women, betraying their respective parties? Probably not, although such alliances are sometimes established when the political regime allows (it is more difficult under Westminster-type parliamentary regimes, but more frequent in American-style presidential regimes, in which the party discipline is weaker; Gertzog 2004). In the final analysis, such alliances are more likely to happen among women in a single party, who, having greater numbers, are no doubt better equipped to defend and promote the "women's cause" within their caucus.

The notion of critical mass leads to the idea of a sort of snowball effect, even a cause-and-effect relationship: more women in politics will lead to more public decisions favourable to women. And yet, increased feminization in an organization may provoke hostility from the members of the majority group, who fear for their influence and power. This is in part what the notion of the "glass ceiling" conveys; it is as if women are admitted to and tolerated in politics as long as there are not enough of them to change the culture, ways of doing things, and priorities. Beyond a certain threshold, they become threatening. Many researchers, international organizations (including the United Nations), and regional organizations set this threshold at 30 per cent – the "critical mass" proportion.

The glass ceiling may thus be understood, at least in part, as a response to critical mass and the contagion effect; it consists of containing the number of women in the name of the status quo. But the defeat of Hillary Rodham Clinton in the US election of 8 November 2016 has added another dimension to the notion of the glass ceiling: in that case, it was also about blocking women's access to the Holy of Holies, the American presidency, no doubt the most powerful political role on Earth. In her concession speech, Clinton said, "Now, I know we have still not shattered that highest and hardest glass ceiling, but someday someone will – and hopefully sooner than we might think right now" (https://www.vox.com/2016/11/9/13570 328/hillary-clinton-concession-speech-full-transcript-2016-presidential-election). That a politician as experienced and battle-hardened as Clinton was not able to "shatter that highest … glass ceiling" inspired a variant on this notion: that of the "glass vault."

Another strategy that perpetuates the gender regime is to restrict female politicians to the sectors traditionally considered appropriate to them (such as education, family, and culture; see question 72). The notion of glass walls conveys this strategy of segregation: to women go the "female" portfolios, and to men the "male" ones. As long as this order rules, the gender regime will endure, even if there are more women in politics.

BIBLIOGRAPHY

Chaney, Paul. 2012. "Critical Actors vs. Critical Mass: The Substantive Representation of Women in the Scottish Parliament." *British Journal of Politics and International Relations* 14 (3): 441–57.

Childs, Sarah and Mona Lena Krook. 2008. "Critical Mass Theory and Women's Political Representation." *Political Studies* 56 (3): 725–36.

– 2009. "Analysing Women's Substantive Representation; From Critical Mass to Critical Actors." *Government and Opposition* 44 (2): 125–45.

Childs, Sarah, Paul Webb, and Sally Marthaler. 2010. "Constituting and Substantively Representing Women: Applying New Approaches to a UK Case Study." *Politics & Gender* 6 (2): 199–223.

"Critical Perspectives on Gender and Politics. Do Women Represent Women? Rethinking the "Critical Mass" Debate." 2006. Special section, *Politics & Gender* 2 (4): 492–530.

Dahlerup, Drude. 1988. "From a Small to a Large Minority. Women in Scandinavian Politics." *Scandinavian Political Studies* 11 (4): 275–99.

Folke, Olle and Johanna Rickne. 2016. "The Glass Ceiling in Politics: Formalization and Empirical Tests." *Comparative Political Studies* 49 (5): 567–99.

Gertzog, Irwin N. 2004. *Women & Power on Capitol Hill: Reconstructing the Congressional Women's Caucus*. Boulder: Lynne Rienner.

Holli, Anne Maria. 2012. "Does Gender Have an Effect on the Selection of Experts by Parliamentary Standing Committees? A Critical Test of 'Critical' Concepts." *Politics & Gender* 8 (3): 341–66.

Kanter, Rosabeth Moss. 1977. "Some Effects of Proportions on Group Life: Skewed Sex Ratios and Responses to Token Women." *American Journal of Sociology* 82 (5): 965–90.

MacDonald, Jason A. and Erin E. O'Brien. 2011. "Quasi-Experimental Design, Constituency, and Advancing Women's Interests: Reexamining the Influence of Gender on Substantive Representation." *Political Research Quarterly* 64 (2): 472–86.

Matland, Richard E. and Donley T. Studlar. 1996. "The Contagion of Women Candidates in Single-Member District and Proportional Representation Electoral Systems: Canada and Norway." *Journal of Politics* 58 (3): 707–33.

Radio Canada 2016. "Vous avez manqué le discours d'Hillary Clinton? Le voici," accessed 31 December 2016, http://ici.radio-canada.ca/nouvelle/813710/transcription-presidentielle-discours-election-defaite-hillary-clinton.

Sawer, Marian. 2012. "What Makes the Substantive Representation of Women Possible in a Westminster Parliament? The Story of RU486 in Australia." *International Political Science Review* 33 (3): 320–35.

Tripier, Pierre. 2010. "De l'esprit pionnier aux plafonds et parois de verre." *Les cahiers du GRIF*, 48 (1): 5–11.

United Nations Development Programme. 1995. *Human Development Report*. New
  York: Oxford University Press, accessed 10 July 2016, http://hdrnet.org/427/1/hdr_
  1995_en.pdf.

40 Why should there be more women in parliaments?

Two types of arguments have been put forward to support the idea of increasing the number of women in politics: those related to justice and
equality, and those related to utilitarianism. The logic of the justice and
equality argument is that because one human being out of two is a woman,
it is only simple justice that the two sexes/genders be equally represented
in politics. This is even truer because democratic governance is not a field
of intervention like any other; it is at the core of life in society. In essence,
politics concerns the means by which a community manages its resources
(usually limited in nature). Politics involves choices and decisions that have
concrete impacts on daily lives, but also on society's longer-term orientations. Excluding women from political representation (or limiting them to
low numerical representation) thus amounts to denying them the right to
participate (fully) in the process of making public decisions that affect
them. If, as citizens, women suffer the consequences of these decisions, it
is only justice that they participate, at the same level as men – that is, with
them – in making those decisions.

There are two types of utilitarian arguments. One concerns the quality
of democratic life and the other, role models. Underrepresentation of
women in political spaces implies that public decision-making processes
are not based on optimal use of all available resources. The inclusion of
women would thus make it possible to enhance the pool of resources upon
which governance draws, notably when it comes to ideas and experiences
associated with women. What is more, the low presence of women among
political elites not only helps promote the idea that women are second-class
citizens, less competent than men, but also undermines the legitimacy of
democracy. Indeed, how can democratic institutions claim to represent the
people's will when half of the human race is obviously so poorly represented (see questions 33 and 34)?

The other has it that there should be more female politicians, and, especially, diverse ones, to offer girls and women models. This argument calls
upon a symbolic conception of political representation: by presence alone,

an idea or entity is evoked (see question 60). For instance, simply having a diverse range of women in politics is enough to show that girls and women may engage in public life. From this point of view, Margaret Thatcher, not well known for her sympathy to women's causes, nevertheless represented them; simply by her presence as head of the British state (a fortiori, in tandem with Elizabeth II), she demonstrated that it was possible for a woman (at least, a white, heterosexual, elitist one) to occupy the highest executive positions. Women's presence in politics also tells boys and men that they do not hold a monopoly on public decision-making positions. Finally, the simple presence of women in politics may constitute an empowerment strategy for women (see question 17), especially if these women come from diversified backgrounds.

To conclude, it is interesting to underline the ideological kinship between arguments in favour of women's suffrage (see question 8) and arguments in favour of increasing the number of women in politics. This kinship flows from the idea, for example, that women are human beings like men and that they therefore must be able to vote and be present equally in parliaments, which is nothing but basic justice; the idea that women are not only equal but different, and they therefore must be able to vote and sit in parliament to represent their interests; and, finally, the idea that by voting and sitting in parliament women will improve all of society.

BIBLIOGRAPHY

Freidenvall, Lenita and Marian Sawer. 2013. "Framing Women Politicians in Old Democracies." In *Breaking Male Dominance in Old Democracies*, edited by Drude Dahlerup and Monique Leyenaar, 260–74. Oxford: Oxford University Press.

Phillips, Anne. 1995. *The Politics of Presence*. Oxford: Clarendon Press. See, in particular, 1–56.

– 1998. "Democracy and Representation; Or, Why Should It Matter Who Our Representatives Are?" In *Feminism & Politics*, edited by Anne Phillips, 224–40. Oxford: Oxford University Press.

Williams, Melissa S. 1998. *Voice, Trust, and Memory: Marginalized Groups and the Failings of Liberal Representation*. Princeton: Princeton University Press. See, in particular, 3–22.

Young, Iris Marion. 1989. "Polity and Group Difference: A Critique of the Ideal of Universal Citizenship." *Ethics* 99 (2): 250–74.

CHAPTER SIX

Strategies for Feminizing Parliaments

41 What international mechanisms are available to promote women's political representation?

International Women's Year (1975), the Decade for Women (from 1976 to 1985), and various international conferences (such as those in Copenhagen in 1980, Mexico City in 1985, Nairobi in 1990, and Beijing in 1995) have offered opportune forums for thinking about and expressing a discourse of legitimization of women's political rights, and their political representation in particular, in terms of human rights. As this discourse states, all human beings have the right to political representation but women are clearly underrepresented, and the consequence is a democratic deficit (see questions 33 and 34). Two types of international mechanisms work to rectify this imbalance: instruments of international law and global organizations.

Since the mid-twentieth century, and particularly since the 1970s, the international community has devised legal instruments regarding women's political rights, and they have had an undeniable – if sometimes indirect – impact on the proportion of women parliamentarians. The Council of Europe, which has made equality between women and men a guiding principle, is particularly active in this area. There are, therefore, a number of international law conventions, declarations, pacts, and other documents that provide for the equality of women and men in general, and the right of women to full participation in the political life of their respective countries in particular: the Universal Declaration of Human Rights (1948), the Convention on the Political Rights of Women (1952), the Convention on the Elimination of All Forms of Discrimination against Women (CEDAW) (1979), the Beijing Platform for Action (1995), the Universal Declaration on Democracy (1997), and the UN General Assembly resolution on women's political participation (2011). On the regional level, there are the Athens Declaration (1992), the Rome Charter (1996), the Treaty of Amsterdam (1997), the South African Development Community Declaration on Gender and Development (1998), the Paris Declaration (1999), and the Protocol to the African Charter on Human and Peoples' Rights on the Rights of Women in Africa (2003), to name just a few.

Adopted on 18 December 1979, by the United Nations General Assembly and coming into effect on 3 September 1981, CEDAW is a powerful instrument of international law for two reasons. The first is that it makes equality between women and men a principle of human rights –no longer a luxury that only a few wealthy states may offer, but an inalienable right for all human beings notwithstanding the cultural, socioeconomic, and political context (at least, theoretically). The second reason is that it legally binds the signatory nations to its conditions.

CEDAW contains a number of provisions that promote the equality of women and men and women's empowerment. Articles 4, 7, and 8 have to do with women's political rights. Article 7 specifies "States Parties shall take all appropriate measures to eliminate discrimination against women in the political and public life of the country and, in particular, shall ensure to women, on equal terms with men," the rights to vote and to run for office in all elections (and to vote in referendums) and participation in the formulation of public policy and in civil society groups that are devoted to the country's public and political life. Article 8 concerns women's right to participate under the same conditions as men in international public activities – that is, "to represent their Governments at the international level and to participate in the work of international organizations." Finally, article 4 stipulates that "adoption by States Parties of temporary special measures aimed at accelerating de facto equality between men and women shall not be considered discrimination." This article opens the door to adoption of quotas in order to increase the presence of women in politics. Under certain conditions, quotas can make an important contribution to feminizing political spaces (see questions 43 to 48).

CEDAW is intended to be a coherent whole, and so its various components are linked to each other. Therefore, although articles 4, 7, and 8 directly concern women's political participation, other articles share this objective. For instance, CEDAW establishes a distinction between equality before the law and equality in fact. This distinction is important. For example, the Universal Declaration of Human Rights (1948) recognizes women's right to participate in state affairs at the same level as men, and yet, in 2016, women constituted only 22.7 per cent of parliamentarians throughout the world, all chambers combined. Similarly, article 5 of CEDAW forces signatory countries to take measures to eliminate sexism against women. Yet, sexism poses serious obstacles to women's full and entire participation in political life (see questions 20, 23, and 28).

An Optional Protocol, which is also a treaty in its own right, is appended to CEDAW, although signatory states are not bound by it. Adopted on 6 October 1999, and coming into effect on 22 December 2000, the Optional Protocol is intended not only to be a tool for interpreting and assessing CEDAW but also to offer recourse to women who feel that their rights under CEDAW have not been respected through two procedures: complaint and investigation. The complaint procedure allows individuals and groups to lodge a complaint with the Committee on the Elimination of Discrimination against Women. If the committee rules that the complaint is well founded – that there seem to have been "grave or systematic" violations of women's rights – it may start an investigation. These two mechanisms, however, can be applied only in Protocol signatory countries. The decisions made by the Committee on the Elimination of Discrimination against Women in the context of the Protocol have no legal force. That is, states are not required to submit to them; their value is moral and symbolic.

These instruments of international law guide the work of a flock of worldwide organizations involved with equality between women and men, promotion of women's political rights, and strengthening their presence in decision-making bodies. The United Nations, the Inter-Parliamentary Union, the International Institute for Democracy and Electoral Assistance (International IDEA), and the International Knowledge Network of Women in Politics (iKNOW Politics) are among the most active organizations in this respect.

Since the mid-1990s, the UN has become an important ally in women's struggle to increase their presence in political institutions. Aside from the 4th World Conference on Women, which resulted in the Platform for Action, the UN oversaw a number of events and conferences on women's participation in public decision making. Significantly, in July 2010, the UN created the United Nations Entity for Gender Equality and the Empowerment of Women (UN Women), an agency devoted to promoting the equality of the sexes/genders and the empowerment of women. UN Women is active in various fields, including women's leadership and political participation, in the context of which it studies the effects of voting systems on women's participation and political representation and takes action to convince parties to be more open to women. In 2011, the UN General Assembly adopted a resolution on women's political participation (A/RES/66/130) that underlines how important it is for women to be involved in their country's political life and asks members states to adopt measures for this purpose. And yet, the UN sometimes makes surprising moves, such as the election of Saudia Arabia to the UN Commission on the Status of Women in April 2017. Given how Saudi women are infantilized – even enslaved – Hillel Neuer, executive director of UN Watch, commented, "Electing Saudi Arabia to protect women's rights is like making an arsonist into the town fire chief" (Murphy and Roth 2017).

The Inter-Parliamentary Union, created in 1889, defines itself as an international organization for parliaments of sovereign states. It has some 140 members. Although the proportion of women in parliaments is not the Union's only focus, it does devote a healthy chunk of resources to the issue. Its statistics on the proportion of women in parliaments are now seen as an authoritative tool in research circles; it also cooperates with academics to conduct studies on women in parliaments, fosters exchanges and networking among female parliamentarians, and offers technical assistance for specific projects.

International IDEA, headquartered in Stockholm, promotes the development of democracy around the world. It does a great deal of research and publishes numerous documents on various aspects of women's participation in democratic institutions and processes. A particularly useful and appreciated tool that it publishes, jointly with the Inter-Parliamentary Union and the University of Stockholm, is the database on quotas for women in politics.

iKNOW Politics was launched in February 2007. It is a joint initiative of UN Women, the United Nations Development Program, International IDEA, and the Inter-Parliamentary Union. Its objective is to promote gender-sensitive political governance and to increase the role and the number of women in politics. To this end, it fosters networking among parliamentarians, political parties, the community of researchers, and actors in the field. Its website offers a long list of publications, and it also hosts a discussion forum that allows people to ask questions of experts, among other things.

Together, these organizations have contributed to creating and promoting a political culture of equality between women and men, which is indispensable to women having a greater presence in politics.

BIBLIOGRAPHY

Baldez, Lisa. 2011. "The UN Convention to Eliminate All Forms of Discrimination Against Women (CEDAW): A New Way to Measure Women's Interests." *Politics & Gender* 7 (3): 419–23.

Byrnes, Andrew and Jane Connors. 2015. *The International Bill of Rights for Women: The Impact of the CEDAW Convention.* Oxford: Oxford University Press.

Cho, Seo-Young. 2014. "International Women's Convention, Democracy, and Gender Equality." *Social Science Quarterly* 95 (3): 719–39.

Freeman, Marsha A., Christine Chinkin, and Beate Rudolf, eds. 2012. *The UN Convention on the Elimination of All Forms of Discrimination Against Women: A Commentary.* Oxford: Oxford University Press.

Hellum, Anne and Henriette Sinding Aasen, eds. 2013. *Women's Human Rights: CEDAW in International, Regional and National Law.* Cambridge: Cambridge University Press.

Inter-Parliamentary Union. "Instruments of International Law Concerning Women," accessed 26 July 2016, http://www.ipu.org/wmn-e/law.htm.

Inter-Parliamentary Union. "Women in National Parliaments," accessed 26 July 2016, http://www.ipu.org/wmn-e/world.htm.

International Institute for Democracy and Electoral Assistance (International IDEA), accessed 26 July 2016, http://www.idea.int/.

International Knowledge Network of Women in Politics (iknow Politics), accessed 26 July 2016, http://iknowpolitics.org/en.

Murphy, Paul P. and Richard Roth. 2017, April 25. "Saudi Arabia's Election to UN Women's Commission Draws Ire." CNN World, accessed June 6, 2017, http://www.cnn.com/2017/04/25/world/saudi-arabia-un-womens-commission-trnd/.

Patkar, Mallika, and Tessa C. Martin. 2013. "International Conventions and Women's Rights." *Washington Report on Middle East Affairs* 32 (7): 53–4.

Quota Database. "Country Overview," accessed 26 July 2016, http://www.quotaproject.org/country.cfm.

Schopp-Schilling, Hanna Beate. 2005. "The Role of UN CEDAW and Its Monitoring Procedures for Achieving Gender Equality in Political Representation." In *The Implementation of Quotas: European Experiences. Quota Report Series,* edited by Julie

Ballington and Francesca Binda. Stockholm: International IDEA. See, in particular, 130–5.

UN Women, accessed 26 July 2016, http://www.unwomen.org/en.

UN Women. "Convention on the Elimination of All Forms of Discrimination against Women," accessed 26 July 2016, http://www.un.org/womenwatch/daw/cedaw/.

Zwingel, Susanne. 2013. "International Feminist Strategies: Strengths and Challenges of the Rights-Based Approach." *Politics & Gender* 9 (3): 344–51.

42 What measures are likely to encourage an increase in women's presence in politics?

Various measures may contribute to more women being involved in politics. These measures would be inserted into the four steps that punctuate the path toward political power: eligibility, recruitment, selection, and election (see question 18). Below, they will be presented as potential measures, not because they are purely theoretical fantasies (on the contrary, a number of them have been implemented) but because their implementation is still more the exception than the rule. It is true that as of June 2016, around 125 countries out of the 190 ranked by the Inter-Parliamentary Union had adopted quotas (in one form or another), but many of these provisions have not had the intended consequences. For instance, Canada is listed in the register of quotas established jointly by International IDEA, the Inter-Parliamentary Union, and the University of Stockholm because in 1985 the New Democratic Party (NDP) adopted a policy to establish 50 per cent female candidates for the federal election, and in 1993 the Liberal Party of Canada (LPC) set a target of 25 per cent seats filled by women. Yet, despite its success in the 2011 election, the NDP remains uncompetitive on the Canadian federal scene (that is, Canada-wide), and the goodwill of its leader is required for the LPC to reach its stated parity goal. Justin Trudeau showed some sensitivity toward the problem of underrepresentation of women in Canadian politics following the 2015 election; as he was unable to affect the feminization rate in the Liberal caucus in the House of Commons, he did so at the executive level, by appointing a parity cabinet (see question 91). In any case, neither target is likely to increase the number of female federal representatives (or, at best, may do so marginally).

With regard to eligibility, which has to do with rights conferred by the state and thus with political citizenship, public information campaigns may be undertaken to present the rights to vote and to run for office as equally legitimate for women and men. Such a measure would make it possible to limit the negative effects of socialization that discourage women's involvement in politics, particularly running for office (see question 28).

Recruitment concerns the composition of a pool of potential candidates for elections. The result of recruitment is analogous to the group of people who respond to a job offer advertised in a newspaper (see question 18). A number of measures might improve the presence and visibility of women within this informal process. These measures may be deployed locally, nationally, or societally, and they are fruitful over the short or the longer term. For example, identifying women interested in political action and forming a bank of potential female candidates is a local (or national) short-term measure; ensuring the presence of women on all levels of parties is a medium-term measure, which may be both local and national; encouraging women's access to university, improving their socioeconomic situation, and adopting family-support measures are long-term societal strategies. A number of other measures are worth mentioning. Political parties might draw their candidates from outside of their usual networks and look instead in spaces where women spend their time (such as community groups and women's groups). They might launch public appeals for candidates in the newspapers, as is done in the Netherlands. The women's movement might be a step ahead of political demand for girls and women, encouraging them to become interested in politics through public lectures, experience with "youth municipal councils," online video capsules on women's political participation, and so on.

Selection is the stage during which the political parties choose their candidates for the elections. To continue with the analogy of the job offer, selection is when the employer takes a closer look at those who responded to the job ad by, for example, interviewing ones who seem the most appropriate (see question 18). A number of studies support the idea that political parties bear primary responsibility for the low proportion of female parliamentarians (see questions 23, 45, and 54). In the vast majority of cases, election to parliament necessitates that a candidate be selected by a political party before an election. But either women are not selected often (enough) by the parties or those who are selected have little chance of being elected. The measures taken at this stage thus aim to ensure that growing numbers of women are selected as candidates, and sometimes they aim to improve (or even assure) their chances at election. These measures vary in strength. For instance, some political parties have expressed their intention to reach a certain proportion of female candidates in vague terms that relieve them of any constraint to act by using the notion of "objective" or target (sometimes called a proviso). According to the database on electoral quotas for women consulted in June 2016, this was how the People's Party–Movement for a Democratic Slovakia expressed its goal of parity. Also in 2016, the New Democratic Party of Canada and the Democrat Party of Thailand made use of the fluid, flexible, and noncommittal notion of "objective." At the other end of the spectrum are robust measures such as formal electoral quotas (see questions 43 and 44). Between these two extremes, a wide range of measures may be implemented. For example, the state may use financial incentives to encourage parties to select women; parties' national leadership may make local leaders responsible for selecting candidates aware of the imperative to choose a greater number of women through consciousness-raising training or tools such as video capsules and online training; the parties may ensure that women sit (in sufficient numbers) on candidate-selection committees; or women's groups may alert public opinion to put pressure on the parties to select more women or set up mentoring opportunities.

At the election stage (which, in the analogy, corresponds to choosing the person to hire; see question 18), a number of measures may encourage women to become candidates. For example, parties that are aware of women's representation deficit could have them run in some of their most promising ridings or place them in the best positions on the lists; they could provide them with particular assistance (financial, human, and material resources, and so on); or they could offer them training, especially on how to handle the media (see question 27). The women's movement may also set up training and funds designed to sustain women's election campaigns (such as the EMILY's Lists in Australia and the United States; see question 21). Although, in general, the electorate is not hostile to women (see question 14), it is not blindly favourable to them, and so it is important to encourage the electorate to vote for a woman. For example, Schmidt (2012) reported that in Peru women's groups promoted the slogan "Of your two preferential votes, cast one for a woman," offering voters who so wished a means to express parity choices. Of course, voters could, if they wanted, cast both of their votes for a female candidate! That said, the most controversial measure aimed at increasing the number of women in politics is the electoral quota.

BIBLIOGRAPHY

Krook, Mona Lena, Joni Lovenduski, and Judith Squires. 2006. "Western Europe, North America, Australia and New Zealand: Gender Quotas in the Context of Citizenship Models." In *Women, Quotas and Politics*, edited by Drude Dahlerup, 194–221. London and New York: Routledge.

Krook, Mona Lena and Pippa Norris. 2014. "Beyond Quotas: Strategies to Promote Gender Equality in Elected Office." *Political Studies* 62 (1): 2–20.

Quota Database. "Country Overview," accessed 11 July 2016, http://www.quotaproject.org/country.cfm.

Schmidt, Gregory. 2012. "Success Under Open List PR: The Election of Women to the Congress." In *Women and Legislative Representation; Electoral Systems, Political Parties, and Sex Quotas*, revised and updated edition, edited by Manon Tremblay, 167–8. New York: Palgrave Macmillan.

43 What is an electoral quota?

According to Dahlerup (2006, 6), "Electoral gender quotas are simply a type of equal opportunity measure that force the nominating bodies, in most political systems the political parties, to recruit, nominate or select more women for political positions." Larserud and Taphorn (2007, 8) describe quotas for women as "a form of affirmative action to help them overcome the obstacles that prevent them from entering politics in the same way as their male colleagues." The Quota Database website defines quotas for women as follows:

Quotas for women entail that women must constitute a certain number or percentage of the members of a body, whether it is a candidate list, a parliamentary assembly, a committee, or a government. The quota system places the burden of recruitment not on the individual woman, but on those who control the recruitment process. The core idea behind this system is to recruit women into political positions and to ensure that women are not only a token few in political life … Today, quota systems aim at ensuring that women constitute a large minority of 20, 30 or 40 per cent, or even to ensure true gender balance of 50-50 per cent. ("About Quotas")

The electoral quota is an equal-opportunity measure that imposes a minimum proportion of women, thus aiming for a more balanced sharing of political roles between women and men.

But there is more: quotas fall within a conception of equality that takes both starting conditions and results into account and is based on the principle that identical treatment does not generate equal, or even fair, results. Treating two long-distance runners the same way, for example, by serving them the same diet, giving them the same shoes, and having them run on the same track is not an egalitarian approach, as it does not take into account the fact that the runners may be of unequal strength: one is an Olympic athlete and the other is an amateur. Quotas for women in politics aim precisely at taking into account the fact that women do not enter electoral competitions endowed with the same resources as men and that, as a consequence, measures must be taken to limit the negative effects of that resource deficit. Quotas intervene at the starting line, but their target is equality (or at least equity) at the finish line.

In short, quotas are a measure designed to compensate, with positive action, for systemic obstacles that keep women from being elected under the same conditions as men. It thus positions political representation on the basis of a physical datum: biological sex. Because of this, it is difficult to escape some degree of essentialism. Electoral quotas target not just the bodies of women but also the number of women, to the detriment of their ideas; the main and manifest objective is to increase the proportion of female politicians and not to influence the content of public decisions in order to, for example, make them more sympathetic to women. However, one does not exclude the other; in fact, one may encourage the other. Certain people believe that in large enough numbers, women may constitute a critical mass that can change politics – an idea that remains to be proved (see question 39).

BIBLIOGRAPHY

"About Quotas," accessed 11 July 2016, http://www.quotaproject.org/aboutQuotas.cfm#what.

Dahlerup, Drude. 2006. "Introduction." In *Women, Quotas and Politics*, edited by Drude Dahlerup, 3–13. Abingdon: Routledge.

Larserud, Stina and Rita Taphorn. 2007. *Designing for Equality: Best-fit, Medium-fit and Non-favourable Combinations of Electoral Systems and Gender Quotas*. Stockholm: International IDEA, accessed 12 July 2016, https://www.ndi.org/files/Designing-for-Equality-PDF.pdf.

Mansbridge, Jane. 2005), "Quota Problems: Combating the Dangers of Essentialism." *Politics & Gender* 1 (4): 622–38.

44 What are the various types of electoral quotas for women?

In 2016, the database on electoral quotas for women listed some 125 countries in which such provisions exist or have existed. Most of these quotas are still in force, but in some countries they have been abolished (for example, Denmark and Ghana). Electoral quotas for women may be characterized in a number of ways: 1) they are formal or informal; 2) they target candidates or people elected; 3) they explicitly name women or refer to both sexes/genders; 4) they are obligatory or voluntary, coercive or incentive, permanent or temporary, or progressive; 5) they involve one or more levels of requirements.

Quotas are formal when they are written into law or result from a party's regulations. They are informal when they result solely from good intentions (which are nevertheless essential to their success). When they are codified in law, quotas are prescribed by either the country's constitution (as was the case, in 2016, in Afghanistan, Argentina, Burundi, France, India at the municipal level, Iraq, Nepal, Pakistan, and Swaziland, for example) or the electoral statute (the former Yugoslav Republic of Macedonia, Guyana, Indonesia, Mongolia, Peru, Portugal, and Senegal, for example). The latter formula is more common than the former: in 2016, some thirty countries had quotas for the single or lower chamber of parliament enshrined in their constitution (many had such provisions in their electoral statute as well), whereas almost seventy countries had quotas written into their electoral statutes (for some, the electoral statute constitutes a response to a constitutional obligation). It is not surprising that the constitutional route is taken less frequently; first, in some countries, fundamental law is very difficult to change; second, the solemn nature of such change may deter legislators. Formal quotas may also arise from partisan regulations: in the absence of legislative constraints (including a constitutional or electoral law provision forcing the parties to adopt or respect quotas), a political party may decide, on its own, to create a representation space for women within its organizational structure, its candidate pool, or its parliamentary delegation. In Malawi, the constitution of the United Democratic Front calls for one quarter of its parliamentary caucus to be composed of women. However, a formula that deals with candidates is much more common: in 2016, about one hundred of the political parties with representation in the 190 national parliaments in the world had quotas to favour women candidates in legislative elections. Of course, the nature of these quotas varies greatly, ranging from equal representation of women and men on electoral lists to a more-than-symbolic presence of women. For example, SWAPO (the South West Africa People's Organization) in Namibia and the Greens in Germany and Austria set out a quota of 50 per cent women on their electoral lists, whereas the proportion is only 20 per cent for the Socialist Party in Hungary and the Labour Party in Malta, and 10 per cent for National Movement for a Society in Development in Niger.

Some parties limit their affirmative action to good intentions. They may state that they want to grant women a more significant place but refuse to commit to legal or regulatory constraints, hoping to retain as great a margin of manoeuvre as possible with regard to their role in feminizing parliament. This amounts to a sort of moral commitment and self-discipline, a way of adopting quotas – without actually saying the word. For example, the New Zealand Labour Party has adopted a "pauses for thought" policy under which its candidate-selection process is punctuated with time to reflect on each bloc of five candidates, in order to ensure diversity in terms of sex/gender, ethnicity, age, and experience (Krook, Lovenduski, and Squires 2006, 213). The effectiveness of these informal quotas clearly depends on the goodwill of the parties' selection committees, though this is also the case for formal quotas.

Electoral quotas, formal and informal, affect candidates or those who are elected. In other words, they may be aimed at recruitment, selection, or election (see question 18). Deployed at the recruitment level, quotas seek to stimulate the supply of female candidates. In this sense, they make it necessary to identify a set of women from among whom a given political party will select its candidates for elections. The use of training to encourage women to enter politics and the compilation of lists of women with the skills to be political actors are examples of informal recruitment quotas. The policy of "women-only short lists" adopted by the British Labour Party from 1992 to 1996 with a view to selecting its female candidates for the 1997 general election is an example of a formal recruitment quota (see question 49).

The government's desire to present female candidates constitutes an informal selection quota. A party leader parachuting female candidates into a given riding is an example of this. No doubt the most widespread type of formal selection quota is that framing the composition of candidate lists. Essentially, such quotas provide that candidate lists in elections must respect a particular numerical balance between women and men. These quotas may be prescribed by law (the constitution or the electoral statute) or by a party's regulations. Kyrgyzstan offers an example of the first type of quota: the electoral statute provides a (minimal) quota of 30 per cent of each sex/gender on the electoral lists presented by the parties; lists that do not satisfy this requirement may be rejected by the electoral commission. In Botswana, the Congress Party and the National Front have a quota of 30 per cent women for their electoral lists (which has not always been attained, apparently without negative consequences for the parties). In Cyprus, the Democratic Rally and the Movement of Social Democrats have similar quotas. The Social Democratic Party of Switzerland has a 40 per cent threshold. The lists are not a prerequisite for parties' adoption of quotas; with a bit of imagination, they may also be used in a majority voting system. For instance, for the Scottish election in 1999, the Labour Party adopted a policy of matching ridings (see question 49).

Finally, informal quotas may apply during elections. That is the case, for example, when winning ridings are reserved for women or when female candidates are placed in eligible positions on the lists (without there being an obligation that they be there), thus guaranteeing their election. Reserved seats are a typical example of a formal election quota: this legal provision sets a given proportion of positions (such as seats in parliament) that must be occupied by women. The national parliaments of Afghanistan, Algeria,

Bangladesh, Eritrea, Jordan, Kenya, Pakistan, Rwanda, Somalia, South Sudan, Tanzania, Uganda, and Zimbabwe, among others, have a policy of seats reserved for women. In Kenya, the constitution adopted in August 2010 reserves forty-seven of the 350 seats in the lower chamber and eighteen of the sixty-eight seats in the upper chamber of the parliament for women. In Rwanda, twenty-four of the eighty seats in the House of Representatives must be occupied by women (see question 36). In Jordan, the seats reserved for women are assigned through a "best losers" formula – that is, for female candidates who lose in their riding but who, on the national scale, have the best (or highest) vote proportions; from six in 2003, the number of seats reserved for women in the lower chamber of the Jordanian parliament was raised to twelve in 2010, then to fifteen in 2012. A similar "best loser" system is used in Samoa to allocate the five seats reserved for women. Sometimes, a policy of seats reserved for women does not apply nationally but does apply at the local or municipal level, as in East Timor, India (where it seems impossible to attain the consensus needed to adopt the *Women's Reservation Bill* in the national parliament), Mauritius, and Vanuatu, among others, or to an (unelected) advisory body, such as the Choura Council in Saudi Arabia.

Quotas, formal or informal, may target women explicitly. For example, the electoral lists may be required to include a given percentage of women. The Front for the Liberation of Mozambique has a rule that women must represent 40 per cent of candidates for election. Similarly, in Uzbekistan, article 22 of the electoral statute stipulates that women may not count for less than 30 per cent of the total number of candidates. More informally, a leader might decree that women must represent a quarter of her or his party's candidates in legislative elections, as Jean Chrétien did when he was prime minister of Canada. The quota may also refer to both sexes/genders. For example, article 3 of the French constitution provides that "the law shall promote equal access of women and men to electoral mandates and elected offices, as well as professional and social responsibilities." Sometimes, as in Bosnia-Herzegovina, the quota covers the underrepresented sex/gender without deliberately naming women. In Djibouti, in 2002, a presidential decree specified that the electoral lists had to be written in such a way that the legislative caucus of each party, after the election, would include a minimum 10 per cent of women or men. In other words, these were seats reserved for women.

In addition, as mentioned above, quotas are obligatory or voluntary, coercive or incentive, and permanent, temporary, or progressive. They are obligatory when prescribed by law or via political party's internal rules, and voluntary when such a constraint does not exist. As of 2016, some thirty countries had only voluntary party quotas; they included Australia, Cameroon, Chile, Germany, Hungary, Israel, Slovakia, Thailand, and Turkey. At least two mechanisms are involved in obligatory quotas. The most common one is simply to prescribe a minimum threshold of presence. This is the case, for example, in Mongolia, where the 2011 electoral law states that at least 20 per cent of candidates of a given political party must be women. However, the electoral law does not say anything about the position of those female candidates, whether it is their registration on the list in the proportional section of the voting system or the competitiveness of the riding in its majority section. To avoid women being at the bottom of the lists and placed in uncompetitive ridings, another mechanism contained in obligatory quotas consists specifically of framing female candidates' positions, for example through strict alternation on the lists between female and male candidates (the "zebra" or "zipper" system). Bolivia, which uses a mixed voting system, offers a brilliant example of this mechanism: the 2010 electoral statute requires that lists of candidates (main and substitute) be composed of an equal number of women and men alternating strictly from top to bottom. Moreover, if a list contains an odd number of candidates, preference goes to a woman. For the majority section, at least half the candidates (main and substitute) selected in all ridings combined must be women. This formula was tested for the first time during the 2014 legislative elections and gave rise to a parliament in which the majority of members (69/130, or 53.1 per cent) were women. Piscopo (2016) sees Bolivia as an example of a country in which the public discourse on women's participation in politics has transitioned from the level of quotas to that of parity.

Even if a quota is obligatory it may not be respected. Indeed, there are many examples of parties flouting quotas or even developing strategies to circumvent them, especially if the electoral statute does not provide – and apply – sanctions when measures are not respected, as is the case in Angola and Nicaragua. Two options are available to make parties play the quota game and to counter this laissez-faire attitude. One is an incentive: it uses encouragements, such as financial gains, to gain compliance. In Burkina Faso, for example, when a political party surpasses, or simply reaches, the quota of 30 per cent female candidates, it receives additional state financial assistance, but if it does not reach the quota, its share of public financing for election campaigns is reduced by half. In Algeria, Georgia, Guinea, and Haiti, among other countries, the parties that have women in their parliamentary caucuses receive a form of bonus under the statute on public financing of political parties. However, the results of the 2013 Guinean election (which resulted in a parliament that was 21.9 per cent feminized) tend to indicate that this incentive may not be enough to make that country's parties respect the quota of 30 per cent female candidates on the lists. The other option is coercive in that it provides sanctions in cases of non-compliance with the electoral statute on quotas. The strength of such sanctions varies widely. A sanction may consist of a simple financial penalty in the form of a fine (as in Albania and the Honduras); a reduction, small or large, in the kitty to which a given party has the right under the terms of public financing of its electoral activities (as in France and Ireland): or full ineligibility for party public financing (as in Cape Verde). But no doubt the most serious penalty consists of rejection by the electoral authorities of lists that do not comply with the law, a scenario adopted by a number of countries (among them Belgium, the Dominican Republic, Montenegro, Morocco, Paraguay, Serbia, and Slovenia).

Whereas some quotas are permanent, others are temporary – they have an expiry date. In Zimbabwe the constitutional provision that reserves sixty seats for women in the National Assembly is limited to two parliaments following adoption of the new constitution in May 2013. And although this quota is not listed in the database on electoral quotas for women, paragraph 3(1) of the Sex Discrimination (Election Candidates) Act, which makes it illegal for a political party in the United Kingdom of Great Britain and Northern Ireland to make a short list composed solely of female candidates, was adopted in 2002 and supposed to expire at the end of 2015. The 2010 Equality Act, however, delayed the expiry to 2030.

Some quotas are progressive – the proportion required increases over time. In Ecuador, the electoral statute provided that the initial proportion of female candidates, set at 20 per cent in 1997, would increase at each election until it reached 50 per cent. Since then, the lists have been compiled according to the principle of parity, with strict alternation of names of female and male candidates from top to bottom. This is another illustration of a country that transitioned from a quota system to a parity system

(Piscopo 2016). In Honduras, the Ley para la Igualdad de Oportunidades para la Mujer, adopted in 2000, set a slightly higher threshold, 30 per cent, which was to increase gradually to 50 per cent. Woman/man parity had not yet been reached in 2016, despite an amendment made to the electoral statute in 2012 to encourage gender balance with regard to candidates for legislative elections.

Finally, quotas provide for one or more levels of requirements. A single level implies that the quota is limited to prescribing a proportion. This is the most common formula. Here are some examples: in Burkina Faso, the electoral statute simply provides for a quota of 30 per cent of female candidates; in Togo it is 50 per cent, but with no other requirement concerning, for example, placement on the lists (which explains, in part, why the Togolese parliament included only 15 per cent women in June 2016); in Nepal, women are supposed to comprise at least one-third of candidates on lists and in ridings, combined; in Brazil, the lists of candidates must have a floor of 30 per cent and a ceiling of 70 per cent of either sex/gender, which, in the absence of any provision concerning placement, means that the first seventy places on a list of one hundred names could be occupied by men. It is to avoid this type of pitfall that quotas are sometimes framed by a number of requirements. These requirements are expressed in various forms, but the placement of candidates on lists (particularly if the lists are closed) is an essential measure because it directly influences the chances of election. A number of formulas exist, from the least to the most constraining. For instance, the Argentine electoral statute stipulated that the electoral lists must have a minimum of 30 per cent female candidates with real chances of election, however, it is not clear how these chances are assessed and by whom. Another formula calls for the organization of names to be based on sublists of candidates. In Armenia, for example, each section of five candidates can have a maximum of four people of the same sex/gender, starting from the second name on the list (2–6, 7–11, 12–16, and so on), a formula that assures a party's leader (usually a man) the top position on the list. In Uruguay, the electoral statute provides "that candidates of both sexes must be represented in every 3 places on electoral lists, either throughout the entire list or in the first 15 places," but without specifying positioning by sex/gender, which means, for example, that women could be placed at positions 3, 6, 9, 12, and 15, and men always at the more competitive positions in each triad (1 and 2 in the case of the 1–2–3 triad; 4 and 5 in the 4–5–6 triad, and so on). In Bosnia-Herzegovina, the electoral statute requires that at least one person from the underrepresented gender be among the first two names on the list, then two out of five, three out of eight, and so on. In Belgium, there are two requirements: the gap between the number of female candidates and the number of male candidates on the list may not be greater than one, and the first two names on the list must be of different sex/gender. In Mexico, for the 200 seats (out of 500) for election by proportional vote in the lower chamber of the Congress of the Union, each group of five names must have two female candidates and two male candidates. There are many more examples, but I will end with the most constricting formula: strict alternation of female and male candidates at the beginning of the list, an alternation based on the principle of parity – in other words, a 50 per cent quota. Bolivia, Costa Rica, Ecuador, Senegal, and Tunisia follow this formula.

In short, electoral quotas for women are a bit like Lego, in that they offer many opportunities for creativity. However, none of the options is a guarantee of success, as the feminization of parliaments depends mainly on the goodwill of the political actors – notably the parties and people – involved (see questions 23, 45, and 54).

BIBLIOGRAPHY

Baker, Kerryn 2014. "Explaining the Outcome of Gender Quota Campaigns in Samoa and Papua New Guinea." *Political Science* 66 (1): 63–83.

Bjarnegård, Elin and Par Zetterberg. 2011. "Removing Quotas, Maintaining Representation: Overcoming Gender Inequalities in Political Party Recruitment." *Representation: The Journal of Representative Democracy* 47 (2): 187–99.

Franceschet, Susan, Mona Lena Krook, and Jennifer M. Piscopo. 2012. "Conceptualizing the Impact of Gender Quotas." In *The Impact of Gender Quotas*, edited by Susan Franceschet, Mona Lena Krook, and Jennifer M. Piscopo, 3–24. New York: Oxford University Press.

Krook, Mona Lena. 2009. *Quotas for Women in Politics: Gender and Candidate Selection Reform Worldwide.* New York: Oxford University Press. See, in particular, 3–56, 207–26.

Krook, Mona Lena, Joni Lovenduski, and Judith Squires. 2006. "Western Europe, North America, Australia and New Zealand: Gender Quotas in the Context of Citizenship Models." In *Women, Quotas and Politics*, edited by Drude Dahlerup, 194–221. London and New York: Routledge.

Krook, Mona Lena and Par Zetterberg. 2014. "Electoral Quotas and Political Representation: Comparative Perspectives." *International Political Science Review* 35 (1): 3–118.

Larserud, Stina and Rita Taphorn. 2007. *Designing for Equality: Best-fit, Medium-fit and Non-favourable Combinations of Electoral Systems and Gender Quotas.* Stockholm: International IDEA, accessed 12 July 2016, https://www.ndi.org/files/Designing-for-Equality-PDF.pdf.

Piscopo, Jennifer M. 2016. "Democracy as Gender Balance: The Shift from Quotas to Parity in Latin America." *Politics, Groups, and Identities* 4 (2): 214–30.

Quota Database, accessed 12 July 2016, http://www.quotaproject.org/en/index.cfm.

45 Under what conditions are quotas most effective?

Matland (2006) identifies three necessary and sufficient conditions under which electoral quotas for women will result in more-feminized parliaments. The first is a proportional voting system (with lists); the second is a large number of seats occupied by a given political party, in a given electoral district; and the third is the political parties' goodwill regarding electoral quotas and their sincere commitment to increasing the presence of women within their legislative delegations.

Studies on factors that influence the proportion of women in parliaments show that proportional voting systems are more likely to result in the election of women than are majority voting systems. However, list proportional voting systems are favourable to women only under certain conditions (see question 21). It is my opinion that list proportional voting systems are not in themselves necessary nor are they sufficient for quotas to result in more feminized parliaments. They are not necessary because majority voting systems with strict electoral quotas in favour of women (reserved seats, a policy of matching ridings – as exists in Scotland and Wales – or parity binomial representation – as proposed in Nunavut and instituted in the new departmental councils in France following adoption of the statute of 17 May 2013; see question 49) may give rise to high proportions of female parliamentarians. They are insufficient because research shows that they do not automatically give rise to highly feminized parliaments (see question 21) even when there are electoral quotas, if these quotas are not very stringent (for example, if they do not set out penalties for non-compliance; see question 44).

Matland's second condition is for a political party to win a large number of seats in a given electoral district, thus indirectly strengthening the first condition. In effect, districts with several seats are very closely linked to list proportional voting systems; very few majority voting systems use such a formula (Mauritius and Tuvalu are examples of countries that use a majority voting system with plurinominal ridings). When a party wins a large number of seats in an electoral district, it is forced to descend low on its list of candidates – where women candidates are often relegated – to fill them.

Matland's third condition is, in my opinion, the most credible: the sincere desire of parties to increase the number of women in parliament and to respect electoral quotas. I would even go so far as to assert that this condition alone is necessary and sufficient to gain more seats for women in parliaments, even under a majority voting system and in the absence of quotas. If the parties want women in parliament, they will be in parliament, and if they do not want them there, they will not be there. The parties are the crafters of parliamentary representation, and it is they – much more than the electorate – that decide who will sit in parliament. It is up to civil society in general, and the women's movement in particular, to pressure parties into showing good faith and deploying strategies for feminizing their legislative wings.

Paxton and Hughes (2007, 312) add three other criteria that seem very relevant for quotas to be truly effective in increasing the number of women in politics: that the proportion of women (or the balance between the sexes/genders) be set at a relatively high level (I would say at least one third [critical mass]; see question 39), that the quota set out strict alternation between women and men on the lists from top to bottom, and that there be severe penalties for parties that do not comply with the quotas.

BIBLIOGRAPHY

Matland, Richard E. 2006. "Electoral Quotas: Frequency and Effectiveness." In *Women, Quotas and Politics*, edited by Drude Dahlerup, 275–92. London: Routledge.

Paxton, Pamela and Melanie M. Hughes. 2007. *Women, Politics, and Power: A Global Perspective*. Los Angeles: Pine Forge Press. See, in particular, 312–14.

Rosen, Jennifer. 2013. "The Effects of Political Institutions on Women's Political Representation: A Comparative Analysis of 168 Countries from 1992 to 2010." *Political Research Quarterly* 66 (2): 306–21.

Tan, Netina. 2014. "Ethnic Quotas and Unintended Effects on Women's Political Representation in Singapore." *International Political Science Review* 35 (1): 27–40.

Verge, Tania and Maria de la Fuente. 2014. "Playing with Different Cards: Party Politics, Gender Quotas and Women's Empowerment." *International Political Science Review* 35 (1): 67–79.

46 Why have a large number of countries implemented quotas to increase the number of women parliamentarians in recent years?

From the start, it is important to mention that quotas were not invented in the 1990s; they go much farther back in time, and – unsurprisingly – they were not first adopted to correct the deficit in women's political representation. In the nineteenth century, countries instituted quotas to enforce legislative representation based on political recognition of historical or identity-related markers. For instance, under the treaty of Waitangi, in 1867, four seats in the New Zealand House of Representatives were reserved for Maoris (in 2016, there were seven such seats). In India, the British colonial power designated seats for representation of the underclasses, a provision that is still in effect: a proportion of the 545 seats in the lower chamber of Parliament (the Lok Sabha, or House of the People) is reserved for Dalits (formerly known as "untouchables").

The first quotas for women were formulated in the second half of the twentieth century; a number of member countries of the Soviet Bloc (such as Hungary and what was then Yugoslavia,) had quotas for the legislative representation of women (and of other groups defined on the basis of criteria such as occupation and ethnic origin). However, under Soviet-type communism, the parliamentary institution was powerless, as the true decision-making centre was the Communist Party and its politburo from which women were notoriously absent. Outside of the Warsaw Pact, in Argentina in 1951, under the influence of Eva Perón, the Peronist Party adopted a policy of quotas designed to foster the feminization of national parliamentary representation. The consequence was that in 1955, there were 22.8 per cent women in the lower chamber of the Argentine National Congress. Two years later, in 1953, Taiwan created a policy reserving 10 per cent of the seats in its legislative assembly for women. Pakistan followed suit in 1954, and Bangladesh in 1972. In 1960 and 1965, Ghana used electoral quotas to elect ten women to parliament, but it did not maintain the practice after that. Thus, although quotas for women in politics have become quite common since the 1990s, they have roots farther back in time.

In 2017, about 125 of the 190 countries recognized by the Inter-Parliamentary Union were registered in the database on electoral quotas for women, a joint initiative of International IDEA, the Inter-Parliamentary Union, and the University of Stockholm. This does not mean that in 2017 this many countries had active electoral quotas for women. In fact, some countries had abandoned quotas: in Denmark quotas disappeared in the mid-1990s; in Egypt, seats were reserved for women in parliament from 1979 to 1986, and then again in 2010, but have once again been abandoned; Ghana used quotas to elect women in parliament in 1960 and 1965. However, such measures are still in force in most of the countries registered in the database. Intensification (or globalization) of the democratization process and the mobilization of the women's movement on the international scale help to explain the large number of countries that have instituted quotas since the 1990s.

The fall of the Berlin Wall in the late 1980s and the propagation of liberal representative democracy accelerated the third wave of democratization that had begun in the 1970s – an acceleration sustained by globalization, notably of means of communication. Not only were the new political communities formed following the dissolution of the Warsaw Pact obliged to reconstruct their political and electoral systems, but long-established democracies (such as Italy, Japan, and New Zealand) reviewed their electoral rules, often in response to internal problems (such as illegitimate electoral results and the ensuing misrepresentation in parliament of wide swaths of the electorate, political corruption, and public cynicism about politics). It was in this context of reengineering representative and electoral democracy that the question of the underrepresentation of women in parliaments was posed.

In addition, the low number of female parliamentarians encouraged the women's movement to mobilize internationally to increase women's access to parliaments (see questions 42 and 55). These mobilizations were encouraged on a broad scale by instruments of international law (such as the Convention on the Elimination of All Forms of Discrimination against Women and the Beijing Platform for Action) and by institutions, both international (such as International IDEA and the Inter-Parliamentary Union) and regional (such as the Council of Europe) favourable to women's rights (see question 41). In short, the strong activism of women's movements around the world and their influence within various international and regional organizations – an influence buttressed by various commitments written into instruments of international law – generated a situation propitious to the equality of women and men. Since the mid-1970s in particular, these institutions have supplied important resources (such as forums and support in the form of training and funding); more important, however, by emphasizing a humanist philosophy that defines women's rights in terms of human rights, they have contributed to legitimizing a discourse on women's full participation in political power – and, more specifically, on the question of electoral quotas – and on placing the issue on the international agenda.

To this international conjuncture, a regional innovation must be added: the exemplary case of Argentina. The country's Ley de Cupos, adopted in 1991, achieved the goal set for it and probably had a contagion effect on other countries in South America and perhaps even beyond. Indeed, the Ley de Cupos resulted in significant feminization of Argentina's Chamber of Deputies; between 1983 and 1991, the average proportion of female representatives was 4 per cent, but it leapt to 21 per cent and then 28 per cent, in 1993 and 1995 respectively, to reach a ceiling of between 35 and 40 per cent in 2006, where, unfortunately, it has remained; this ceiling seems unbreakable.

On the domestic scale, Krook (2009) identifies four scenarios in which national, majority male political elites adopt quotas for women in politics. In the first scenario, adoption of electoral quotas is the result of pressure exerted by women, whether by the women's movement on the national scale or by feminist activists within political parties or the state administration. This scenario is not dissimilar to Krook's fourth scenario, in which adoption of quotas results from mobilizations by the women's movement on the international scale, along with rapid dissemination of knowledge and experiences, good and bad – in short, a kind of quota contagion effect. The second scenario has it that quotas are adopted because the political class gauges that it will make gains, both electoral (such as broadening its electoral base among women) and nonelectoral (such as recrafting its image on the international scene or responding to the requirements of international financial backers). In this scenario, the political class does not necessarily intend to promote the political representation of women; one example of this is the signature of the Convention on the Elimination of All Forms of Discrimination against Women by the Taliban government (but never ratified by the United States). The third scenario is that in which electoral quotas are part of a larger undertaking – that of achieving equality of women and men or improving representative democracy. It goes without saying that these scenarios are not mutually exclusive and that various national situations follow several of them simultaneously.

BIBLIOGRAPHY

Baker, Kerryn. 2014. "Quota Adoption and the Exogenous Track Model: The Parity Laws in the French Pacific Collectivities." *Representation* 50 (3): 295–306.

Dubrow, Joshua Kjerulf. 2011. "The Importance of Party Ideology: Explaining Parliamentarian Support for Political Party Gender Quotas in Eastern Europe." *Party Politics* 17 (5): 561–79.

Krook, Mona Lena. 2009. *Quotas for Women in Politics: Gender and Candidate Selection Reform Worldwide.* New York: Oxford University Press. See, in particular, 20–5.

Murray, Rainbow, Mona Lena Krook, and Katherine A.R. Opello. 2012. "Why Are Gender Quotas Adopted? Party Pragmatism and Parity in France." *Political Research Quarterly* 65 (3): 529–43.

Quota Database. "Country Overview," accessed 14 July 2016, http://www.quotaproject.org/country.cfm.

47 What are the arguments for and against quotas?

Table 4 presents some arguments for and against electoral quotas for women in politics. Although listed separately, these arguments are not mutually exclusive; on the contrary, they are closely related, overlap, and combine to reinforce each other.

1. Representation is subject to conflicting interpretations. One common reading of representation is based on territory: parliaments represent a territory, whether it is an entire country (such as Israel or the Netherlands) or part of one (a riding or electoral district, for example). However, other

Table 4

Some arguments for and against quotas

Arguments for	*Arguments against*
1. Representation reflects the diversity of the population	Representation is based on territory
2. Equality in difference	Equality in similarity, in "sameness"
3. Women share experiences and interests	Women do not form a cohesive group
4. Sex and gender are significant identity markers	Identities are plural and fluid
5. Women are not a social minority like others	Women are a social minority like others
6. Fair sharing of political roles	Quotas are an injustice to men
7. Skills result from a particular social structure modelled, among other things, by the gender system	Skills are independent of sex/gender
8. Quotas end a system that protects men	Women do not want protectionist measures, which are insulting to them
9. Quotas bring changes that can be gradual	Quotas cause an upheaval
10. Quotas constitute one rule of the electoral game among others, neither more nor less constraining	Quotas inhibit the freedom of the parties and, in turn, that of the electorate
11. Quotas are strategies to create balance among different interests within parties	Quotas may be a source of conflict within parties
12. Candidate-recruitment and -selection processes must be reviewed	There are not enough "skilled" female candidates to fill quotas
13. Quotas must be neutral	Women elected through quotas will be ostracized
14. Quotas not only are compatible with democracy, but they strengthen it	Quotas are contrary to democracy

Source: Tremblay (2010), 157.

readings of representation dwell on the importance of taking account of the diversity of the population, which features a multitude of identifying markers (in terms of experience, sociodemographic traits, and ideological affiliations); in these cases, quotas allow representation to be sensitive to the composition – notably by sex, ethnicity, or religion – of the population. For example, of the 458 seats in the single chamber of the Ugandan parliament, 112 are reserved for women; as well as those, ten are reserved for the Uganda People's Defence Force (two of which must go to women), five for young people (including one woman), five for handicapped people (one woman), and five for workers (at least one woman).

2. Today it is generally agreed that women and men are equal. The problem is how to negotiate the distinctions between them: should those differences be understood according to abstract models of the human being that value the similarities (or "sameness") of the genders or their differences, and, in the latter case, ensure that these do not become the source of discrimination? In other words, should women and men be treated the same (with the risk of treating women according to criteria defined by and for men) or in ways that are sensitive to their particular experiences? The first perspective excludes quotas, whereas the second requires them.

3. The question of whether women form a politically significant group – a group that could be the subject of specific representation in the political space – is highly controversial (see questions 12, 52, and 60). On the one hand, to consider that women do not form such a group, whether because they do not share experiences and interests in common or because the very identity of "woman" poses a problem, excludes, de facto, the adoption of electoral quotas designed to represent them (that is, represent what exactly?). On the other hand, to consider that women share experiences and interests that make them a politically significant group implies that they should be effectively represented (that is, on the quantitative and qualitative levels) in parliaments. According to this reasoning, the low presence of women in politics becomes problematic because women are best positioned to represent women (see questions 60 and 63), even if it is not clear whether women elected to office – who, by definition, form an elite – actually represent the spectrum of women's multiple and diverse experiences. Certainly, their numerical underrepresentation leads to their misrepresentation with regard to public decisions (see question 34). In this light, quotas are seen

as a way to increase not only their numbers (and, it is hoped, their diversity) in politics but also public policies favourable to a broad spectrum of their experiences and interests as a group.

4. Electoral quotas for women are based on the postulate that sex/gender is a significant identity marker both collectively (see preceding paragraph) and individually (that is, for the person to whom it applies). Yet, each person is shaped by multiple identities that include not only sex/gender, but also ethnicity, nationality, sexual preference, political party affiliation, and so on. These identities are not organized in a fixed way (for example, the label "woman" always the most decisive, followed by "ecologist," then "feminist," and so on); rather, their importance varies depending on the situation (see questions 12 and 52). Quotas for women in politics, argue those who oppose them, not only fix women in their sex/gender identity but give priority to this label to the detriment of the others.

5. Why should there be quotas for women and not for other social minorities? Although electoral quotas and parity are two different issues (see question 50), debates on parity in France offer a partial answer to this question. Women must be able to benefit from measures encouraging their access to parliaments because they are not a minority like others; they form half of the human species, which is not the case for cultural, ethnic, sexual, and other minorities. Furthermore, the differences between women and men structure all other social minorities: there are Maori women and men, lesbians and gays, black women and men, and so on. This reasoning is not above criticism. For example, aside from its essentialism, it presumes that sexual diversity involves only two sexes/genders, thus ignoring the increasing numbers of people who are refusing to identify as one or the other sex/gender and prefer to identify with fluid sex/genders (see question 52).

6. People who plead in favour of electoral quotas for women maintain that these measures make it possible for women and men to fairly share political roles. In effect, one human being out of two is a woman, and so it is just simple justice that women and men should enjoy equal political representation (see questions 50 and 53). The opposing side responds that electoral quotas for women are unfair to men because they limit the political field that men could occupy under the laws of the political free market. Furthermore, quotas divide men among themselves; not only do younger men not have the resources of their elders to get elected but they do not

benefit from the same systemic benefits (being male, being white, being heterosexual, for example) from which their elders did.

7. Quotas, according to their detractors, relegate skills to a secondary position, and it is skills, rather than sex/gender, that should be favoured in responsible democratic governance. However, the other camp replies, skills are not an absolute value; they are part of a particular social structure modelled, among other things, by the gender regime. More specifically, the skills considered relevant for performing in politics must meet various criteria, such as time and space (the effects of which are different for women and men, and differ among women depending on their identity markers and their experiences) and the themes on the agenda (women are seen as more skilled in dealing with social questions, whereas men are considered more skilled in military matters; see question 13). In short, the skills for performing in politics are not universal but circumstantial, and thus the argument that invokes them as a reason to reject electoral quotas for women is not very credible.

8. Another argument has it that electoral quotas are a protectionist measure for women – although many women do not want them, and some view them as insulting. The contrary argument is that implementation of quotas for women would have the consequence of ending the protection of men in a system historically defined by them for their benefit. Another way to rebut the accusation that quotas are a protectionist measure for women is to define them neutrally. For example, some quotas provide that there may be no more than 70 per cent of people of the same sex/gender on electoral lists or that one or another sex/gender may not occupy less than 30 per cent of positions on parties' lists. This neutrality is also a way of answering the argument that women elected through quotas will be ostracized; if a quota targets both sexes/genders and not only women, they cannot legitimately be tarnished with the brush of protectionism.

9. Some people think that quotas cause an upheaval, and that it would be better to let change occur naturally over time. However, it is naïve to think that time and patience alone will result in parliamentary parity (see question 31). It is true that electoral quotas favouring women create disruption, including the breakup of men's virtual monopoly on politics, but in the context in which political representation mirroring the population is valued, many feel that such a shift is desirable. Finally, for those who prefer things to move slowly – like a tortoise rather than a hare – some coun-

tries have opted for gradual increases in quota percentages from election to election (see question 44).

10. One of the most tenacious arguments against quotas is that they impede parties', and therefore the electorate's, freedom: parties must be free to make their own choices and act according to their values, objectives, and priorities, especially with regard to their choice of candidates to present to voters. More specifically, parties should not be required to select, for example, 30 per cent women as candidates, if that is not part of their philosophy or one of their campaign objectives. By this argument, quotas are not only the unwarranted interference by the state in the affairs of a private organization but an obstacle to voters' freedom of choice. A number of arguments counter this reasoning. First, the freedom of political parties to run their affairs as they wish cannot be absolute – and, in fact, it is not. Parties may be private organizations, but they are subject to their country's laws. Second, by extension, the state already intervenes heavily in the affairs of political parties, among other things through providing public financing for their activities (in countries where such programs exist). Third, and again by extension, to the extent that political parties receive public funding and the state values equality of women and men, it is only consistent with the state's principles to require the parties to respect the values of the society that they seek to govern. Fourth, the constraint posed by quotas for women on the freedom of parties is minimal in light of their other obligations (an election campaign, for example, is extremely constraining and seriously limits parties' freedom). Fifth, the idea that voters have "free choice" in liberal democracies is deceptive; the electorate's freedom is in fact limited to voting for the candidates put forth by the political parties (see question 48). Finally, it is my opinion that the costs engendered by electoral quotas for women are more than compensated for by the gains that society in general and the parties in particular will derive from their implementation, whether it is with regard to the quality of democratic life or to electoral support.

11. Some maintain that quotas would lead to conflicts within parties. If there is conflict, it is perhaps because those with the upper hand do not want change. In fact, electoral quotas for women actually offer the possibility of settling disputes, notably by responding to pressure exerted by women on parties – pressure that comes as much from civil society (from the women's movement, among others) as from party activists. What is more, quotas provide a crystal clear formula (for example, no less than 30

per cent of candidates from one sex/gender on the list) to balance and accommodate diverse interests within a political party.

12. Another antiquota argument is that the supply of "skilled" female candidates would not be sufficient to meet the requirements. As mentioned above, the criterion of skill is not neutral; rather, it reflects a state of social relations in time and space modelled, among other things, by the gender regime and other structures of oppression based, for example, on social class, sexual preference, and skin colour. Thus, by some strange coincidence, many of the personality traits associated with leadership (such as rationality, strength of character, and the capacity to sustain a power relationship) are also those valued in male socialization. Further, when it comes to the supply of female candidates, how can it be seriously suggested that, in a country such as Canada, for example, a political party cannot find 169 female candidates (half of all of its candidates) for election to the House of Commons, which has 338 ridings? If the parties cannot find enough female candidates, they are either looking in the wrong places or are going through the motions without really seeking qualified women. This brings us back to the prerequisite for feminization of parliaments: the sincere desire of parties to increase the number of women within their legislative delegations (see questions 23, 45, and 54).

13. Women elected through quotas, argue some detractors, will be ostracized. This is possible, but it depends on the nature of the quota. Such a problem should not arise when a quota is defined neutrally – that is, when it targets both sexes/genders and not specifically women. For example, a quota requiring that at least forty of the one hundred seats in parliament must be occupied by one sex/gender and at least sixty by the other does not specify women, and, therefore, should not lead to their being ostracized. True, a number of female researchers have noted that quotas that consist of reserving seats for women in parliaments often result in undesirable effects for those women (Tamale 1999: 114–31, Tripp 2000: 219–20, Yoon 2011), and yet, seats reserved for women are not uniformly negative in their effects. Burnet (2011) ventures to establish a link between the seats reserved for women in the Rwandan parliament and an enhancement of the social capital of Rwandan women – and thus of their social citizenship. Bhavnani (2009) notes that seats reserved for women in local Indian elections seem to generate a contagion effect: the probability that a female candidate will win a riding not reserved for women but that was reserved in the previous

election is five times higher than that of a woman running in a riding that does not have such a history.

14. A final argument concerns democracy: some of the people who oppose electoral quotas for women in politics feel that such quotas are contrary to democracy, whereas other people who are in favour of them argue, on the contrary, not only that quotas are compatible with democracy but that they strengthen it. This argument, clearly, depends on one's conception of democracy (see question 48).

BIBLIOGRAPHY

Bacchi, Carol. 2006. "Arguing for and against Quotas: Theoretical Issues." In *Women, Quotas and Politics*, edited by Drude Dahlerup, 32–51. Abingdon: Routledge.

Bhavnani, Rikhil. 2009. "Do Electoral Quotas Work after They Are Withdrawn? Evidence from a Natural Experiment in India." *American Political Science Review* 103 (1): 23–35.

Burnet, Jennie E. 2011. "Women Have Found Respect: Gender Quotas, Symbolic Representation, and Female Empowerment in Rwanda." *Politics & Gender* 7 (3): 303–34.

Htun, Mala N. and Mark P. Jones. 2002. "Engendering the Right to Participate in Decision-Making: Electoral Quotas and Women's Leadership in Latin America." In *Gender and the Politics of Rights and Democracy in Latin America*, edited by Nikki Craske and Maxine Molyneux, 32–56. Houndmills: Palgrave.

Murray, Rainbow. 2010. "Second Among Unequals? A Study of Whether France's 'Quota Women' are Up to the Job." *Politics & Gender* 6 (1): 93–118.

O'Brien, Diana Z. 2012. "Quotas and Qualifications in Uganda." In *The Impact of Gender Quotas*, edited by Susan Franceschet, Mona Lena Krook, and Jennifer M. Piscopo, 57–71. New York: Oxford University Press.

Squires, Judith. 1996. "Quotas for Women: Fair Representation?" *Parliamentary Affairs* 49 (1): 71–88.

Tamale, Sylvia. 1999. *When Hens Begin to Crow: Gender and Parliamentary Politics in Uganda*. Kampala: Fountain Publishers.

Tremblay, Manon. 2010. *Quebec Women and Legislative Representation*, translated by Käthe Roth. Vancouver: UBC Press. See, in particular, 157.

Tripp, Aili Mari. 2000. *Women & Politics in Uganda*. Madison: University of Madison Press.

Yoon, Mi Yung. 2011. "More Women in the Tanzanian Legislature: Do Numbers Matter?" *Journal of Contemporary African Studies* 29 (1): 83–98.

48 Are quotas for women democratic?

In my opinion, quotas are democratic. People who do not agree say that quotas damage the principle of individual freedom upon which representative democracy is based. This vision of democracy draws its coherence from the logic of the free market: on the one hand, there is the supply of candidates; on the other hand, there is the demand of political elites (see question 18). According to this reading, supply and demand interact in total freedom, determined only by merit: people who wish to be elected compete in an electoral system through which they make their ideas and skills known thanks to, among other things, freedom of expression. The people (that is, the electorate) will decide the winner – in essence, their wisdom will sort the wheat from the chaff. In other words, anyone who wishes may run for election, and whomever the electorate deems worthiest will win. However, this is simply not how things work – maybe in theory, but not in practice.

Under the law, everyone has the right to run for election. In practice, though, not everyone has the resources that would enable her or him to participate in politics. These resources correspond to various forms of oppression conditioned by sex/gender, social class, ethnic origin, language, and other factors. Furthermore, these intertwine, which intensifies their effects. These cleavages generate systemic discrimination – that is, types of discrimination inscribed in the very structures of social organization. For example, socialization may significantly affect an individual's capacity to perform in politics by sending the message either that men are fitter than women for politics (the evidence being, would argue some populists, that there are many more men than women in politics) or that people from minorities cannot represent the majority due to the specificities that define them. Socialization takes place in a given socioeconomic context: a privileged social background will confer a sense of political effectiveness (the feeling, or even the conviction, that a person with power can change things) that many people from more modest backgrounds will not be equipped to feel. In other words, a sense of political effectiveness is not distributed evenly throughout the population; rather, it reflects societal class structure. In short, contrary to the myth of free access that representative liberal democracy promotes, not everyone is equipped to become involved in politics.

It is precisely to minimize the negative effects of systemic discrimination against women who wish to be active in politics that electoral quotas exist (see questions 43 to 47). Quotas aim to remove certain invisible barriers that impede women's path to political power. They also enable women to catch up by accelerating the process of bringing them to parity in the sharing of political power. For example, a quota providing that parties must present at least 30 per cent women candidates makes it possible to overcome the negative effects of the idea in certain political elites that men win elections more easily because the electorate is not ready to vote for a woman (see questions 14, 15, 20, 21, and 23). In addition, because a quota requires parties to recruit women in order to fill a space of representation created for them, it may encourage women to become active in civil society organizations from which parties draw their candidates (see question 18).

Electoral quotas for women are democratic – that is, they are compatible with the individual freedoms inherent to representative democracy. Indeed, quotas make it possible to move from theory to practice by offering empirical conditions under which the theoretical freedom to run for office in an election becomes a truly conceivable option for a growing number of people (in this case, women). Quotas, which proceed from a logic of inclusion, thus broaden the potential pool of people hoping to assume a role of representation. In this sense, not only are electoral quotas for women compatible with democracy but they also strengthen it.

Other debates call upon different conceptions of democracy. One of these debates has to do with the still unresolved dilemma of the nature of representative democracy: does it concern ideas or identities? If the former, representation is a question of collective rather than individual interests. The members of parliament as a group represent the nation – that is, its interests, understood in their totality. This reading of representative democracy is opposed to any particularism – and thus to electoral quotas, which draw their raison d'être from such particularism. In the latter case representation is based on identities and, notably, on the experiences that they generate. It postulates that 1) parliament must reflect society, and 2) women are best represented by women, as they share a group of common societal experiences (see questions 12, 60, and 63). Quotas are willingly accepted under this interpretation. Historically, the representation of interests has dominated parliaments, even though representation based on identities has been gaining more and more support, especially since the 1970s, with the affirmation of new social movements (including the women's movement).

Another debate underlines the polysemy of democracy according to political cultures in which it is deployed. In other words, democracy is a fluid concept whose components fluctuate over time and in space. Although, today, it might be considered antidemocratic to refuse women the right to vote, this was not the case in the early twentieth century. Indeed, "one person, one vote" is a generally accepted principle today, but at one time suffragists had to fight the idea that women were represented by their husbands; granting suffrage, it was argued, was tantamount to giving husbands two votes (see question 8). Democracy also varies in space, as illustrated by the diversity of electoral rules. In a one-round majority vote, the fact that the party that forms the government does not necessarily obtain an absolute majority of votes or that the one that obtains the most votes does not necessarily form the government is not perforce antidemocratic – an idea that would be unacceptable in countries that use proportional voting systems (although these systems have their own paradoxes). These comparisons help us understand why electoral quotas are adopted after a long period of resistance and also why some countries use them while others categorically oppose them.

In short, I feel that electoral quotas for women are democratic in that they involve a reading of representation according to which parliament must reflect as well as possible the diversity of the population. Fundamentally, I find it problematic that women, who constitute half of the human species, occupied only 22.7 per cent of parliamentary seats in June 2016 (lower chambers, upper chambers, and single chambers combined) worldwide. Given that women are subjected to laws, they must also participate fully in the writing and adoption of those laws. Because the goal of quotas is to be inclusive, they strengthen democracy.

49 What measures other than quotas are advocated for countries with majority voting systems?

A number of strategies may be adopted in countries with majority voting systems to increase the number of women in politics: short lists of female candidates, matching of ridings, parity binomial woman–man representation, seats in parliament reserved for women, and financial incentives.

Between 1992 and 1996, the British Labour Party adopted a policy of "short lists of women only" in order to recruit its female candidates for the 1997 election. This measure, officially adopted by Labour, consisted of making short lists composed exclusively of aspiring female candidates; these lists were used in half of the seats left vacant by a Labour member of parliament and in ridings that offered good potential for electoral success. Despite its effectiveness in feminizing the Labour caucus, this measure was deemed contrary to the equality of women and men under the Sex Discrimination Act (1975); as a consequence, the Labour Party had to abandon their short lists in 1996. The party then applied the principle of alternating women and men to form short lists of candidates in ridings left vacant by the incumbent. However, in 2002, the British Parliament adopted the Sex Discrimination (Election Candidates) Act, which exempted the candidate-selection process within parties from the Sex Discrimination Act (1975). As a consequence, the Labour Party is again applying its "short lists of women only" policy, as it did for the 2015 election. Although the exemption is valid until 2030, it does not seem to have been very effective in feminizing the British House of Commons, and some are asking that more coercive measures be adopted, such as legislative quotas or even parity.

For the elections in Scotland and Wales in 1999, the Labour Party adopted a policy of matching ridings. This consisted of linking two neighbouring ridings with equivalent competitiveness. Each riding selected one woman and one man, and then the Labour organizations of the matched ridings got together and chose (we don't know by what criteria) a female candidate from between the two women selected and a male candidate from between the two men selected. Since there had to be one woman and one man, the matching policy was in fact a formal 50 per cent quota applying to candidate selection. However, it did not guarantee female–male parity in parliament, as fewer women than men might be elected (or vice-versa) even if the competitiveness of the respective riding was taken into account when a candidate of one or the other sex/gender was selected to run.

The New Democratic Party of Canada offers another (more flexible) interpretation of the strategy of matching ridings, this time to favour the emergence not of female candidates but of diversified candidates – among whom female candidates would also be found. This involves creating groups of ridings and establishing, for each group, an objective of balanced candidacies in terms of women, nonheterosexual sexual orientation, people with handicaps, visible and linguistic minorities, and so on. At least three-fifths of ridings the party deems "winnable" have to be assigned to female candidates. It is possible that this interpretation of the riding-matching strategy simply expresses the ethos of Canadian multiculturalism. It does seem debatable, however, as it is not certain that sex/gender is a difference like all others (see questions 51 and 52).

A strategy not dissimilar to riding matching is that of parity binomial woman–man representation – a strategy that guarantees parity between women and men with regard to parliamentary representation. It consists of the election of two people – a woman and a man – to represent an electoral district. Such an arrangement was proposed in Canada in 1995, when the territory of Nunavut was created: each of the eleven ridings would be represented in the legislative assembly by a female and a male representative. This proposal was rejected by referendum, however, in May 1997 (see question 95). In May 2013, France adopted this representation mechanism for the new departmental councils. Binomial parity, as it is called, forces political parties to present in each riding in the departmental elections a pair of candidates consisting of a woman and a man. Tested for the first time in March 2015, this mechanism resulted in parity of female and male councillors. However, the parity rule was not imposed on the presidencies of departmental councils, which, after the elections, had a miserable feminization rate of 10 per cent.

The policy of reserving seats for women prescribes that only women may occupy certain seats in parliament. This measure generates a number of difficulties; the proportion of seats prescribed is interpreted as a maximum (or a ceiling) rather than a minimum (or "floor"); "general" seats are more highly valued than "specific" seats; women who occupy the reserved seats sometimes lack credibility, especially if they are replacing an eminent politician from their party or are perceived as puppets of powerful male politicians; a policy of reserved seats for women smacks of paternalism and marks them as second-class citizens; reserved seats do not transform the political culture – which is the source of misrepresentation of women in politics. However, all of these objections are debatable (see question 47).

Finally, utilizing monetary incentives is an easily implemented strategy. Essentially, such incentives recognize parties' efforts to make room for women: for instance, the state may allocate funding to parties according to the proportion of their female candidates or elected representatives or it may cut funding to parties with a deficit of female candidates or elected representatives. Canada, New Brunswick, and Quebec considered implementing the former formula but did not (see question 95), and France and Ireland have implemented the latter formula (see question 44).

In sum, majority voting systems are not incompatible with the adoption of measures to increase the number of women in politics. However, it is certainly more difficult to adopt such measures under a majority system than under a proportional voting system – or, seen from another angle, such measures may require stronger political will among the political elites of a majority voting system.

BIBLIOGRAPHY

Chaney, Paul. 2006. "Women and Constitutional Reform: Gender Parity in the National Assembly for Wales." In *Representing Women in Parliament: A Comparative Study*, edited by Marian Sawer, Manon Tremblay, and Linda Trimble, 188–203 Abingdon: Routledge.

Childs, Sarah and Elizabeth Evans. 2012. "Out of the Hands of the Parties: Women's Legislative Recruitment at Westminster." *Political Quarterly* 83 (4): 742–48.

Childs, Sarah and Mona Lena Krook. 2012. "Labels and Mandates in the United Kingdom." In *The Impact of Gender Quotas*, edited by Susan Franceschet, Mona Lena Krook, and Jennifer M. Piscopo, 89–102. New York: Oxford University Press.

Cutts, David and Paul Widdop. 2013. "Was Labour Penalised Where It Stood All Women Shortlist Candidates? An Analysis of the 2010 UK General Election." *The British Journal of Politics and International Relations* 15 (3): 435–55.

Kayuni, Happy M. and Ragnhild L. Muriaas. 2014. "Alternatives to Gender Quotas: Electoral Financing of Women Candidates in Malawi." *Representation* 50 (3): 393–404.

Krook, Mona Lena and Pippa Norris. 2014. "Beyond Quotas: Strategies to Promote Gender Equality in Elected Office." *Political Studies* 62 (1): 2–20.

Lexier, Roberta. 2013. "Waffling Towards Parity in the New Democratic Party." In *Mind the Gaps: Canadian Perspectives on Gender and Politics*, edited by Roberta Lexier and Tamara A. Small, 64–75. Halifax and Winnipeg: Fernwood.

Mackay, Fiona. 2006. "Descriptive and Substantive Representation in New Parliamentary Spaces; The Case of Scotland." In *Representing Women in Parliament: A Comparative Study*, edited by Marian Sawer, Manon Tremblay, and Linda Trimble, 171–87. Abingdon: Routledge.

Mackay, Fiona and Laura McAllister. 2012. "Feminising British Politics: Six Lessons from Devolution in Scotland and Wales." *Political Quarterly* 83 (4): 730–4.

Murray, Rainbow. 2012. "French Lesson: What the United Kingdom Can Learn from the French Experiment with Gender Parity." *Political Quarterly* 83 (4): 735–41.

Norris, Pippa and Mona Lena Krook. 2014. "Women in Elective Office Worldwide; Barriers and Opportunities." In *Women and Elective Office: Past, Present, and Future*, 3rd ed., edited by Sue Thomas and Clyde Wilcox, 288–305. New York: Oxford University Press.

Tremblay, Manon and Jackie F. Steele. 2006. "Paradise Lost? Gender Parity and the Nunavut Experience." In *Representing Women in Parliament: A Comparative Study*, edited by Marian Sawer, Manon Tremblay, and Linda Trimble, 221–35. Abingdon: Routledge.

50 Are electoral quotas and French-style parity the same thing?

Electoral quotas and parity are two different concepts, although they are not completely unrelated. An electoral quota is a positive action that aims to counteract some of the systemic obstacles impeding women's capacity to perform in politics at the same level as men (see question 43). Parity, a notion attributed to the French feminist activist Hubertine Auclert (1848–1914), concerns a goal expressed as an ideal: the presence in equal numbers of women and men in the institutions of representative democracy. It was imposed in French politics in the early 1990s as a consequence of a 1982 ruling by the Conseil constitutionnel (the constitutional council, a French state body devoted to examining the constitutionality of laws) that declared electoral quotas for representation unconstitutional. In Lépinard's (2007) view, parity is a fundamental principle, a concept of political philosophy, whereas electoral quotas are simply a legal notion and a technical means of achieving parity (the presence in equal numbers of female and male representatives). In fact, it is unlikely that parity will be achieved without the adoption of quotas. As an ideal and a goal to attain, parity is a definitive measure, an actual characteristic of democracy, whereas quotas are usually (though not always) circumstantial measures that can be fashioned to fit particular situations (see question 44). However, the difference between parity and quotas seems less clear today. Indeed, the definition of parity offered in 2014 by the Haut Conseil à l'Égalité entre les femmes et les hommes presents it as both philosophical and practical: "Parity is both a tool and the goal of equal sharing of representative and decision-making power between women and men. It is a requirement of justice and democracy" (7; our translation). Parity is philosophical because of its "requirement of justice and democracy," and practical because it is "a tool."

Parity and electoral quotas diverge in various respects. Parity is based on a fundamental fact: the human species is composed of women and men. In other words, one human being out of two is a woman. This is a universal phenomenon but not an absolute; in China and India, for instance, there are fewer women than men because those profoundly patriarchal cultures value men over women and legitimize the abortion of female embryos and foetuses and the murder of girls, thus creating a gender imbalance within their borders. Nevertheless, the primary, foundational proportion is that of humanity formed of two equal components: women and men. This is why parity requires an equal number of women and men in politics, rejecting any other ratio (such as 30–70 or 40–60), such as those proposed in quotas. Indeed, if we accept the principle that one human in two is a woman and that this principle should dictate the composition of legislative assemblies, it is not possible to accept a woman–man proportion in politics other than 50–50.

A second divergent element is that parity is claimed in the name of the primary division of the human species (that is, sex as determined by the organs of generation), whereas quotas might involve social categories (resembling more closely the concept of gender). According to the discourse of parity, human beings are universally either female or male, and therefore women cannot be considered a category on the same level as, for example, cultural, ethnic, or sexual minorities. What is more, sex is the primary identifier, assigned at birth, the substrate of the human species; anatomical duality – female or male – precedes, intersects with, and marks every other social cleavage, all other differences. There are women and men in every culture and in every ethnic group, among the sexual minorities of lesbians and gays, in all linguistic minorities, among all social classes, and so on. In contrast, quotas target social categories (such as young people, Maoris in New Zealand, people with disabilities in Uganda, and so on), the proportion of which within the population most frequently guides the proportion in parliament.

Finally, the concept of parity, although it is of European origin, was claimed by French activists as being a perfect fit with the universalist fundaments of republicanism; parity made it possible to establish true universalism. Whereas quotas divide society, shattering it into a myriad of categories and interests (the United States being the model to avoid as well as, no doubt, Canada with its multiculturalism), parity affirms the universality of the difference between the sexes; human beings are, universally, female or male – a universality that does not concern other social divisions (for example, human beings are not universally heterosexual). The universality of the difference between the sexes also marks the republican individual, who is universal by definition; it means that this individual cannot evade the difference between the sexes. The principle of universalism, the bedrock of the Republic, is preserved. In short, parity has made it possible to "sex" the abstract and universal individual of the Republic in order, paradoxically, to "desex" this individual in practice.

It may seem that the rooting of the parity argument in the universalist foundations of French republicanism makes it more difficult to apply it outside of France, but it is only the argument's ideological edifice that is specific to France; the notion of parity could be applied elsewhere. For example, the abstract and universal republican citizen, stripped of all identity-related markers, is not a political actor in North America in general or in Canada more particularly. To the contrary, in fact: in the United States the myth of the "melting pot" prevails, whereas the Canadian "mosaic" of citizenship is defined by a multitude of traits, including sex/gender, age, sexual preference, race, national or ethnic origin, skin colour, and religion. Thus, in the context of Canadian multiculturalism, it is possible that the idea that the difference between the sexes is a social division more significant than all others would be roundly criticized.

Although parity and electoral quotas diverge in several ways, they nevertheless share some common ground. First, neither parity nor quotas address the question of the presence of women in politics from the angle of substantive representation (or women's experiences or interests; see questions 43, 44, 50 to 52). Both are limited to a quantitative, or numerical, perspective on women's representation, with things such as total benefits in terms of decisions and public policies favourable to women being simple incidentals. Second, the debates over parity and electoral quotas have drawn on a common pool of arguments (see questions 47, 51, and 53). Third, beyond philosophical debates, Ms and Mr Everybody see parity as a 50 per cent quota. Finally, neither parity nor quotas guarantee a higher rate of feminization of parliament in the absence of a real political desire to attain this objective.

BIBLIOGRAPHY

France (Premier ministre, Haut Conseil à l'Égalité entre les femmes et les hommes). 2014. *Guide de la parité: Des lois pour le partage à égalité des responsabilités politiques, professionnelles et sociales*, Paris: Haut Conseil à l'Égalité entre les femmes et les hommes, accessed 15 July 2016, http://www.haut-conseil-egalite.gouv.fr/IMG/pdf/ hcefh_guide_de_la_parite_version_longue__10_02_2014.pdf.

Haut Conseil à l'Égalité entre les femmes et les hommes. "Parité," accessed 15 July 2016, http://www.haut-conseil-egalite.gouv.fr/parite.

Lépinard, Éléonore. 2007. *L'égalité introuvable: La parité, les féministes et la République*. Paris: Presses de sciences po. See, in particular, 77–99.

Urbinati, Nadia. 2012. "Why *Parité* Is a Better Goal than Quotas." *International Journal of Constitutional Law* 10 (2): 465–76.

51 What arguments have been advanced to promote parity?

The background argument for debates over parity is the following: the universality of the republican individual means that this individual also represents the universality of the difference between the sexes. This difference, ultimately, is primary and foundational, in that it precedes, intersects with, and marks all other societal cleavages. This reasoning is apropos to the French debate on parity because it reflects the ideology of republicanism – that of a single, indivisible nation, upon which rests the organization of the French state and society. The discourse in favour of parity thus consists of bringing the idea into line with the values of the republic. It could not, in my opinion, be applied elsewhere – for example, in Canada, where multicultural (characterized by multiplicity and diversity) citizenship prevails.

A number of the arguments advanced to promote quotas have also been employed to serve the parity cause (see questions 47, 51, and 53). Here are just a few examples. The principle of equality between women and men justifies women's access in greater numbers to political institutions, through equality that is not formal (that is, inscribed in law, thus undifferentiated, which has already been achieved) but real (that is, takes into account the differences between the sexes/genders and is far from being achieved, as demonstrated by the low proportions of female politicians). Equality that is sensitive to differences would make it possible to change politics, to stamp it with women's ways of being, speaking, and doing (see questions 64 and 65). The argument of simple justice also arises in rationales developed to support parity and quotas: it is simply justice for women to be better represented in decision-making bodies because they form half the population; simply justice for them to have the right to be in politics because they are citizens; simply justice for them to participate alongside men in writing laws because they are equally subject to those laws (see question 40). The idea that the low presence of women in politics constitutes a democratic deficit and shows a crisis in representative democracy also feeds into debates on quotas and parity (see questions 33, 34, and 40). The entry of a greater number of women into legislative assemblies would make it possible not only to respond to this malaise but also to improve democracy, even to complete it.

In sum, aside from the argument linked to the republican citizen bearing the universal difference of the sexes, debates on parity have evolved not in a vacuum but in relation to the arguments deployed to justify quotas.

BIBLIOGRAPHY

Achin, Catherine, et al. 2007. *Sexes, genre et politique*. Paris: Economica. See, in particular, 19–54.

Gaspard, Francoise, Claude Servan-Schreiber, and Anne Le Gall. 1992. *Au pouvoir, citoyennes! Liberté, Égalité, Parité*. Paris: Seuil.

Lépinard, Éléonore. 2007. *L'égalité introuvable: La parité, les féministes et la République*. Paris: Presses de sciences po. See, in particular, 77–183.

Scott, Joan W. 2005. *Parité! L'universel et la différence des sexes*. Paris: Albin Michel. See, in particular, 21–60, 89–126.

Sénac-Slawinski, Réjane. 2008. *La parité*. Paris: PUF, coll. Que sais-je?, no 3795. See, in particular, 59–71.

52 What should we think of the parity argument of universality and the primacy of the difference between the sexes?

In my view, the argument that the difference between the sexes is universal and more significant than all other social cleavages is neither credible nor legitimate. In fact, it is dangerously essentialist. The difference between the sexes that parity proponents identify is biological: the human species is divided between female and male. First, this standardizes women (that is, the group of human beings defined as female from the physiological point of view) even though they do not form a monolithic group but are divided in a number of ways and by various oppositions (see questions 12, 60, and 63). Second, it ignores the fluidity of sexes/genders manifested, for example, in phenomena related to third sex, intersexuality, and transgenderism. Each year a significant number of intersex people are born; the medical profession rushes to assign either a female or male sex to all babies as soon as possible after birth, a manifestation of the totalitarian discourse and practices of heteronormativity. It also ignores the considerable number of trans (transsexual and transgender) people whose very existence represents a challenge to the female/male and feminine/masculine binaries. Finally, the idea that the differences between the sexes are universal reinforces an essentialist vision of heterosexuality; because the human species needs relations between a woman and a man for reproduction, this pairing should also mark the re/production of society in all of its manifestations, notably the management of the state.

The argument that the difference between the sexes is a more fundamental cleavage than, for example, the difference between people belonging to the ethnic and cultural majority and those who belong to ethnic and cultural minorities or between LGBT and straight people is also, in my opinion, unfounded. Indeed, how is saying "It's a girl!" or "It's a boy!" when a child is born more significant than celebrating the baby's skin colour? The fact that a person is black or bisexual is certainly no less consequential in a racist and bi-phobic society than is being a woman in a patriarchal society. But there is more. In decreeing the primacy of the difference between the sexes over all other social cleavages, the parity movement in France not only rejected solidarity with groups bearing these "other differences" but clearly foreclosed even the possibility for them to claim the right to legislative representation; sex would be the only difference worthy of representation because it is inherent and primary to the universal individual – who also has no identity-related markers in terms of skin colour or sexual preference. Taking into consideration these "other differences" would pose the risk of splintering the universal individual (universal because universally female or male), the only political actor authorized by the republic.

In short, in my view, the argument of universality of the difference of the sexes and its monopoly over the field of political meaning is absolutely indefensible.

53 What arguments have been raised against parity?

Three basic arguments have been advanced against parity: equality between the sexes (which remains open to interpretation), division of popular sovereignty into categories, and protection of national identity against foreign influences.

Equality has at least two positions: formal equality and equality in fact (see question 43). Parity proponents see parity as an objective to attain: achieving equality between women and men in practice. People who oppose parity do not challenge the principle of equality of women and men (at least, not publicly) but advocate a formal interpretation of this principle. Of course, parity embodies equality in the form of presence in equal numbers of women and men in institutions of representative democracy. Its opponents allow this, although they claim, in the same breath, that the means used to achieve it are contrary to republican equality, as they involve preferential treatment for women (although they do not see that the current political system is organized in such a way that it results in preferential treatment for men). Moreover, the antiparity side fears that parity will discriminate against men. What is certain, says the antiparity side, is that both scenarios are contrary to the principle of equality of women and men. In sum, the antiparity camp endorses the goal (that of equal sharing of political roles between women and men) but not the means (inevitably quotas, though without mentioning them) of getting there.

The second argument invoked against parity is that of division of popular sovereignty into categories. According to the republican perspective, the people is sovereign and, above all, indivisible; each member of parliament represents the people – and not part of the people – which, in turn, is represented by all members of parliament. Parity might mean that female politicians would represent only female citizens, male politicians only male citizens, female politicians from Alsace only female citizens from Alsace, women elected by a cultural and ethnic minority only female citizens of that minority, lesbian politicians only lesbian citizens, and so on. In this way, parity will fracture the unity of the people and lead to the representation of particular interests rather than the nation's common good. It will encourage the formation of politicized identities that will, in turn, claim access to political representation. Will sexual minorities have the right to representation quotas in the National Assembly? And why not people with blue eyes? How far will these demands go? In short, parity will lead to an avalanche of specific demands, signing, in the short or the long term, the death warrant of the universal citizen, and even of the republic.

The third argument, that of protection of national identity against foreign influences, flows from the second argument; it consists of preserving French political culture from values and practices that come from abroad – notably the United States, a communitarian country rife with identity-related claims and quotas, government by judges and judicial activism, political correctness, and so on.

BIBLIOGRAPHY

Achin, Catherine, et al. 2007. *Sexes, genre et politique*. Paris: Economica. See, in particular, 19–54.

Amar, Micheline, ed. 1999. *Le piège de la parité. Arguments pour un débat*. Paris: Hachette Litteratures.

Lépinard, Éléonore. 2007. *L'égalité introuvable. La parité, les féministes et la République*. Paris: Presses de sciences po. See, in particular, 77–183.

– 2013. "For Women Only? Gender Quotas and Intersectionality in France." *Politics & Gender* 9 (3): 276–98.

Scott, Joan W. 2005. *Parité! L'universel et la différence des sexes*. Paris: Albin Michel See, in particular, 21–60, 89–126, 169–208.

Sénac-Slawinski, Réjane. 2008. *La parité*. Paris: PUF, coll. Que sais-je?, no 3795. See, in particular, 59–71.

54 Can we say that parity in France is a failure?

A flippant answer would be, "It depends how you define failure." In general, parity has only partially reached its target of egalitarian sharing of electoral mandates and political functions between women and men in France. More specifically, a relative balance between women and men has been reached where the provisions on parity set out strict legal constraints, but men clearly dominate where such constraints do not exist. In other words, the imposition of legal constraints is key to the success of parity – a lesson that architects of quotas should take into account. This observation emerges from the data compiled by Mossuz-Lavau and Sénac (2014) and synthesized in table 5 (the table has been modified to present the proportions of women rather than of men).

As Mossuz-Lavau and Sénac summarize (2014, 1, our translation), "French democracy presents two contrasting faces between territorial collectivities and a government composed of equal numbers of women and men, on the one hand, and the executive leaders embodying 'exclusive democracy,' on the other." Furthermore, in the view of Mossuz-Lavau and Sénac, parity cannot be assessed solely in terms of percentages but must also take into account the nature of the portfolios given to women. At the moment, they still occupy positions deemed compliant with their gender assignment, thus doubly distorting the ideal of parity: vertically, for these portfolios are often considered less powerful, and horizontally, because the state missions are unequally divided among women and men. Together, these dynamics re/produce the gender system in a way that contradicts parity.

This relative failure of parity cannot be attributed to legislative inactivity. Since it was adopted in 2000, the "parity" law has been amended a number of times to make it a better tool for attaining its goal of equal distribution of women and men in positions of power. For instance, regional elections have been subjected to a system of strict alternation of women and men on the lists since the 2003 reform, and in municipal elections (in communes with a population of 3,500 or more) since the 2007 reform. In addition, the law of January 2007 specifies that the prefecture will not register lists that do not alternate the order of women and men candidates. The law made three other important changes. First, it introduced an obligation of parity within regional and municipal executives (in communes

Table 5

Proportion of women in French local and national political assemblies and in executive councils, prior to and after the adoption of gender parity laws, April 2015

	Before 1999 (%)	Most recent election (%)
NO LEGAL CONSTRAINT		
Presidents of regional councils	11.5	9.1
Presidents of departmental councils	1.0	9.9
Presidents of intercommunal councils	5.2	7.7
Deputy presidents of intercommunal councils	–	19.9
Chair of city council (undifferentiated in terms of size)	7.5	16.0
Town councillors in towns > 3,500 inhabitants (1995) and > 1,000 (2014)	21.0	34.9
PARTIAL LEGAL CONSTRAINT OR INCENTIVES		
Senators	5.3	25.0
Members of parliament (lower house)	10.9	26.9
STRICT LEGAL CONSTRAINT		
French members of the European Parliament	40.2	43.2
Regional councillors	27.5	47.9
Vice-presidents of regional councils	15.1	48.4
Departmental councillors	9.2	50.1
Vice-presidents of departmental councils	–	48.3
Deputies to the chair of the city council > 3,500 inhabitants (1995) and > 1,000 (2014)	21.8	47.5
Town councillor > 3,500 inhabitants (1995) and > 1,000 (2014)	21.7	48.2

Source: Haut Conseil à l'Égalité entre les femmes et les hommes (2016), 5.

with a population of 3,500 or more). Second, it imposed a parity tandem in cantonal elections – that is, the incumbent–replacement pairing must be composed of a woman and a man. Third, it raised from 50 per cent to 75 per cent the financial holdback incurred by parties that do not respect parity, calculated on the basis of the gap between the percentage of female and male candidates. For example, if a party presents 40 per cent female candidates and 60 per cent male candidates, the gap is 20 per cent, and the holdback, which had been 10 per cent (half of 20 per cent) before the 2007 reform would now be 15 per cent (three quarters of 20 per cent). The 17 May 2013 law changed the voting system for election of councillors in communities, municipalities, and departments. For election of commune and municipal councillors, parity lists with strict alternation of women and men were now to be used in centres with a population of more than 1,000 (previously 3,500). For departmental elections, the lists had to have a pair of parity female/male candidates for each canton. The law of 2 August 2013 reformed the voting system for senatorial elections; from now on, in communes with a population of 1,000 or more, municipal councils elect their delegates (responsible for electing senators) from lists made with woman–man (or man–woman) alternation. Finally, the law of 4 August 2014 doubles the penalties for political parties that do not respect parity in legislative elections.

BIBLIOGRAPHY

Baudino, Claudie. 2003. "Parity Reform in France: Promises and Pitfalls." *Review of Policy Research* 20 (3): 385–400.

France (Premier ministre, Haut Conseil à l'Égalité entre les femmes et les hommes). 2015. *Guide de la parité. Des lois pour le partage à égalité des responsabilités politiques, professionnelles et sociales.* Paris: HCE|fh, April 16, 2015, version, accessed 16 July 2016, http://www.haut-conseil-egalite.gouv.fr/IMG/pdf/guide_parite-2015.pdf.

– 2016. *Guide to Gender Parity. Laws Aiming at a Gender Equal Sharing of Political, Professional and Social Responsibilities.* Paris: HCE|fh, updated in February 2016, accessed on 16 July 2016, http://www.haut-conseil-egalite.gouv.fr/IMG/pdf/hce_s_synthesis_about_parity.pdf.

Haut Conseil à l'Égalite entre les femmes et les hommes, "Parité," accessed 16 July 2016, http://www.haut-conseil-egalite.gouv.fr/.

Mossuz-Lavau, Janine and Réjane Sénac. 2014. *Élections municipales 2014. Les enjeux.*

1944–2014: les élections municipales et intercommunales au prisme de la parité.
Paris: CEVIPOF, accessed 15 July 2016, https://hal.archives-ouvertes.fr/hal-01064755/
document.

55 Is a women's (or feminist) party an effective strategy for increasing the number of women in politics?

In general, the creation of a women's (or feminist) political party is not an effective strategy for increasing the number of women in politics. To begin with, it is important to distinguish between a women's political party and a feminist party; the former is composed of women and is not necessarily inspired by feminism, whereas the second, composed mainly of women but also admitting men among its activist base, makes feminism its source of inspiration and mobilizations. Women of Russia is an example of the first type, and the Belgian Parti féministe unifié is an example of the second. On the other hand, a feminist party may want to avoid the "feminist" label by presenting itself as a women's party.

It is tempting to see a women's (or feminist) political party as a strategy for getting more women elected to parliament. Indeed, because political parties raise the highest barriers to the election of women (see questions 18 to 20 and 23), it is logical to think about getting around them by setting up a party devoted to the election of women. A number of women's (or feminist) political parties have been created since the late nineteenth century in, for example, Afghanistan, Armenia, Australia, Belarus, Belgium, Bulgaria, Canada, Denmark (Greenland), France, Georgia, Germany, Great Britain and Northern Ireland, Greece, Iceland, India, Japan, Kyrgyzstan, Lithuania, Mauritius, Moldova, the Philippines, the Poland, Russia, Ukraine, and the United States. Although incomplete, this list illustrates the diversity of countries in which women's (or feminist) political parties have been formed: world economic powers and countries with little wealth, some countries with a proportional voting system and others with a majority voting system, countries in which equality of women and men is almost a reality and others marked by a strong patriarchal tradition.

Women's (or feminist) parties do not increase the number of women in politics simply because their candidates tend not to win elections. Of course, the electoral success of a political party depends in part on the type of voting system used, with a list proportional system supposedly more favourable to women than a majority voting system (see question 21). Yet, even under a list proportional voting system, the results for women's (or feminist) political parties are negative (Matland 2003). First, often these parties do not get a single female candidate elected and thus remain unrepresented in parliament. Their poor electoral performance indicates to other parties that the women's question is not important, that it is not an electoral issue, and that they can therefore ignore it. Worse, when no female candidates are elected, those who voted for candidates from these parties are not represented in parliament, even in a list proportional voting system. Furthermore, if they attain parliamentary representation, these parties usually play only a situational and limited role in public governance. Second, they siphon off human resources (female activists, notably) that might be used more effectively if they were involved in a truly competitive party on the electoral and parliamentary levels. Third, women's (or feminist) political parties not only deplete the limited resources of the feminist movement between the electoral and extra-electoral scenes but they demonstrate its weakness in the sense that the movement seems incapable of influencing the important parties represented in parliament (Moser 2003). Fourth, the presence of a women's (or feminist) political party may send the message that this party has a monopoly on women's representation and encourage other political parties to ignore, completely legitimately, the female electorate and the problems linked to the female status. Women's (or feminist) political parties thus help to ghettoize women and the questions related to their living conditions.

Women's (or feminist) political parties nevertheless present certain positives. For instance, they can promote debates of ideas, foster women's (and feminist) mobilizations, and popularize a feminist reading of governance and political processes – that is, a reading in which feminism is not confined to "women's questions" but is posed as a transversal reading of public debates. Women's (or feminist) political parties may thus contribute to the socialization of girls and women, even encourage them to become active in a political organization (composed of feminists, or women only, or women and men). These functions can, however, be performed by vehicles other than a women's (or feminist) party, such as civil society groups or parties that are not labelled "women's" or "feminist" but are completely open to women and feminism. This last option raises another question: rather than setting up women's (or feminist) political parties, could women's political representation (descriptive and substantive; see questions 55 and 60) not take place through women's and feminists' participation in mixed political parties?

In conclusion, the electoral balance sheet of women's (or feminist) political parties is not unremittingly negative. The clearest example is the Women's Alliance in Iceland. In four national elections held between 1983 and 1995, the party saw some success, obtaining between 4.9 per cent and 10.1 per cent of the votes and filling between three and six seats in the Althingi. At one point during this period, the Women's Alliance even held the balance of power. Yet, I suspect that the success of this experiment is overestimated and that, in the end, its function is essentially symbolic – offering a legendary episode in the history of women's movement mobilization on the political and electoral scenes. There is nothing negative about this – far from it; the symbols and the hopes that they crystallize are essential to action. *I have a dream …*

BIBLIOGRAPHY

Ishiyama, John T. 2003. "Women's Parties in Post-Communist Politics." *East European Politics and Society* 17 (2): 266–304.

Matland, Richard. 2003. "Women's Representation in Post-Communist Europe." In *Women's Access to Political Power in Post-Communist Europe*, edited by Richard E. Matland and Kathleen A. Montgomery, 321–42. New York: Oxford University Press.

Moser, Robert G. 2003. "Electoral Systems and Women's Representation: The Strange Case of Russia." In *Women's Access to Political Power in Post-Communist Europe*, edited by Richard E. Matland and Kathleen A. Montgomery, 153–72. New York: Oxford University Press.

Nechemias, Carol. 2001. "The Women of Russia Political Movement." In *Encyclopedia of Russian Women's Movements*, edited by Norma C. Noonan and Carol Nechemias, 356–59. Westport: Greenwood/Praeger.

Purvis, June. 2016. "The Women's Party of Great Britain (1917–1919): A Forgotten Episode in British Women's Political History." *Women's History Review* 25 (4): 638–51.

Styrkársdóttir, Auður. 1999. "Women's Lists in Iceland – A Response to Political Lethargy." In *Equal Democracies? Gender and Politics in the Nordic Countries*, edited by Christina Bergqvist et al., 88–96. Oslo: Scandinavian University Press.

– 2013. "Iceland: Breaking Male Dominance by Extraordinary Means." In *Breaking Male*

Dominance in Old Democracies, edited by Drude Dahlerup and Monique Leyenaar, 124–5. Oxford: Oxford University Press.

Zaborszky, Dorothy. 1987. "Feminist Politics: The Feminist Party of Canada." *Women's Studies International Forum* 10 (6): 613–21.

56 What should we think of the practical strategies implemented to increase the number of women in parliaments?

These strategies are a necessary evil. To the extent that it is imperative that more women sit in parliaments (see question 40) and given that time and patience are no guarantee that women will eventually occupy half of the seats in parliaments (see question 31), practical strategies such as short lists of female candidates, the pairing of ridings, targeted financial incentives, quotas and seats in parliament reserved for women, and parity or parity binomial woman–man representation are proving essential to accelerating matters and attaining more-feminized parliaments. Up to now, the laissez-faire policy has not been successful; as of June 2016, only 22.7 per cent of parliamentarians (all chambers combined) around the world were women. If, beyond discourse, we want equality of women and men, simple justice, and the quality of democratic life really to mean something, it is important to intervene. From this point of view, such strategies are not only legitimate but necessary, especially as they encourage women to mobilize within civil society and with respect to electoral politics.

Having said that, the strategies employed seem problematic to me because they involve a certain amount of essentialism, as they aim for representation based on a physical marker: biological sex. This is particularly true of parity, which poses the difference between the sexes as a universal truth (see questions 50 to 52), a primary distinction that has precedence over all others. The strategies for increasing the number of women in politics confine identities to a rigid naturalist straitjacket; women form a group because they are of the same anatomical sex, which differentiates them from men. The body justifies and legitimizes male access to political representation. And the body serves to justify and legitimize the idea that women should represent women because they share common experiences modelled on their belonging to one sex/gender (see questions 12, 60, and 63). Such strategies do not target substantive representation of women, except indirectly. It is the presence of bodies labelled "female/women/feminine" in political assemblies that is important.

In short, I am not saying that strategies to increase the presence of women in politics are not necessary. They are. However, I maintain that these measures are based on an essentialist vision of women and of the difference between the sexes/genders, a vision that they reinforce and spread.

CHAPTER SEVEN

Political Representation

57 Who are the women elected to political office?

Women elected to political office are exceptional; their profile does not match that of "Ms Everywoman." Studies show that, in general, female politicians are more highly educated than the general female population. Not surprisingly, they usually hold positions at the top of the hierarchy in the job market, such as lawyer, executive director, businesswoman, doctor or other healthcare professional, professor, and social sciences professional (economist, psychologist, sociologist, and so on). They also have substantially higher incomes than most women. More female than male politicians are single – a reminder of the weight that family responsibilities may place on the shoulders of some women (see question 24). Many come from politicized families, and some take over the seat of a male relative (a father or husband); this phenomenon was once quite common in the United States and remains so in Asia (see question 70). As a rule, before entering parliament, women have long experience with engagement in civil society (for example, in sociocommunity or cultural groups or in unions) and at other political levels (municipal councils or school boards).

On the other hand, it would be a mistake to believe that women and men in politics form monolithic and opposed blocs – in other words, that these women resemble each other and are different from all men (see question 12). In fact, research tends to show that although female and male politicians were once relatively polarized in terms of characteristics, today they tend to be more alike: women have adopted traits traditionally held by men and men have taken on a few of the traits associated with women. In the past women entered politics at a more advanced age than men, but the age gap between women and men at time of first election has now shrunk. Increasing numbers of women who make the leap into the parliamentary arena are lawyers, a profession that was long closed to them (for example, until 1906 in New Brunswick, 1912 in British Columbia, and as late as 1941 in Quebec). More and more male politicians complain about having to juggle their family and political responsibilities. Nevertheless, some major differences persist (notably with regard to the authority that women exercise in politics; see Murray 2010; Vanlangenakker et al. 2013).

Female politicians share with their male colleagues a sense of identity and membership in an elite. It is my opinion that they are closer in profile to their fellow politicians than to other women: both the career path and the profile of politicians are elitist in comparison to those of the general population. In addition, politicians, female and male, are participating in society's exemplary elitist activity, an activity for which the selection procedure – election – is accessible to a very small number of people with exceptional resources (resources that are not exclusively economic in nature but also involve networks, influence, and family reputation, among other factors). What is more, studies have shown that women who are members of elitist circles have profiles that distance them more from other women in the population than is the case for men in a similar situation. This is not surprising because female politicians are just as qualified and competent as their male counterparts (often even more so; see Anzia and Berry 2011; Fulton 2012), whereas women in general are disadvantaged in comparison to men in terms of factors such as annual income, access to networks, and schedule flexibility. From this point of view, it is paradoxical to expect female politicians to represent women, as they have little in common with them except anatomical sex (see questions 60 and 63).

BIBLIOGRAPHY

Anzia, Sarah F. and Christopher R. Berry. 2011. "The Jackie (and Jill) Robinson Effect: Why Do Congresswomen Outperform Congressmen?" *American Journal of Political Science* 55 (3): 478–93.

Franceschet, Susan and Jennifer M. Piscopo. 2014. "Sustaining Gendered Practices? Power, Parties, and Elite Political Networks in Argentina." *Comparative Political Studies* 47 (1): 85–110.

Fulton, Sarah A. 2012. "Running Backwards and in High Heels: The Gendered Quality Gap and Incumbent Electoral Success." *Political Research Quarterly* 65 (2): 303–14.

Murray, Rainbow. 2010. "Linear Trajectories or Vicious Circles? The Causes and Consequences of Gendered Career Paths in the National Assembly." *Modern & Contemporary France* 18 (4): 445–59.

Schwindt-Bayer, Leslie A. 2011. "Women Who Win: Social Backgrounds, Paths to Power, and Political Ambition in Latin American Legislatures." *Politics & Gender* 7 (1): 1–33.

Tremblay, Manon and Linda Trimble. 2004. "Still Different After All These Years? A Comparison of Female and Male MPs in the 20th Century." *Journal of Legislative Studies* 10 (1): 97–122.

Trimble, Linda and Manon Tremblay. 2003. "Women Politicians in Canada's Parliament and Legislatures, 1917–2000: A Socio-demographic Profile." In *Women and Electoral Politics in Canada*, edited by Manon Tremblay and Linda Trimble, 37–58. Don Mills: Oxford University Press.

Vanlangenakker, Ine, Bram Wauters, and Bart Maddens. 2013. "Pushed Toward the Exit? How Female MPs Leave Parliament." *Politics & Gender* 9 (1): 61–75.

58 Where are women situated in the political space?

The position of women in the political space is commonly analyzed along two axes: vertical and horizontal. The vertical axis concerns the positions occupied by women in the political hierarchy: are they backbenchers or ministers, and, in the latter case, are they junior, intermediate, or senior ministers? Up to the 1990s, women usually found themselves at the bottom of the political hierarchy – that is, in junior ministerial positions. This was explained by their relatively recent access to pools of executive recruitment – either legislative assemblies in parliamentary systems or other spaces of specialized skills (the legal and medical professions, academe, and so on) in presendential systems. Since the 1990s, more women have been intermediate and senior ministers (minister of defence or finance, for example). Because they have been in parliaments longer and have developed sociopolitical capital, they can no longer be ignored as candidates for the highest-level positions in state power. It is also possible that they now assume such functions because public attitudes, especially those in the male political class, have evolved.

The horizontal axis concerns the types of portfolios assigned to female politicians. Traditionally, women's portfolios were confined to sectors deemed compatible with female roles, such as culture, education, and car-ing for others (children, the elderly, and other groups). Today, this ghettoization is much less obvious; it is no longer unusual for a woman to be a minister of defence (for example, Michelle Bachelet held this position in the Chilean government from 2002 to 2004; Kim Campbell, in Canada in 1993; Michèle Alliot-Marie, in France from 2002 to 2007; Ursula von der Leyen, in Germany since 2013; and Andreja Katič, in Slovenia since 2015), minister of finance (such as Ellen Johnson-Sirleaf, in Liberia from 1979 to 1980 and Christine Lagarde, in France from 2007 to 2011; in Canada, women have been ministers of finance in a number of provinces: for example, in Alberta, Shirley McClellan, from 2004 to 2006, and Iris Sylvian Evans, from 2008 to 2010; in British Columbia, Carole Taylor, from 2005 to 2008; in Ontario, Janet Ecker, from 2002 to 2003; in Quebec, Pauline Marois, from 2001 to 2003, and Monique Jérôme-Forget, from 2007 to 2009), or foreign minister (examples are Maite Nkoana-Mashabane, in South Africa, since 2009; María Ángela Holguín, in Colombia, since 2010; and Sushma Swaraj, in India, since 2014). Similarly, women participate in a much wider variety of legislative committees than previously.

In short, an analysis of the positioning of women in politics reflects that of their identity, opinions, and actions: previously polarized, women and men have become more similar.

BIBLIOGRAPHY

Davis, Rebecca H. 1997. *Women and Power in Parliamentary Democracies: Cabinet Appointments in Western Europe, 1968–1992*. Lincoln: University of Nebraska Press.

Jalalzai, Farida. 2013. *Shattered, Cracked, or Firmly Intact? Women and the Executive Glass Ceiling Worldwide*. New York: Oxford University Press.

List of elected and appointed female heads of state, accessed 20 July 2016, https://en.wikipedia.org/wiki/List_of_elected_and_appointed_female_heads_of_state.

Paxton, Pamela and Melanie M. Hughes. 2007. *Women, Politics, and Power: A Global Perspective*. Los Angeles: Pine Forge Press. See, in particular, 96–100.

Tremblay, Manon and Gretchen Bauer. 2011. "Conclusion." In *Women in Executive Power: A Global Overview*, edited by Gretchen Bauer and Manon Tremblay, 171–90. London: Routledge.

59 Do female politicians think and act differently from male politicians?

Worded this way, this question would lend itself to the assumption that women form a uniform group, which is not the case – never mind that it poses men as a standard against which women should be evaluated. That being said, a large number of studies show that women in politics tend to have different opinions than do their male colleagues. In general, they are situated farther to the left on the ideological spectrum. They are apparently more in favour of an interventionist state that seeks to redistribute the collective wealth through public policies in the social field as a whole – for example with regard to culture, assistance to the elderly and vulnerable, education, the environment, family, health, and community services. However, they are apparently more hostile to state spending in the sectors of nuclear energy, infrastructure (the road network, for example), and the military. Studies also show that female politicians are more open on questions of ethics and minority rights. For example, they are less inclined to adopt a repressive attitude with regard to "homosexuality" and the death penalty. They are in favour of gun control, and they believe that rehabilitation should be stressed in sentencing for criminal matters. They are also more flexible with regard to sex education and access to contraceptives for young people. Unsurprisingly, female politicians are more likely than their male colleagues to support women's rights with regard to equal pay, access to abortion, affirmative action policies, daycare centres, shelters for victims of conjugal violence, and similar matters.

Research also indicates that although female and male politicians have different opinions, there are many nuances to this finding. On the one hand, in statistical studies on opinions, sex often emerges as a factor of secondary (and sometimes no) importance, in comparison to other factors – which should not be surprising given that women have multiple identities. On the other hand, each political party exerts a decisive influence on the opinions of its members. Women are often elected under the banner of a left-leaning party (in general, these parties are more open to women), which provides a more credible explanation of their ideological positions than does their sex. Identification with feminism is another strong determinant of opinions expressed in politics: in general, people who call themselves feminist will also be ideologically to the left, more favourable to state interventionism in social affairs, more hostile to economic free-market laws and military spending, and so on. This means that men who identify as feminist and belong to left-wing parties are sometimes better substantive representatives of the "women's cause" than are women who reject the feminist label and belong to right-wing parties (on substantive representation, see question 60). Aside from party and identification with feminism, variables such as seniority in parliament and political ambition also exert an influence on the opinions that women express in politics.

Similarly, the results of a number of studies support the idea that women in politics behave differently from their male colleagues. For example, they place a higher value on exchanges with the population and make themselves more available than men do. It is in relation to the status of women, however, that women's attitudes apparently diverge most significantly from men's. In general, female politicians, more than their male colleagues, become involved in activities intended to represent women – that is, to change and improve the collective experiences of the greatest number of diverse women (see questions 60 and 63). For example, female politicians are more likely to be in contact with women's groups than are male politicians and to perform legislative actions of all kinds (for example, table a bill, make a motion, or submit a petition) regarding the status of women. Such actions may involve themes that have spurred feminist demands (such as abortion, pay equity, and violence against women) or are related to more traditional issues of equality between women and men (equal pay, equality in marriage, equal division of assets in case of divorce, legal access to education and healthcare, and so on). Women elected to office are also apparently more involved than their male colleagues in legislative committees that deal with questions that have an impact on women's living conditions.

However, like their opinions, women's behaviours in politics do not evolve in a vacuum; research has brought to light a wide range of personal and institutional factors that shape their actions. Personal factors affecting their identity and their status in politics involve, among other things, identity markers (such as ethnicity and language spoken); their party and its ideology; political experience and, notably, longevity of political career; whether they have been a member of a women's group; the rural or urban nature of their riding; the margin of electoral victory; and political ambitions. The institutional factors likely to influence the behaviours of female politicians concern the rules of the game that frame their political activities, such as party discipline (see question 61) and ministerial solidarity, the proportion of women elected (or critical mass; see question 39), the existence of a women's caucus within the party, and the existence of legislative or executive bodies devoted to women's representation (such as a department or a parliamentary committee; see question 68).

In short, studies indicate that female politicians have opinions and behaviours distinct from those of male politicians. However, variables other than sex, including identity, political party, and affinities with feminism, shape their opinions, actions, and gestures.

BIBLIOGRAPHY

Hancock, Ange-Marie. 2014. "Intersectional Representation or Representing Intersectionality? Reshaping Empirical Analysis of Intersectionality." In *Representation: The Case of Women*, edited by Maria C. Escobar-Lemmon and Michelle M. Taylor-Robinson, 41–57. New York: Oxford University Press.

Htun, Mala, Marina Lacalle, and Juan Pablo Micozzi. 2013. "Does Women's Presence Change Legislative Behavior? Evidence from Argentina, 1983–2007." *Journal of Politics in Latin America* 5 (1): 95–125.

Rosenthal, Cindy Simon, ed. 2002. *Women Transforming Congress*. Norman: University of Oklahoma Press.

Swers, Michele L. 2002. *The Difference Women Make: The Policy Impact of Women in Congress*. Chicago: University of Chicago Press.

– 2014. "Representing Women's Interests in a Polarized Congress." In *Women and Elective Office: Past, Present, and Future*, edited by Sue Thomas and Clyde Wilcox, 3rd ed., 162–80. New York: Oxford University Press.

Tremblay, Manon. 1998. "Do Female MPs Substantively Represent Women? A Study of Legislative Behaviour in Canada's 35th Parliament." *Canadian Journal of Political Science* 31(3): 435–65.

Tremblay, Manon and Rejean Pelletier. 2000. "More Women or More Feminists? Descriptive and Substantive Representations of Women in the 1997 Canadian Federal Election." *International Political Science Review* 21 (4): 381–405.

60 Do women represent women?

I have researched this issue extensively, but I am still unable to provide a clear and definitive answer. I must therefore answer yes and no. But before going any further, it is important to understand what "represent" means.

Although it was published half a century ago, Hanna Fenichel Pitkin's book *The Concept of Representation* (1967) is still authoritative when it comes to concepts of political representation, even if Pitkin's interpretation can be questioned and enhanced (see the discussion on works by Saward and Squires below). Pitkin distinguishes four types of political representation: symbolic, formal, descriptive, and substantive.

When it embodies an idea or an entity, representation is called symbolic (see the excellent book by Lombardo and Meier [2014] on this subject); for instance, a cross refers to the Christian religion, a red rose embodies love, and a flag evokes a country. In the field of political institutions, symbolic representation supports the myth that the election of a person from a social minority helps to represent that minority. For instance, the election of the first woman, lesbian, or Indigenous person not only becomes the proof that women, lesbian, gay, bisexual, and trans (LGBT) communities, and Indigenous communities are represented in politics but at the same time legitimizes political institutions by making them seem accessible to anyone, notwithstanding her or his homosocial (see question 20) and sociopolitical capital. Finally, symbolic representation helps to socialize girls and women by allowing them to see themselves as contributing to governance (although the capacity to recognize oneself in an elected official may vary depending on the identities: would a black woman recognize herself more in Barack Obama or in Hillary Rodham Clinton?); it does the same thing for the general population by challenging certain tenacious prejudices with regard to the roles of women in politics.

Representation is formal when it is written into law. For instance, women and men must enjoy the same political rights, notably the rights to vote and to run for election. This is equality at the starting line: women and men benefit from the same rights – that is, they have identical status when it comes to participation in political life. For decades, this principle has been inscribed in instruments of international law, such as the 1948 Universal Declaration of Human Rights (in articles 2 and 21) and the 1952 Convention on the Political Rights of Women (in articles I, II, and III; see question 41).

Women's political rights are interpreted as human rights: because they are human beings like men and, invested with inalienable rights inherent to this fact, women may (and must) participate, like men, in the political life of their country. Today, women and men have the same political rights in almost all countries – at least formally, for in fact a number of difficulties may keep women, particularly those who are less well endowed in terms of homosocial and sociopolitical capital, from exercising these rights (see questions 6, 18, and 20).

Descriptive representation concerns the composition of parliaments: one human being out of two being a woman, one seat out of two in parliament should be occupied by a woman. In this perspective, parliament constitutes a small-scale model of society, but in which these women themselves must be diversified to reflect their heterogeneity in the population (Dovi 2002). To the possession of human rights as a criterion for representation is added that of the identity of the people elected. According to this perspective, it is clear that women and men are not equal with regard to representation: whereas they form about half of the population, as of June 2016 women did not hold even one quarter of the seats in the lower or single chambers of national parliaments around the world. This idea about equality of representation inspires national and international women's movement mobilizations and strategies to push for parliaments to become more feminized (see questions in chapter 6 and questions 38, 41, and 98). It also explains the willingness shown by many governments and political parties, since the early 1990s, to enact quota measures designed to increase the presence of women in politics (see questions 32 to 48). Similar to the principle of formal representation, that of descriptive representation is found in instruments of international law such as the 1995 Beijing Platform for Action. For example, article 181 provides that "achieving the goal of equal participation of women and men in decision-making will provide a balance that more accurately reflects the composition of society and is needed in order to strengthen democracy and promote its proper functioning." Article 182 observes that "although women make up at least half of the electorate in almost all countries and have attained the right to vote and hold office in almost all States Members of the United Nations, women continue to be seriously underrepresented as candidates for public office." These two articles spell out the disconnection between the proportion of women in the population and their (low) level of participation in legislative power: although one human being in two is a woman, one parliamentarian in two is not – an injustice to women with regard to representation (see question 40).

Finally, substantive representation concerns the content of public decisions. This perspective on equal representation of women and men starts from the principle that public policies are not neutral. In contrast to the liberal and republican premise that people elected to office elevate themselves above individual interests to devote themselves to representation of what is discursively posed as the "common good," the substantive perspective postulates that the identity of elected people is not unrelated to how they will approach their mandate of representation because the body (female or male) influences their daily experiences and guides how they integrate into society. A car salesperson might not address a woman and a man in the same way but might highlight the vehicle's comfort to her and the engine's performance to him. Many more women than men fear walking alone at night because female bodies are more often subjected to sexual assault than are male bodies; the result is the subtle control of women's mobility in the public space. Thus, in the substantive perspective, equality between women and men in representation is conveyed through the election of women who will defend the needs, demands, and interests of the female population. This is because they understand these needs, demands, and interests better than men do, as Young (2000, 143–4) explains: "To the extent that what distinguishes social groups is structural relations, particularly structural relations of privilege and disadvantage, and to the extent that persons are positioned similarly in those structures, then they have similar perspectives both on their own situation and on other positions in the society." Of course, this positioning is not uniform and varies according to women's identities; nevertheless, it is possible to believe that because of their gender women understand societal experiences that are essentially foreign to men. In this sense, substantive representation is not thought of in isolation from descriptive representation, as it envisages a connection between identity (and its diverse components) and public decisions. This idea is stated, for example, in article 181 of the Beijing Platform for Action: "Women's equal participation in decision-making is not only a demand for simple justice or democracy but can also be seen as a necessary condition for women's interests to be taken into account." This quote links the descriptive and substantive perspectives on equality of women and men with regard to representation, which amounts to parity of participation in making decisions and formulating public policies favourable to women. The notion of "critical mass" makes the connection between presence and ideas (see question 39).

So, we return to the initial question: do women represent women? Yes, from a symbolic and descriptive point of view, for these two readings of representation depend upon presence. Symbolically, the presence of female politicians demonstrates that politics is an activity accessible to women. These officeholders send a message to girls and women that they, too, can assume an electoral mandate of representation. In this perspective, Kim Campbell, Hillary Rodham Clinton, Indira Gandhi, Ana Jara, Cissé Mariam Kaïdama Sidibé, Angela Merkel, and Margaret Thatcher, for example, have all represented women. The number or proportion of women in a political assembly is another criterion by which women represent women and so is their presence in numbers that encourage diversity among female politicians and political participation by diverse women. In fact, this is one of the arguments used by the women's movement to demand that politics include more women. With an average proportion of around 23 per cent of legislators worldwide, as opposed to 50 per cent in the world population as a whole, women suffer from a 27 per cent deficit in representation in parliaments. In other words, men are overrepresented to the tune of 27 per cent. It must also be mentioned that women belonging to minorities have a deficit in representation even more marked than do those from the majority (Hughes 2013), a deficit that epistemological and methodological traditions of research on women and politics do not always fully reveal (Hancock 2014).

Conversely, women do not represent women from the formal and substantive points of view, which are based on ideas rather than on presence alone. Regardless of the nature of the voting system, women are not elected to represent women; they are elected to represent an electoral district. The possible exceptions to this rule are women's (or feminist; see question 55) political parties and seats reserved for women (see question 44), but this is not a foregone conclusion: it all depends on how the structures are designed. For example, does a women's or feminist party only represent women or does it contribute a feminist interpretation of all issues involved in living in a community? Women elected under the banner of a women's or feminist party have a privileged, but not exclusive, relationship with the female population; it is essentially female voters who vote for female candidates in these types of parties, and their programs are concerned with equality of the sexes/genders. However, once elected, these "women" or "feminists," although they pay special attention to the female population, must also take positions on broader themes, such as the budget and infrastructure, which they may certainly address from a "women's" or feminist" angle. As for reserved seats, do they simply represent women or might they make it possible for those who have been historically discriminated against to participate in and enhance sociopolitical governance (Phillips 1995: 57–83)? In Rwanda, women's groups play a prominent role in the election of the holders of these seats (see question 36). However, although reserved seats offer a platform for historically marginalized voices to be heard, representing only women would be equivalent to marginalizing these elected women even more, both in the political space and in society as a whole (see question 47).

From a substantive point of view, there is no evidence that women represent women. Of course, in general, female politicians, more than male politicians, are likely to act in a way that improves the collective experiences of the greatest number of diverse women. However, it is not possible to say there is a cause-and-effect connection between the presence of women in politics and public policies favourable to women. Women's political representation does not hew blindly to the criterion of sex – or of gender; it is related first and foremost to the parties, their programs, and their electoral opportunities; the political and electoral conjuncture and the influence of the women's movement on the political class; and female politicians' ambitions, career plans, and identification with feminism, among other things (see questions 16, 23, 45, 54, and 63). Too many factors shape the representation activity of female politicians to conclude that they represent women substantively in parliament. That being said, much research shows that female politicians feel invested in the responsibility of representing women in a substantive perspective.

As mentioned above, Pitkin's (1967) book, though published five decades ago, is still the basis for all thought about political representation, if only to revisit and propose alternatives to the concepts that it contains. A number of works have been published to those ends in recent years, including those by Saward (2010) and Squires (2008). The former proposes that political representation is a creative process inscribed in a performative discourse: to represent is to declare to do so. This declaration generates the very subject of the representation to the extent that, according to Dryzek and Niemeyer (2008, 482), "Discourses help constitute identities and their associated interests." Squires (2008) concurs with this reasoning: by claiming to represent women, female representatives constitute at the same time what women are and what they are not – whence the imperative that women elected to political office be aware of the multiple and diversified identities of women. This perspective is particularly enlightening because it gives meaning to Monique Wittig's prescient comment about the gender system (long before the subject was in fashion) to the effect that lesbians are not women as soon as they escape the regime of heteronormative hegemony. In fact, my research on women in politics over the years has enabled me to observe that the women whom female politicians are said to represent are eminently heterosexual and living within heterofamilies. This fact, which not only excludes lesbians but associates women's representation with heterofamily problems, risks essentializing women (Baldez 2011). Through such a discursive and constitutive activity, we can understand how conservative women can claim to represent women, whose interests are seen not as universal but as built discursively by politically situated female representatives (Osborn and Kreitzer 2014). For example, for left-wing female officeholders, representing women may mean advocating access to free abortion services; for right-wing female officeholders, it may mean advocating for a broader array of services to be offered to pregnant women so that they do not consider having an abortion. Today, substantive representation of women is complex and expressed in several variants – feminist, nonfeminist, even antifeminist (Childs and Celis 2012).

Taking Celis et al. (2008) as a springboard, Dahlerup (2014) seeks to summarize knowledge on the political representation of women through four questions: Who? What? How? Where? The "who" refers to female elected officials, of course, but Saward (2010) shows that nonparliamentary actors (such as the feminist movement) also represent women if they claim to do so and if a public accepts this claim. The "what" refers to the delicate question of "women's interests": do they exist and, if they do, what do they consist of (Beckwith 2014)? The "how" refers to the mechanisms of democracy that structure and frame representation – the mechanisms that provide inclusion in, and exclusion from, representation. Finally, the "where" brings to light the many sites in which representation takes place, inside or outside the legislature; local, national, or international – and, I would add, material or virtual.

In short, the question of whether women in politics represent women does not have a definitive answer – except that this question is, as always, complex.

BIBLIOGRAPHY

Baldez, Liza. 2011. "The UN Convention to Eliminate All Forms of Discrimination Against Women (CEDAW): A New Way to Measure Women's Interests." *Politics & Gender* 7 (3): 419–23.

Barnes, Tiffany D. 2012. "Gender and Legislative Preferences: Evidence from the Argentine Provinces." *Politics & Gender* 8 (4): 483–507.

Barnes, Tiffany D. and Stephanie M. Burchard. 2013. "'Engendering' Politics: The Impact of Descriptive Representation on Women's Political Engagement in Sub-Saharan Africa." *Comparative Political Studies* 46 (7): 767–90.

Beckwith, Karen. 2007. "Numbers and Newness: The Descriptive and Substantive Representation of Women." *Canadian Journal of Political Science* 40 (1): 27–49.

– 2014. "Plotting the Path from One to the Other: Women's Interests and Political Representation." In *Representation: The Case of Women*, edited by Maria C. Escobar-Lemmon and Michelle M. Taylor-Robinson, 19–40. New York: Oxford University Press.

Campbell, Rosie and Sarah Childs. 2015. "Conservatism, Feminisation and the Representation of Women in UK Politics." *British Politics* 10 (2): 148–68.

Celis, Karen and Sarah Childs, eds. 2014. *Gender, Conservatism and Political Representation*. Colchester: ECPR Press.

Celis, Karen, Sarah Childs, Johanna Kantola, and Mona Lena Krook. 2008. "Rethinking Women's Substantive Representation." *Representation* 44 (2): 99–110.

Childs, Sarah and Karen Celis. 2012. "The Substantive Representation of Women: What to Do with Conservative Claims?" *Political Studies* 60 (1): 213–25.

"Critical Perspectives on Gender and Politics: Hanna Pitkin's 'Concept of Representation' Revisited." 2012. Special section, *Politics & Gender* 8 (4): 508–47.

Dahlerup, Drude. 2014. "Representing Women: Defining Substantive Representation of Women." In *Representation: The Case of Women*, edited by Maria C. Escobar-Lemmon and Michelle M. Taylor-Robinson, 58–75. New York: Oxford University Press.

Dovi, Suzanne. 2002. "Preferable Descriptive Representatives: Will Just Any Woman, Black, or Latino Do?" *American Political Science Review* 96 (4): 729–43.

Dryzek, John S. and Simon Niemeyer. 2008. "Discursive Representation." *American Political Science Review* 102 (4): 481–93.

Escobar-Lemmon, Maria C., and Michelle M. Taylor-Robinson. 2014. "Dilemmas in the Meaning and Measurement of Representation." In *Representation: The Case of Women*, edited by Maria C. Escobar-Lemmon and Michelle M. Taylor-Robinson, 1–16. New York: Oxford University Press.

– 2014. "Does Presence Produce Representation of Interests?" In *Representation: The Case of Women*, edited by Maria C. Escobar-Lemmon and Michelle M. Taylor-Robinson, 227–47. New York: Oxford University Press.

Hancock, Ange-Marie. 2014. "Intersectional Representation or Representing Intersectionality? Reshaping Empirical Analysis of Intersectionality." In *Representation: The Case of Women*, edited by Maria C. Escobar-Lemmon and Michelle M. Taylor-Robinson, 41–57. New York: Oxford University Press.

Hughes, Melanie M. 2013. "The Intersection of Gender and Minority Status in National Legislatures: The Minority Women Legislative Index." *Legislative Studies Quarterly* 38 (4): 489–516.

Lombardo, Emanuela and Petra Meier. 2014. *The Symbolic Representation of Gender: A Discursive Approach*. London and New York: Routledge.

Mansbridge, Jane. 1999. "Should Blacks Represent Blacks and Women Represent Women? A Contingent 'Yes.'" *Journal of Politics*, 61 (3): 628–57.

Osborn, Tracy L. 2012. *How Women Represent Women: Political Parties, Gender, and Representation in the State Legislatures*. New York: Oxford University Press.

Osborn, Tracy and Rebecca Kreitzer. 2014. "Women State Legislators: Women's Issues in Partisan Environments." In *Women and Elective Office: Past, Present, and Future*, 3rd ed., edited by Sue Thomas and Clyde Wilcox, 181–98. New York: Oxford University Press.

Pearson, Kathryn and Logan Dancey. 2011. "Speaking for the Underrepresented in the House of Representatives: Voicing Women's Interests in a Partisan Era." *Politics & Gender* 7 (4): 493–519.

Phillips, Anne. 1995. *The Politics of Presence*. Oxford: Clarendon Press.

Pitkin, Hanna Fenichel. 1967. *The Concept of Representation*. Berkeley: University of California Press.

Saward, Michael. 2010. *The Representative Claim*. New York: Oxford University Press.

Schreiber, Ronnee. 2008. *Righting Feminism: Conservative Women and American Politics*. New York: Oxford University Press. See, in particular, 56–116.

Squires, Judith. 2008. "The Constitutive Representation of Gender." *Representation: The Journal of Representative Democracy* 44 (2): 187–204.

UN Women, *Fourth World Conference on Women, Platform for Action*, accessed 9 October 2016, http://www.un.org/womenwatch/daw/beijing/platform/decision.htm.

Wittig, M. 1992. *The Straight Mind and Other Essays*. Boston: Beacon Press.

Young, Iris Marion. 2000. *Inclusion and Democracy*. Oxford: Oxford University Press.

61 Does party discipline pose an obstacle to representation of women?

An idea often advanced is that party discipline poses an obstacle to the political representation of women. Party discipline is a rule of the political game in which parliamentarians belonging to a political party close ranks, for example by all voting the same way on bills that are tabled. In parliamentary systems based on the British tradition (such as those in Great Britain, Australia, Canada, and New Zealand), party discipline is particularly strong, which means that, in some contexts, parliamentarians who break away from their party's official line may be severely reprimanded. In presidential systems such as that in the United States, in contrast, party discipline is much less constraining. This is because the US president does not need the support of a majority of members of Congress to stay in the White House, whereas in a parliamentary system (particularly in the British tradition), governments must have the support of a majority of parliamentarians to remain at the helm of the state.

Does party discipline pose an obstacle to the political representation of women? Once again, I must answer yes and no. It does, for example, if a party forces the members of its parliamentary wing to vote against a progressive bill or support a regressive bill with regard to women's rights and not in the contrary case (if the party line requires endorsement of a progressive bill and rejection of a regressive bill). For instance, suffragists' struggles for the vote in Quebec would not have been successful if the leader of the Liberal Party of Quebec, Adélard Godbout, had not forced his members of the Legislative Assembly – all men – to vote in favour of female suffrage on 18 April 1940 (a bill that many of them had rejected in the past). That being said, if a measure to change and improve women's collective experience does not benefit from the strength of party discipline, it will be dead on arrival.

Some argue that party discipline keeps female politicians from forming a common front beyond their party affiliation in order to get bills favourable to women adopted. Evidence of this is that in the United States, where party discipline is more relaxed, Democratic and Republican female lawmakers have worked together, notably within the Congressional Caucus for Women's Issues (Gertzog 2004). Nevertheless, it is not impossible under the parliamentary system for women to collaborate, in the view of Louise Harel, member of the National Assembly of Quebec from 1981 to 2008. Harel believes, to the contrary, that "in the last twenty-five years of parliamentary life in Quebec, there has been great female solidarity, beyond party lines, in all portfolios fighting discrimination and in laws in favour of women's equality" (Tremblay 2005, xiv; our translation). In other words, it is possible for representatives from different political horizons to work together to defend and promote women's rights, even in a British-style parliamentary system. Structures such as the Standing Committee on the Status of Women in Canada and the Status of Women Policy Committee within the Parliamentary Labor Party in Australia offer an illustration of this.

In short, just as I have argued that the supposedly positive impacts of a list proportional voting system and a critical mass of women in politics should be assessed with caution (see questions 21 and 39), I also argue that the role of party discipline in the political representation of women should be apprehended in a nuanced way. Party discipline may raise barriers to representation of women, but it may also be a springboard.

BIBLIOGRAPHY

Clark, Jennifer Hayes and Veronica Caro. 2013. "Multimember Districts and the Substantive Representation of Women: An Analysis of Legislative Cosponsorship Networks." *Politics & Gender* 9 (1): 1–30.

Gertzog, Irwin N. 2004. *Women and Power on Capitol Hill: Reconstructing the Congressional Women's Caucus*. Boulder: Lynne Rienner.

Sawer, Marian. 2012. "What Makes the Substantive Representation of Women Possible in a Westminster Parliament? The Story of RU486 in Australia." *International Political Science Review* 33 (3): 320–35.

– 2016. "Specialised Parliamentary Bodies: Their Role and Relevance to Women's Movement Repertoire." *Parliamentary Affairs* 69 (4): 763–77.

Sawer, Marian and Joan Grace. 2016. "Special Section: Specialised Parliamentary Bodies and Gender Representation." *Parliamentary Affairs* 69 (4): 745–875.

Tremblay, Manon. 2005. *Québécoises et représentation parlementaire*. Quebec City: Presses de l'Université Laval.

62 Are parliamentary committees an effective tool for representing women?

Parliamentary committees may certainly contribute to the political representation of women, although their impacts must be assessed carefully. In recent years, parliaments around the world have created legislative committees devoted to the broad field of "status of women." In 2006, the Inter-Parliamentary Union listed such structures in some forty countries, including Canada, Croatia, France, Israel, Kosovo, Kuwait, Macedonia, Niger, Pakistan, Serbia, South Africa, Ukraine, Uruguay, and Zimbabwe. The status of these legislative structures within the state apparatus varies greatly, as do their roles, powers, composition, and nature, the scope of their work, and their recommendations. The wide range of titles given these committees testifies to this diversity: Committee on Health, the Environment, Social Work, Labour, Former Combatants, Families, Children, and the Advancement of Women (Angola); House Standing Committee on Equal Opportunities for Men and Women (Cyprus); Committee on the Empowerment of Women (India), Committee on Women's Affairs (Kuwait); Committee on Family, Equal Opportunities and Youth (Luxembourg); Committee on Equality and Gender (Mexico); and Committee on Women Development (Pakistan). In some cases, the titles would lead us to believe that women are at the core of these committees' mandate (such as in India), but in other cases women are drowned in a sea of categories (as in Angola), and sometimes they are not even mentioned (as in Luxembourg).

It is undeniable that parliamentary committees offer women's movements a forum for expressing their demands to the political class, which, in turn, cannot then pretend to ignore the demands of women in civil society. In a sense, legislative committees transform women's groups into pressure groups. They also make better communication possible between the state and civil society, by integrating women's movements into the public decision-making process. Many fear, however, that "status of women" parliamentary committees help to make women's claims less radical. Indeed, it is likely that women's groups that deal with these parliamentary committees endorse the rules of the political game, and it is very possible that they also endorse a liberal and reformist reading of feminism. Others also see parliamentary committees as a mechanism that enable the state to co-opt women's movements (and even individual feminists, by appointing them to senior positions) or, worse, to appropriate and profit from their initiatives. However, the state has a diversity of actors, and their perspectives on the "status of women" are certainly not unanimous.

In short, I believe that it would be wrong to reject the contribution of legislative bodies to a broader project of women's representation, on the pretext that this is a form of distortion by the state. The women's movement really cannot afford to thumb its nose at any strategy aimed at changing and improving the collective experiences of women.

BIBLIOGRAPHY

Gertzog, Irwin N. 2004. *Women & Power on Capitol Hill: Reconstructing the Congressional Women's Caucus*. Boulder: Lynne Rienner.

Grace, Joan. 2016. "Presence and Purpose in the Canadian House of Commons: The Standing Committee on the Status of Women." *Parliamentary Affairs* 69 (4): 830–44.

Holli, Anne Maria. 2012. "Does Gender Have an Effect on the Selection of Experts by Parliamentary Standing Committees? A Critical Test of 'Critical' Concepts." *Politics & Gender* 8 (3): 341–66.

Inter-Parliamentary Union. 2006. *The Role of Parliamentary Committees in Mainstreaming Gender and Promoting the Status of Women*. Geneva: IPU, accessed 20 June 2016, http://www.ipu.org/pdf/publications/wmn_seminar06_en.pdf.

Lovenduski, Joni, et al. (2005). *State Feminism and Political Representation*. Cambridge: Cambridge University Press.

Palmieri, Sonia. 2013. *A Comparative Study of Structures for Women MPs in the OSCE Region*. Warsaw: OSCE Office for Democratic Institutions and Human Rights, accessed 6 August 2017, http://www.osce.org/odihr/105940?download=true.

Sawer, Marian. 2012. "What Makes the Substantive Representation of Women Possible in a Westminster Parliament? The Story of RU486 in Australia." *International Political Science Review* 33 (3): 320–35.

Sawer, Marian and Joan Grace, eds. 2016. "Special Section: Specialised Parliamentary Bodies and Gender Representation." *Parliamentary Affairs* 69 (4): 745–875.

Tremblay, Manon and Stephanie Mullen. 2007. "Le Comité permanent de la condition féminine de la Chambre des communes du Canada: un outil au service de la représentation politique des femmes." *Canadian Journal of Political Science* 40 (3): 1–23.

63 Is it better to elect women or feminists?

The answer to this question is not black or white: the best would be to elect feminist women, but it is also important to elect women who are not feminists and men who are feminists.

Feminist women must be elected because they fulfil a conception of women's representation that is descriptive, substantive, and symbolic (see question 60). In fact, it is only simple justice that there be more women in politics, in the name of equal representation of the sexes/genders (see question 40). In addition, feminist identity is an extremely important determinant of substantive representation: a female politician who is a feminist is more likely to act to improve the collective experiences of diverse women (see question 60). Finally, only women can, through their presence in politics, encourage girls and women to see and think of themselves in relation to politics. On the other hand, the election of feminist men and of women who are not feminists is not insignificant: the former contribute to substantive representation (in its feminist variant; see question 60) of women and the latter to their descriptive and symbolic representation (perhaps also to substantive representation but in a nonfeminist variant). In the end, only nonfeminist men apparently cannot serve the cause of women's representation. The problem is that at the moment they are the ones filling most of the seats in parliaments.

Aside from the influence of their simply being present in parliament, the election of women who are not feminists is important because it reflects the fact that not all women are feminists. Indeed, in the population there are feminist women, of course, but also women who are not feminist, and some who are even antifeminist. It is, to say the least, condescending to assume that it would be desirable for feminists to have a monopoly on representing women because, in essence, this implies that only feminists know what is "good" for women – a little like Marxists knowing what is good for the working class. Because women adopt a variety of positions with regard to feminism, their representation must reflect this reality, including positions that reject it as an ideological guide for women's representation. In other words, there is no justification for a monopoly by feminism on the political representation of women.

BIBLIOGRAPHY

Rhodebeck, Laurie A. 1996. "The Structure of Men's and Women's Feminist Orientations: Feminist Identity and Feminist Opinion." *Gender & Society* 10 (4): 386–403.

Schreiber, Ronnee. 2014. "Conservative Women Run for Office." In *Women and Elective Office: Past, Present, and Future*, 3rd ed., edited by Sue Thomas and Clyde Wilcox, 111–25. New York: Oxford University Press.

Tremblay, Manon and Rejean Pelletier. 2000. "More Women or More Feminists? Descriptive and Substantive Representations of Women in the 1997 Canadian Federal Election." *International Political Science Review* 21 (4): 381–405.

64 Do women change politics?

Because women and men have divergent opinions and behaviours on various levels (see chapter 3), it is certainly reasonable to think that women do change politics: the fact that they are being elected suggests that opinions and behaviours different to men's are accessing the political arena. But we must not assume that women and men have mutually exclusive opinions and behaviours. Some female politicians support an increase in military expenditures, and some male politicians believe that the welfare state should be strengthened rather than dismantled. What is more, it is not possible, beyond any reasonable doubt, to attribute responsibility for transformations that emerge – inevitably, I would say – in politics to the presence of women. Too many factors model political governance. Finally, it seems to me that responding only in the affirmative to the question of whether women change politics amounts to endorsing the myth of a "political Mother Teresa," because the idea underlying this question is that women would change politics for the better (see question 65), which remains to be proven.

That being said, the results of numerous studies support the idea that women do change politics on three levels: the political agenda, public policy, and parliamentary style. The agenda consists of the subjects addressed by political governance – in other words, what the political class is interested in. Women apparently put on the agenda questions that, in their absence, would remain unasked. Female politicians thus bring into the political arena experiences once considered relevant to the private sphere under the traditional division of gender roles. Women also change public policies – that is, the content of legislation and the perspectives that they convey. Female politicians add the criterion of gender to the examination of laws and might even enrich laws with points of view arising from the women's movement. For example, female politicians in certain countries have been successful in making assessment of the benefits of public policies to women and men an integral part of the formulation of these policies. What is more, female legislators may table policies deliberately designed to improve the life experiences of the diverse female population. Finally, women may transform political ways of being, saying, and doing. With more women in politics, the political class may conduct itself in a more civilized way, political language may be less rude, and governance may be closer to people and their everyday concerns.

In short, a number of studies support the idea that women change politics. Yet, I resist this proposal for two reasons: first, too many factors mould governance and it is not possible to attribute to women, beyond all doubt, any beneficial changes; second, it seems to me that this idea promotes a moralizing conception of "woman" as the redemption of politics – a conception that I do not endorse.

BIBLIOGRAPHY

Bicquelet, Aude, Albert Weale, and Judith Bara. 2012. "In a Different Parliamentary Voice?" *Politics & Gender* 8 (1): 83–121.

Catalano, Ana. 2009. "Women Acting for Women? An Analysis of Gender and Debate Participation in the British House of Commons 2005–2007." *Politics & Gender* 5 (1): 45–68.

Pearson, Kathryn and Logan Dancey. 2011. "Elevating Women's Voices in Congress: Speech Participation in the House of Representatives." *Political Research Quarterly* 64 (4): 910–23.

– 2011. "Speaking for the Underrepresented in the House of Representatives: Voicing Women's Interests in a Partisan Era." *Politics & Gender* 7 (4): 493–519.

Rosenthal, Cindy Simon, ed. 2002. *Women Transforming Congress*. Norman: University of Oklahoma Press.

65 Would politics be better if there were more female politicians?

In some ways, yes; in some ways, no. Yes, to the extent that the perception of politics might be improved, for three reasons. First, with a more balanced number of women and men, politics would appear fairer and more egalitarian with regard to the two sexes/genders. Some people might perceive it as less elitist and more accessible. Second, one of the causes (though certainly not the only one) of the population's cynicism about the political class has to do with the fact that they cannot see themselves as part of it. A political class that includes more women and fewer men might be easier for the general public to identify with. This is particularly true for girls and women, who currently lack models of women involved at the highest echelons of state power (see questions 17 and 68). Third, over the last few years, a descriptive conception of political representation – that is, one that reflects the population – has become more valued on the international scene (see questions 41 and 60). Although an increase in the number of women in the halls of power is not enough on its own to satisfy the criterion of diversity, the resulting representation cannot ignore this imperative.

And no, because I reject the notion that women are better than or superior to men. Such a perspective promotes an essentialist conception of the "woman" politician according to which women are naturally altruistic, good, generous, and so on because they give and maintain life (even though not all women realize this potential). I describe this type of magical thinking as the myth of "political Mother Teresa," which leads to untenable statements that begin with "If there were more women in politics": "… there would be fewer wars in the world and peace would reign"; "… there would be no more misery, no more famine, everyone would eat their fill and their basic needs would be satisfied"; "… pollution and climate change would slow, as women are in harmony with Mother Nature"; "… political governance would be fairer, as women are more concerned with the wellbeing of the weakest and most disadvantaged"; "… people wouldn't be very rich or very poor, and everyone would be equal." Not only does the "political Mother Teresa" myth inspire farfetched ideas with regard to the benefits of the presence of women in politics but it also plays right into the gender system. It can go so far as to shut women's citizenship into the prison of their biology, as if women and men have utterly distinct ways of being, speaking, and doing deeply rooted in their female and male genes. Such a conception of the political role of women is simply not compatible with modern democracy.

CHAPTER EIGHT

Participation in Cabinet

66 What steps must women take to gain access to the cabinet?

The first three steps that women must take to gain access to the cabinet are similar to those that they must take to gain access to parliament (see question 18): eligibility, recruitment, and selection. In this case, though, the fourth step is appointment rather than election.

Eligibility is the legal capacity to be a cabinet member. Citizenship is an essential criterion: to be a member of the Australian cabinet, for example, one must be an Australian citizen (and decline all other citizenships). In addition, in British-inspired parliamentary governments (such as those in Australia, Bangladesh, Canada, India, and New Zealand), a person must be a member of parliament (or quickly become one) to be eligible for appointment to the cabinet. This is not the case in regimes with separation of powers, such as the United States, where an elected representative must resign from the legislature to become a cabinet secretary (the equivalent, roughly, of a minister in British-tradition parliamentary regimes).

Recruitment consists of identifying, from among a given pool of people, those who have the resources to assume the very demanding role of cabinet member. In the American presidential regime, this pool is very large, as the leader of the executive branch (the president) is free to recruit people from any walk of life (for example, the business world, the art field, or academe) to be members of her or his cabinet. It is thus reasonable to assume that a low feminization rate in the legislature would not necessarily lead to a low feminization rate in the cabinet. In British-style parliamentary regimes, the leader must limit recruitment not only to members of parliament but to members of her or his own party; a reduced supply of

Figure 2

Steps to access cabinet (in the Canadian parliamentary system)

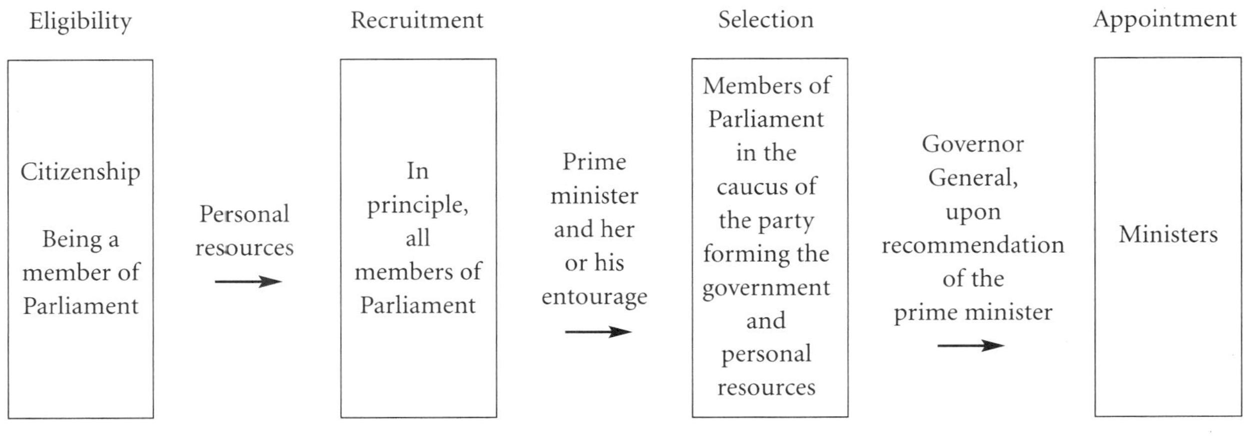

female officeholders (particularly within the caucus of the party in power) will thus legitimize weak demand for women; as a consequence, the cabinet may be not very feminized. In this perspective, Studlar and Moncrief (1997, 1999) found that the proportion of women in the governing party exerts a stronger influence on the proportion of female ministers than does the overall feminization rate in parliament, but Davis (1997, 63–4) reached the opposite conclusion. In any case, leaders cannot ignore the women in their caucus (especially if there are a healthy number or they are organized in a "women's group") or resist both the crosswinds and the quicksand of the pressure exerted by their party (which may want to project an image of openness and progressiveness).

Through selection, leaders of the executive branch choose the people who will form the cabinet. In a presidential regime, in which cabinet members are often specialists, selection is usually based on the recruit's expertise, reputation, and, of course, commitment to the party and ideological affinities with the leader. In a parliamentary regime, in which cabinet members must sit in parliament and are often generalists, expertise and reputation may also play a role in selection (particularly for the finance, justice, and health portfolios), but other, more political considerations will also be taken into account, such as representation by identity marker (language, culture and ethnicity, region, and others), a context of crisis that necessitates great political tact, or the leader's expressed desire to make changes to her or his governance team. Leaders may also find it difficult to ignore people who were cabinet members when the election was called and were reelected. Davis (1997, 87), Siaroff (2000), and Claveria (2014) have shown that cabinets of specialists are more feminized than are cabinets of generalists. However, in both types of regime, networking is an essential criterion for selection: a person must move in the same circles as the leader (or be in her or his inner circle) to be chosen by her or him. In other words, selection is the leader's prerogative: as a rule, no one can aspire to be in the cabinet if she or he is not in the leader's good graces (although constraints may sometimes force the leader to select a candidate who is essential for other reasons; for instance, Jean Chrétien could not ignore Paul Martin even though they did not always agree on things). In France, Édith Cresson's appointment to the position of prime minister was often interpreted as a direct result of President Mitterrand's wish. As women do not necessarily move in the same circles as the leader, they may suffer from some discrimination in terms of selection. This is a hypothesis that remains to be explored.

Finally, appointment is the official procedure through which the people selected by the leader become cabinet members. Formally, this step does not pose particular difficulty to women; the challenge for them is to pass the selection test – that is, to be noticed by the leader. As Franceschet and Thomas (2015) note, appointing female ministers is not a politically insignificant decision: the leader is sending a message regarding her or his comprehension of the gender regime and where women fit with regard to political representation (see question 1).

BIBLIOGRAPHY

Annesley, Claire. 2015. "Rule of Ministerial Recruitment." *Politics & Gender* 11 (4): 618–42.

Bauer, Gretchen and Manon Tremblay. 2011. "Introduction." In *Women in Executive Power: A Global Overview*, edited by Gretchen Bauer and Manon Tremblay, 1–9. London: Routledge.

Bego, Ingrid. 2014. "Accessing Power in New Democracies: The Appointment of Female Ministers in Postcommunist Europe." *Political Research Quarterly* 67 (2): 347–60.

Claveria, Silvia. 2014. "Still a 'Male Business'? Explaining Women's Presence in Executive Office." *West European Politics* 37 (5): 1156–76.

Davis, Rebecca H. 1997. *Women and Power in Parliamentary Democracies: Cabinet Appointments in Western Europe, 1968–1992*. Lincoln: University of Nebraska Press. See, in particular, 63–5, 84–91.

Franceschet, Susan and Gwynn Thomas. 2015. "Resisting Parity: Gender and Cabinet Appointments in Chili and Spain." *Politics & Gender* 11 (4): 643–64.

Siaroff, Alan. 2000. "Women's Representation in Legislatures and Cabinets in Industrial Democracies." *International Political Science Review* 21 (2): 197–215.

Studlar, Donley T. and Gary F. Moncrief. 1997. "The Recruitment of Women Cabinet Ministers in the Canadian Provinces." *Governance: An International Journal of Policy and Administration* 10 (1): 67–81.

– 1999. "Women's Work? The Distribution and Prestige of Portfolios in the Canadian Provinces." *Governance: An International Journal of Policy and Administration* 12 (4): 379–95.

67 What positions do women occupy in cabinets around the world?

My analyses of data published jointly by the Inter-Parliamentary Union and UN Women (2015) show that in January 2015, women occupied an average of 18.5 per cent of ministerial positions in 191 government cabinets and sat in 22.4 per cent of the seats in single or lower chambers in 191 national parliaments. Five countries had cabinets in which at least half the members were women: Finland (62.5 per cent), Cape Verde (52.9 per cent), Sweden (52.2 per cent), and France and Liechtenstein (50 per cent). However, eight countries were led by cabinets devoid of any female presence: Bosnia-Herzegovina, Brunei, Hungary, Saudi Arabia, Slovakia, Tonga, and Vanuatu. The last two stood out as the only ones in which both the legislative and executive branches (parliament and cabinet) were composed solely of men. In eighteen countries, the feminization rate of the cabinet ranged between one third and less than one half, whereas in 142 countries this proportion was less than one quarter. In short, although there are currently women in almost all cabinets in the world, the proportion varies widely, and in few cabinets do they form a critical mass (see question 39).

Nevertheless, the number of women in cabinets has expanded considerably in recent years. In a study published in 1980, Blondel estimated that women accounted for 0.5 per cent of leaders of executive branches in the world (116). Looking at cabinets in fifteen countries in Western Europe, Davis (1997, 13, 16) observed that their feminization rate had risen from 3 per cent in 1968 to 13 per cent in 1992. The Centre for Social Development and the Humanitarian Affairs of the United Nations Office at Vienna (1992, 3) estimated that in 1987, 3.5 per cent of ministers in the cabinets of some 155 countries were women. In his study of the cabinets of some 180 countries in 1998, Reynolds (1999) found that almost 8.7 per cent (302 out of 3,486) of their members were women; thirty-eight had absolutely no female members (this number dropped to eight by 2015). According to a study conducted by Mathiason (2006), in 2005 women comprised 10.6 per cent of cabinet members around the world, whereas they represented 16 per cent of parliamentarians. Finally, in January 2010, 16.9 per cent of the approximately 4,100 cabinet ministers in 188 countries were women (Tremblay and Bauer 2011: 172).

Although more women have made their way into cabinets and parliaments in recent decades, it is not clear whether progress has been greater within the executive or the legislative branch. Mathiason (2006) notes that the proportion of female cabinet ministers was 6.8 per cent in 1994 and 10.6 per cent in 2005; the corresponding figures for female parliamentarians were 11.6 per cent (in 1995) and 16 per cent. The proportion of women in cabinets therefore rose by 3.8 per cent between 1994 and 2005, compared to 4.4 per cent in parliaments over the same period. Tremblay and Bauer (2011) also observe that the proportion of women has grown more in parliaments than in cabinets. Based on the data compiled by the Inter-Parliamentary Union in January 2010, women represented 19 per cent of parliamentarians worldwide (of single or lower chambers) and 16.9 per cent of ministers; in January 2015, they represented 22.4 per cent and 18.5 per cent, respectively – increases of 3.4 per cent in legislatures and 1.6 per cent in cabinets. Analyzing the feminization rates of cabinets and parliaments in the world from 1979 to 2009, Jacob, Scherpereel, and Adams (2014) conclude, on the contrary, that the proportion of women has risen more in the executive than the legislative branch. Their explanation is that international norms with regard to the equality of women and men have taken hold more in cabinets than parliaments. However, this explanation is not entirely satisfactory. Indeed, one mechanism flowing precisely from these international norms for equality of women and men – electoral quotas for women, which have spread like wildfire since the 1990s – has targeted parliaments but not cabinets (even though the formation of a cabinet is often based on compliance with informal quotas in terms of representation of diverse ethnic, linguistic, regional, and other minorities). That being said, as recent research by Claveria (2014, 1156) shows, "Women are more likely to receive a ministerial post when the governing party has adopted gender quotas." It is as if electoral quotas for women form a conduit between parties and parliament, on the one hand, and between parliament and cabinet, on the other hand, implying that there may be a contagion effect from the former to the latter (see questions 20 and 39). At any rate, it seems that the process of spreading international norms with regard to equality of women and men plays a complex role in the feminization of spaces of power – including cabinets.

The proportion of female cabinet members also varies from region to region around the globe. Analyzing the data published by the Inter-

Parliamentary Union on the feminization rates of some 190 cabinets in the world in January 2010, Tremblay and Bauer (2011) painted the following portrait: women represented 7.6 per cent of ministers in the cabinets of nineteen Arab countries, 8.4 per cent in thirty-one countries in Asia, 11.1 per cent in the fourteen countries forming Oceania (but 26 per cent in Australia and New Zealand), 20 per cent in the thirty-four countries of North and South America, 20.2 per cent within the forty-four cabinets of countries in sub-Saharan Africa, and 22.7 per cent in the forty-six countries of Europe (49.7 per cent in the five Nordic countries). My analysis of the data published jointly by the Inter-Parliamentary Union and UN Women (2015) shows that as of 1 January 2015, the feminization rates of cabinets in these regions are 11.5 per cent among the nineteen governments in Arab countries, 10 per cent in Asia (thirty-one countries), 12.8 per cent in the fourteen countries of Oceania (but 25.3 per cent in Australia and New Zealand), 21.9 per cent in the Americas (thirty-five countries), 19.7 per cent in sub-Saharan Africa (forty-six countries), and 25.8 per cent in Europe (forty-six countries; 46.5 per cent in the Nordic countries). In comparison with 2010, there were more women in cabinets in 2015, except in sub-Saharan Africa (−0.5 per cent), Australia and New Zealand (−0.7 per cent), and the Nordic countries (−3.2 per cent). The drop in average feminization rates of cabinets in the five Nordic countries not only gives the lie to the idea that the proportion of women in politics can only increase (see questions 30 and 31) but also mitigates the Nordic countries' reputation for progressiveness – even in these countries, women may face a backlash. Looking farther back in time, advances achieved by women in cabinets become clearer. In his study of 180 governments in 1998, Reynolds (1999) established these proportions as follows: 20 per cent in Western Europe, 14.7 per cent in North America and the West Indies, 10.5 per cent in South and Central America, 7.8 per cent in Africa, 5.9 per cent in Asia, 5.3 per cent in Central and Eastern Europe, 3.9 per cent in Oceania, and 2.1 per cent in the Middle East. In 1987, the Centre for Social Development and Humanitarian Affairs of the United Nations Office at Vienna noted, in its study of governments of some 155 countries, that women represented 6.8 per cent of ministers and senior civil servants in industrialized Western countries (8.6 per cent in North America), 6 per cent in South America and the West Indies, 3.7 per cent in Eastern Europe, 3.6 per cent in Africa, and 2 per cent in Asia and the Pacific (United Nations Office at Vienna 1992, 63).

We can make some observations from these data. First, although the figures vary widely from study to study, in general the proportion of women in cabinets rose in all regions of the world between 1987 and 2015, even if this progress may be seen as insufficient. Second, the low feminization rate in cabinets in Asia contrasts with the not insignificant number of female presidents and first ministers in that part of the world (see question 70). Third, level of economic development does not seem to correlate strongly with feminization of cabinets, which is also the case for parliaments (see questions 19 and 35). Finally, the few declines recorded (notably in the Nordic countries), although slight, are a reminder that women can take nothing for granted and suggest that they must continue their fight.

BIBLIOGRAPHY

Annesley, Claire and Susan Franceschet. 2015. "Gender and the Executive Branch." *Politics & Gender* 11 (4): 613–17.

Blondel, Jean. 1980. *World Leaders: Heads of Government in the Postwar Period*. Beverly Hills: Sage.

Claveria, Silvia. 2014. "Still a 'Male Business'? Explaining Women's Presence in Executive Office." *West European Politics* 37 (5): 1156–76.

Davis, Rebecca H. 1997. *Women and Power in Parliamentary Democracies: Cabinet Appointments in Western Europe, 1968-1992*. Lincoln: University of Nebraska Press.

Inter-Parliamentary Union and UN Women. 2015. "Women in Politics: 2015," accessed 20 July 2016, http://www.ipu.org/pdf/publications/wmnmap15_en.pdf.

Jacob, Suraj, John A. Scherpereel, and Melinda A. Adams. 2014. "Gender Norms and Women's Political Representation: A Global Analysis of Cabinets, 1979–2009." *Governance: An International Journal of Policy and Administration* 27 (2): 321–45.

Mathiason, John with Loveena Dookhony. [2006]. *Women in Governmental Decision-Making in the Early 21st Century. What Has – and Has Not – Been Achieved in the Post-Beijing Period*, accessed 20 July 2016, http://intlmgt.cipa.cornell.edu/sessions/women/Women%20in%20governmental%20decision-making%20publication.pdf.

Reynolds, Andrew. 1999. "Women in the Legislatures and Executives of the World: Knocking at the Highest Glass Ceiling." *World Politics* 51 (4): 547–72.

Tremblay, Manon and Gretchen Bauer. 2011. "Conclusion." In *Women in Executive Power: A Global Overview*, edited by Gretchen Bauer and Manon Tremblay, 171–90. London: Routledge.

United Nations Office at Vienna, Centre for Social Development and Humanitarian Affairs. 1992. *Women in Politics and Decision-Making in the Late Twentieth Century*. Dordrecht: Martinus Nijhoff Publishers. See, in particular, 58–72.

68 Who are the female presidents and prime ministers?

Table 6 presents a (nonexhaustive) list of women who have been president or prime minister of a country between 1960 and December 2016. Excluded from this list are leaders of subnational units such as states and territories in the United States and India, the German *länder*, and provinces in Argentina and Canada. Temporary mandates (interim or transitional) are not considered; only regular mandates of at least one month are listed. For example, Ellen Louks Fairclough was prime minister of Canada on 19 and 20 February 1958, but she does not appear in the table because her mandate ended before 1960; in any case, her mandate was less than one month. Also not appearing in the table because her mandate lasted less than one month is Florence Duperval Guillaume, prime minister of Haiti from 21 December 2014, to 16 January 2015.

The following observations can be made about table 6.

1. One hundred and two women have been a president or prime minister. Two of them – Chandrika B. Kumaratunge (Sri Lanka) and Janet Jagan (Guyana) – had a mandate in each position, for a total of 104 female presidents and prime ministers. These 102 women, distributed among seventy-one countries, fulfilled a total of 121 mandates.

2. Almost two fifths of these prime ministers and presidents (forty-one of 104) led an executive branch in a European country, twenty-five in the Americas (one in North America, ten in South America, and fourteen in Central America and the Caribbean), twenty in Asia, fourteen in Africa, and four in Oceania. Although Europe has had the greatest number of female heads of government, it wasn't until 1979 that a woman reached the leadership position for the first time (Margaret Thatcher in Great Britain). It was in Asia – more precisely, Sri Lanka (Ceylon at the time) – that a woman was first a government leader: Prime Minister Sirimavo Bandaranaike, in

Table 6

Female presidents and prime ministers, 1960–2016

Country	Name	Role*	Period (mandates)
Sri Lanka	Sirimavo Bandaranaike	PM	1960–65; 1970–77; 1994–2000
India	Indira Gandhi	PM	1966–77; 1980–84
Israel	Golda Meir	PM	1969–74
Argentina	Isabel Martínez de Perón	P	1974–76
Central African Republic	Elisabeth Domitien	PM	1975–76
Great Britain	Margaret Thatcher	PM	1979–90
Bolivia	Lidia Gueiler Tejada	P	1979–80
Portugal	Maria de Lourdes Pintasilgo	PM	1979–80
Dominica	Mary Eugenia Charles	PM	1980–95
Iceland	Vigdís Finnbogadóttir	P	1980–96
Norway	Gro Harlem Brundtland	PM	1981; 1986–89; 1990–96
Yugoslavia	Milka Planinc	PM	1982–86
Malta	Agatha Barbara	P	1982–87
Dutch Antilles	Maria Liberia-Peters	PM	1984–86; 1988–93
Philippines	Corazon Aquino	P	1986–92
Pakistan	Benazir Bhutto	PM	1988–90; 1993–96
Haiti	Ertha Pascal-Trouillot	P	1990–91
Lithuania	Kazimiera D. Prunskiene	PM	1990–91
Nicaragua	Violeta Barrios de Chamorro	P	1990–97
Ireland	Mary Robinson	P	1990–97
(ex-)German Democratic Republic	Sabine Bergmann-Pohl	P	1990
Bangladesh	Khaleda Zia	PM	1991–96; 1996; 2001–06
France	Édith Cresson	PM	1991–92
Poland	Hanna Suchocka	PM	1992–93
Canada	Kim Campbell	PM	1993
Burundi	Sylvie Kinigi	PM	1993–94

Table 6

Continued

Country	Name	Role*	Period (mandates)
Rwanda	Agathe Uwilingiyimana	PM	1993–94
Dutch Antilles	Susanne Camelia-Römer	PM	1993; 1998–99
Turkey	Tansu Çiller	PM	1993–96
Sri Lanka	Chandrika B. Kumaratunge	PM	1994
Sri Lanka	Chandrika B. Kumaratunge	P	1994–2005
Bulgaria	Renata Indzhova	PM	1994–95
Haiti	Claudette Werleigh	PM	1995–96
Bangladesh	Sheikh Hasina Wajed	PM	1996–2001; 2009–present**
Guyana	Janet Jagan	PM	1997
Guyana	Janet Jagan	P	1997–99
Ireland	Mary McAleese	P	1997–2011
Bermuda	Pamela Gordon	PM	1997–98
New Zealand	Jenny Shipley	PM	1997–99
Bermuda	Jennifer Smith	PM	1998–2003
Switzerland	Ruth Dreifuss	P	1999
Latvia	Vaira Vike-Freiberga	P	1999–2007
Panama	Mireya Elisa Moscoso de Arias	P	1999–2004
New Zealand	Helen Elizabeth Clark	PM	1999–2008
Finland	Tarja Kaarina Halonen	P	2000–12
Philippines	Gloria Macapagal-Arroyo	P	2001–10
Senegal	Mame Madior Boye	PM	2001–02
Indonesia	Megawati Sukarnoputri	P	2001–04
Sao Tome and Principe	Maria das Neves Ceita Batista de Sousa	PM	2002–03; 2003–04
Finland	Anneli Jäätteenmäki	PM	2003
Peru	Beatriz Merino	PM	2003
Mozambique	Luísa Días Diogo	PM	2004–10
Bahamas	Cynthia A. Pratt	PM	2005
Ukraine	Yulia Tymochenko	PM	2005; 2007–10
Sao Tome and Principe	Maria do Carmo Silveira	PM	2005–06
Germany	Angela Merkel	P	2005–present
Republic of Korea	Han Myung-sook	PM	2006–07
Liberia	Ellen Johnson-Sirleaf	P	2006–present
Chile	Michelle Bachelet	P	2006–10; 2014–present

Table 6

Continued

Country	Name	Role*	Period (mandates)
Jamaica	Portia Simpson-Miller	PM	2006–07; 2012–16
Switzerland	Micheline Calmy-Rey	P	2007; 2011
Federation of Bosnia and Herzegovina	Borjana Kristo	P	2007–11
India	Pratibha Patil	P	2007–12
Argentina	Cristina Fernández de Kirchner	P	2007–15
Moldova	Zinaida Greceanîi	PM	2008–09
Haiti	Michèle Pierre-Louis	PM	2008–09
Iceland	Jóhanna Sigurðardóttir	PM	2009–13
Croatia	Jadranka Kosor	PM	2009–11
Lithuania	Dalia Grybauskaité	P	2009–present
Switzerland	Doris Leuthard	P	2010
Costa Rica	Laura Chinchilla	P	2010–14
Kyrgyzstan	Roza Otounbaïeva	P	2010–11
Trinidad and Tobago	Kamla Persad-Bissessar	PM	2010–15
Finland	Mari Kiviniemi	PM	2010–11
Australia	Julia Gillard	PM	2010–13
Slovakia	Iveta Radičová	PM	2010–12
Brazil	Dilma Rousseff	P	2011–16
Peru	Rosario Fernández	PM	2011
Mali	Cissé Mariam Kaïdama Sidibé	PM	2011–12
Kosovo	Atifete Jahjaga	P	2011–16
Thailand	Yingluck Shinawatra	PM	2011–14
Denmark	Helle Thorning-Schmidt	PM	2011–15
Switzerland	Eveline Widmer-Schlumpf	P	2012
Guinea-Bissau	Adiato Djaló Nandigna	PM	2012
Malawi	Joyce Banda	P	2012–14
Republic of Korea	Park Geun-hye	P	2013–present
Slovenia	Alenka Bratušek	PM	2013–14
Senegal	Aminata Touré	PM	2013–14
Norway	Erna Solberg	PM	2013–present
Latvia	Laimdota Straujuma	PM	2014–16
Malta	Marie-Louise Coleiro Preca	P	2014–present

Table 6

Continued

Country	Name	Role*	Period (mandates)
Peru	Ana Jara	P M	2014–15
Poland	Ewa Kopacz	P M	2014–15
Switzerland	Simonetta Sommaruga	P	2015
Croatia	Kolinda Grabar-Kitarovi	P	2015–present
Namibia	Saara Kuugongelwa-Amadhila	P M	2015–present
Mauritius	Ameenah Gurib	P	2015–present
Nepal	Bidhya Devi Bhandari	P	2015–present
Poland	Beata Szydło	P M	2015–present
Marshall Islands	Hilda Cathy Heine	P	2016–present
Myanmar	Aung San Suu Ky	P M	2016–present
Taiwan	Tsai Ing-wen	P	2016–present
Great Britain	Theresa May	P M	2016–present
Estonia	Kersti Kaljulaid	P	2016–present

71 COUNTRIES	102 WOMEN		121 MANDATES

* P: president; P M: prime minister.
** "Present": 31 December 2016.
Sources: Inter-Parliamentary Union (n.d.), *Women in Politics: 1945–2005. Information Kit*, data sheet no. 4 (Geneva: Inter-Parliamentary Union); "Female Heads of State and Government Currently in Office," accessed 31 December 2016, http://www.guide2womenleaders.com/Current-Women-Leaders.htm; "List of Elected and Appointed Female Heads of State," accessed 31 December 2016, https://en.wikipedia.org/wiki/List_of_elected_and_appointed_female_heads_of_state.

1960. And until 1974, only in Asia had women acceded to leadership of the executive branch.

3. About fifteen women were prime ministers and presidents in the 1960s, 1970s, and 1980s. In the 1990s, the number of female heads of state began to grow – as did the number of female parliamentarians and ministers.

4. More women have been prime minister than president: sixty-three and forty-one, respectively. Jalalzai (2013, 1–3) posits that it is easier for women to access the role of prime minister than of president because the former position requires more collaboration and consensus, and thus involves less power and authority.

5. Some women have more than once been prime minister (among others, Sirimavo Bandaranaike in Sri Lanka, Benazir Bhutto in Pakistan, Gro

Harlem Brundtland in Norway, Susanne Camelia-Römer and Maria Liberia-Peters in the Dutch Antilles, Helen Elizabeth Clark in New Zealand, Indira Gandhi in India, Portia Simpson-Miller in Jamaica, Margaret Thatcher in Great Britain, and Khaleda Zia in Bangladesh) or president (including Michelle Bachelet in Chile, Vigdís Finnbogadóttir in Iceland, Tarja Kaarina Halonen in Finland, Ellen Johnson-Sirleaf in Liberia, Chandrika B. Kumaratunge in Sri Lanka, Mary McAleese in Ireland, and Vaira Vike-Freiberga in Latvia).

6. Some countries have had at least two female presidents (including Argentina, Ireland, Malta, the Philippines, and Switzerland) or prime ministers (Bangladesh, Bermuda, Dutch Antilles, Great Britain, Haiti, New Zealand, Norway, Peru, Poland, Sao Tome and Principe, and Sri Lanka).

7. Finally, Finland offers an exceptional model of female leadership. During Tarja Kaarina Halonen's tenure as president (from 2000 to 2012), there were two female prime ministers: Anneli Jäätteenmäki in 2003 and Mari Kiviniemi in 2010–11. Finland thus continues its progressiveness with regard to women's political rights: Finnish women gained the right to vote in legislative elections in 1906 and 10 per cent of Finnish parliamentarians were women in 1907 (see questions 3, 4, and 37).

What table 6 does not show is a fact that underlines the eminently gendered nature of the path to assuming the highest responsibilities of the state. In a recent study, O'Brien (2015) reveals that women access power under conditions that are often more difficult than those that face men — via minor opposition parties that are losing popularity.

BIBLIOGRAPHY

"Female Heads of State and Government Currently in Office," accessed 20 July 2016, http://www.guide2womenleaders.com/Current-Women-Leaders.htm.

Genovese, Michael A. 1993. *Women as National Leaders*. Newbury Park: Sage.

Inter-Parliamentary Union. N.d. *Women in Politics: 1945–2005. Information Kit*. Geneva: Inter-Parliamentary Union, data sheet no. 4.

Jalalzai, Farida. 2013. *Shattered, Cracked, or Firmly Intact? Women and the Executive Glass Ceiling Worldwide*. New York: Oxford University Press. See, in particular, 1–3.

– 2014. "Gender, Presidencies, and Prime Ministerships in Europe: Are Women Gaining Ground?" *International Political Science Review* 35 (5): 577–94.

Jensen, Jane S. 2008. *Women Political Leaders: Breaking the Highest Glass Ceiling*. New York: Palgrave MacMillan.

"List of elected and appointed female heads of state," accessed 20 July 2016, https://en.wikipedia.org/wiki/List_of_elected_and_appointed_female_heads_of_state.

O'Brien, Diana Z. 2015. "Rising to the Top: Gender, Political Performance, and Party Leadership in Parliamentary Democracies." *American Journal of Political Science* 59 (4): 1022–39.

Paxton, Pamela and Melanie M. Hughes (2007). *Women, Politics, and Power: A Global Perspective*. Los Angeles: Pine Forge Press. See, in particlular, 80–100.

Skard, Torild. 2014. *Women of Power: Half a Century of Female Presidents and Prime Ministers Worldwide*. Bristol: Policy Press.

69 What is the profile of female presidents and prime ministers?

The studies by Jalalzai (2013) and Jensen (2008) are particularly relevant for answering this question. However, other than that they are from elites and exceptional, it is difficult to draw a single profile into which all female presidents and prime ministers fit because these women are diverse – as diverse as their male colleagues in executive positions, their female co-parliamentarians, and women in general. Nevertheless, some observations do emerge.

In general, female presidents and prime ministers are in their early fifties when they begin their mandate. Some, however, begin much younger (Benazir Bhutto became prime minister of Pakistan at age thirty-five; Isabel Martinez de Perón was president of Argentina at age forty-three) and others much older (Golda Meir became head of state at age seventy; Janet Jagan, at age seventy-seven). Unsurprisingly, these women had an education better than the average among women in their respective countries and generations. They studied a wide variety of disciplines, but many of them took law and economics courses. A number attended universities abroad – some of them prestigious – particularly those from Africa (for example, Ellen Johnson-Sirleaf of Liberia has a master's degree in public administration from Harvard University), Latin America (Peruvian prime minister Beatriz Merino graduated in economics from the London School of Economics and earned a master's degree in law at Harvard), and Asia (Benazir Bhutto studied at Oxford and Yingluck Shinawatra, prime minister of Thailand, studied in the United States). Some have a master's degree (including Luísa Días

Diogo, prime minister of Mozambique and Pratibha Patil, president of India) or a doctorate (such as Gloria Macapagal-Arroyo, president of the Philippines; Tansu Çiller, prime minister of Turkey; and Angela Merkel, German chancellor). Few of them had not gone to college or been homemakers; before acceding to executive power, they were employed, usually in elite jobs (as managers, senior civil servants, professionals, or businesswomen). They are not novice politicians; they have years of activism and political experience behind them. In Asia (and, to a lesser extent, in South America), many are members of political dynasties, with a father or husband who is a politician (see question 70). Yet, as Jalalzai (2013, 93) notes, despite their impressive résumés, women remain largely underrepresented in the very small circle of heads of state or government. What is more, it is not possible to explain this deficit by an insufficient supply of competent women (see question 18).

In short, female heads of state and of government have an eminently elitist profile – as do their male colleagues. This observation raises the question of whether, with such a profile, they can provide substantive representation of women in the population (see question 60).

BIBLIOGRAPHY

Genovese, Michael A. 1993. *Women as National Leaders.* Newbury Park: Sage.

Jalalzai, Farida. 2013. *Shattered, Cracked, or Firmly Intact? Women and the Executive Glass Ceiling Worldwide.* New York: Oxford University Press.

Jensen, Jane S. 2008. *Women Political Leaders: Breaking the Highest Glass Ceiling.* New York: Palgrave MacMillan.

Skard, Torild. 2014. *Women of Power: Half a Century of Female Presidents and Prime Ministers Worldwide.* Bristol: Policy Press.

70 How can the importance of the political dynasty in Asia be explained?

Although Asia is one of the regions with the lowest feminization rate of parliaments and cabinets (see questions 29 and 67), this continent also stands out for the large number of women who have reached leadership in the executive branch through family lines. In fact, Paxton and Hughes (2007, 87) estimate that three quarters of the countries that have had a female leader of government more than once are in Asia.

The well-marked path taken by a number of female Asian heads of government can be described in relation to their association with three types of male leaders: a political figure tied to decolonization and struggles for national independence (Sheikh Hasina Wajed in Bangladesh, Aung San Suu Kyi in Myanmar, Indira Gandhi in India, and Megawati Sukarnoputri in Indonesia), a figure rising in opposition to an authoritarian regime (Corazon Aquino in the Philippines and Wan Azizah Wan Ismail in Malaysia), or a figure who has stood out during a crisis or turning point in national history (Khaleda Zia in Bangladesh and Benazir Bhutto in Pakistan). For instance, Sirimavo Bandaranaike, prime minister of Sri Lanka three times between 1960 and 2000, was married to Solomon Bandaranaike, prime minister assassinated in 1959. Their daughter, Chandrika B. Kumaratunge, was also prime minister, in 1994. A few months later, she became president, a position she held until 2005. Indira Gandhi, prime minister of India from 1967 to 1984 (with an interruption between 1977 and 1980), was the daughter of Prime Minister Nehru. Corazon Aquino, president of the Philippines from 1986 to 1992, had been the spouse of Benigno Aquino Jr, assassinated opposition leader. Benazir Bhutto, Pakistani prime minister from 1988 to 1990, then from 1993 to 1996, and assassinated in 2007, was following in the footsteps of her father, Zulfikar Ali Bhutto, Pakistani prime minister from 1973 to 1977. Khaleda Zia, the spouse of Ziaur Rahman, Bangladeshi president assassinated in 1981 and often described as a martyr, was prime minister of Bangladesh from 1991 to 1996 and again from 2001 to 2006. The father of Sheikh Hasina Wajed, prime minister of Bangladesh at the time of publication (2018) and between 1996 and 2001, is considered the country's founder, and he also assumed the positions of president and prime minister. Similarly, Megawati Sukarnoputri, president of Indonesia from 2001 to 2004, is the daughter of the country's first president, Sukarno. Gloria Macapagal-Arroyo, president of the Philippines from 2001 to 2010, is the daughter of that country's former president, Diosdado Macapagal. To this list must be added Sonia Gandhi, daughter-in-law of Indira Gandhi and widow of her son Rajiv. Gandhi might have become prime minister of India after the 2004 election, but she declined the invitation.

One explanation often advanced to account for the importance of the family line in Asia is that of the "female substitute," according to which these women benefit from the aura of a man (father or spouse), often a martyr or hero, whose values they embody and whose struggle they pursue.

In a way, these women become genderless, symbolic beings, freed of the significant sexist prejudices that weigh against women who want to be active in politics in traditional and strongly patriarchal societies. This reading, though convincing, does not explain why the "female substitute" path is not taken more often in other countries hostile to the political participation of women, such as those in Africa, the Pacific region, and the Arabian Peninsula. Moreover, the conclusions reached by Jalalzai (2013), Jensen (2008), and Skard (2014) from analyses of the biographies of female heads of state and government leaders through the world (including Asia) indicate that although many of these women benefited from the family line in their climb to the leadership level, they undeniably acquired skills and were socialized with a view to assuming power, if only because they had lived since childhood in highly politicized environments.

Although Asia has seen the greatest number of women who have acceded to political leadership through the family route, the "dynasty" phenomenon is also seen in South America. Isabel Martínez de Perón, president of Argentina from 1974 to 1976, succeeded her spouse, Juan Perón. The spouse of Violeta Barrios de Chamorro, president of Nicaragua from 1990 to 1997, was Pedro Joaquín Chamorro Cardenal, a journalist known for his opposition to the Somoza family regime. The president of Panama from 1999 to 2004, Mireya Elisa Moscoso de Arias, was the widow of president Arnulfo Arias. Michelle Bachelet, president of Chile elected in 2006 (and reelected in 2014) was the daughter of Alberto Bachelet, an air force general accused of treason and tortured by the Pinochet regime. Finally, Cristina Fernández de Kirchner succeeded her spouse, Néstor Kirchner, as leader of Argentina in October 2007. Although she has an impressive political curriculum vitae of her own, her husband's shadow seems to loom large.

BIBLIOGRAPHY

Fleschenberg, Andrea. 2008. "Asia's Women Politicians at the Top: Roaring Tigresses or Tame Kittens?" In *Women's Political Participation and Representation in Asia: Obstacles and Challenges*, edited by Kazuki Iwanaga, 23–54. Copenhagen: Nias Press.

– 2011. "South and Southeast Asia." In *Women in Executive Power: A Global Overview*, edited by Gretchen Bauer and Manon Tremblay, 23–44. London: Routledge.

Jalalzai, Farida. 2013. *Shattered, Cracked, or Firmly Intact? Women and the Executive Glass Ceiling Worldwide*. New York: Oxford University Press.

Jensen, Jane S. 2008. *Women Political Leaders: Breaking the Highest Glass Ceiling.* New York: Palgrave MacMillan.

Paxton, Pamela and Melanie M. Hughes. 2007. *Women, Politics, and Power: A Global Perspective.* Los Angeles: Pine Forge Press. See, in particular, 80–100.

Skard, Torild. 2014. *Women of Power: Half a Century of Female Presidents and Prime Ministers Worldwide.* Bristol: Policy Press. See, in particular, 121–95.

71 Who were the first women to sit in a cabinet?

In November 1917, Alexandra Mikhailovna Kollontai (1872–1952) became People's Commissioner for Social Welfare in the Soviet government, thus becoming the first woman in the world to be a cabinet member. In the non-communist world, it was in Denmark in 1924 that a woman, Nina Bang, first became a minister. However, she was not in position for long – just two years. In 1926, a third woman, Miina Sillanpää, became a minister in the Finnish government, a position she held for twenty years. Finally, another Nordic country, Sweden, was the first to form a parity government, from 1986 to 1991, under the leadership of Ingvar Carlsson.

BIBLIOGRAPHY

Raaum, Nina C. 1999. "Women in Parliamentary Politics; Historical Lines of Development." In *Equal Democracies? Gender and Politics in the Nordic Countries,* ed. Christina Bergqvist et al., 27–47. Oslo: Scandinavian University Press.

72 What portfolios have women held in governments?

Female cabinet members tend to hold portfolios in areas traditionally considered to match their private roles: family, children and youth, culture and education, health, social and community affairs, and, of course, "status of women." In other words, governments are structured along a horizontal segregation of skills as a function of gender. Tripier (2010) uses the notion of "glass walls" to describe the distribution of portfolios by gender: some portfolios are given to women and others to men, without any contact between them, as if glass walls are keeping them apart. In its study on the governments of 155 countries in the late 1980s, the Centre for Social Development and Humanitarian Affairs of the UN Office at Vienna (1992, 69) observed that ministerial responsibilities usually handed to women had to do with social affairs, followed by the law and justice portfolios – which should not be surprising because, like the social sector, this sector draws on skills that require certain values traditionally defined as feminine, such as compassion and empathy (see question 13). In her study of women's participation in the governments of fifteen Western European countries between 1968 and 1992, Davis (1997, 16) made a similar observation: about half of the 438 ministerial portfolios given to women over that period concerned social welfare and consumption, culture, education, family, and health. Reynolds (1999) also noted that women were responsible for portfolios of a sociocultural nature rather than for the prestigious economic development and finance, national security, or foreign affairs portfolios. In the conclusion to their major regional inquiry on female cabinet ministers around the world published in 2011, and in line with other recent research on the subject (Connolly 2013; Krook and O'Brien 2012), Tremblay and Bauer note the general tendency to give women "pink portfolios." They remark, however, that this custom is falling into disrepute as women gain access to governments in greater numbers and take on portfolios traditionally held by men. In Borrelli's (2010) view, by taking on portfolios traditionally assigned to men, female members of the executive branch are helping to redraw the boundaries between private and public, and in doing so they are also redefining the contours of gender.

Why are women confined to social portfolios? The gender regime is largely responsible. First, it is the prerogative of heads of state to assign portfolios to the people in their cabinets. Such assignments are determined, in part, by the expertise and skills of officeholders, even in a parliamentary regime in which ministers are generalists rather than specialists. Another aspect of assigning portfolios, however, is determined by the leader's perceptions and the composition of her or his inner circle: can the prime minister envisage a woman being responsible for finance, economic development, fisheries, or mines? Does the president believe that women, due to their life experiences, are more skilled in social affairs? Does the prime minister feel that the population, or the military establishment, will view with suspicion the appointment of a woman to international relations or defence, especially if the country is undergoing a wave of terrorist attacks? It is also possible that female candidates for ministerial functions aspire to taking on responsibilities of a social nature because they feel more competent in these areas given their socialization, expertise, and experience, or because they feel some pressure to conform with what is expected of them in order to be better integrated into and accepted on the government team. Finally, portfolios with an economic and international vocation are usually the most coveted and influential within the government apparatus and their assignment must also take account of criteria such as seniority. As a rule, women have fewer years of experience in politics than do men – although this will change over time.

And in fact, things are changing. Analyzing the appointments to US cabinets since Jimmy Carter was president, King and Riddlesperger (2015, 101) conclude, "Without question, the history of women's and minorities' appointments to the cabinet reflects desegregation more than inclusion but recent trends point toward cabinet integration." More and more women are holding portfolios traditionally associated with male skills. For example, defence ministers include Michèle Alliot-Marie (France), Michelle Bachelet (Chile), Sirimavo Bandaranaike (Sri Lanka), Kim Campbell (Canada), Andreja Kati (Slovenia), Portia Simpson-Miller (Jamaica), and Ursula von der Leyen (Germany); foreign affairs ministers, Julie Bishop (Australia), Patricia Espinosa Cantellano (Mexico), María Ángela Holguín (Colombia), Maite Nkoana-Mashabane (South Africa), Ana Pauker (Romania), and Sushma Swaraj (India); ministers of finance, Luísa Días Diogo (Mozambique), Ellen Johnson-Sirleaf (Liberia), and Christine Lagarde (France), who became managing director of the International Monetary Fund in 2011. As secretary of state for a global political, economic, and military power, Madeleine Albright, Condoleezza Rice, and Hillary Rodham Clinton played an important role in American foreign policy. It is important that women be ministers because they offer role models to girls and women interested in politics (see question 40). But for women to assume responsibilities traditionally entrusted to men (and vice versa) is even more important because it pushes against the constraints of gender roles that ghettoize women in cultural and social portfolios – and men in defence, economics, finance, and international relations. However, it must be recognized that women and men are not ghettoized in equivalent ways: the former have less influence, power, and prestige than do the latter.

To sum up, although there is always a horizontal segregation of skills resulting from the gender regime, it is not absolute. In addition, this cleavage does not mean that portfolios traditionally associated with women are necessarily devoid of power. Education and health, which mobilize a substantial share of budgets in modern states, are responsibilities often handed to women. However, these are positions of expenditures and not revenues, which make them distasteful to the neoliberal *doxa* that guides Western governments.

BIBLIOGRAPHY

Borrelli, MaryAnne. 2010. "The Contemporary Presidency: Gender Desegregation and Gender Integration in the President's Cabinet, 1933-2010." *Presidential Studies Quarterly* 40 (4): 734–49.

Connolly, Eileen. 2013. "Parliaments as Gendered Institutions: The Irish Oireachtas." *Irish Political Studies* 28 (3): 360–79.

Davis, Rebecca H. 1997. *Women and Power in Parliamentary Democracies: Cabinet Appointments in Western Europe, 1968–1992.* Lincoln: University of Nebraska Press. See, in particular, 11–28.

King, James D. and James W. Riddlesperger. 2015. "Diversity and Presidential Cabinet Appointments." *Social Science Quarterly* 96 (1): 93–103.

Krook, Mona Lena and Diana Z. O'Brien. 2012. "All the President's Men? The Appointment of Female Cabinet Ministers Worldwide." *Journal of Politics* 74 (3): 840–55.

Reynolds, Andrew. 1999. "Women in the Legislatures and Executives of the World: Knocking at the Highest Glass Ceiling." *World Politics* 51 (4): 547–72.

Tremblay, Manon and Gretchen Bauer. 2011. "Conclusion." In *Women in Executive Power: A Global Overview*, edited by Gretchen Bauer and Manon Tremblay, 171–90. London: Routledge.

Tripier, Pierre. 2010. "De l'esprit pionnier aux plafonds et parois de verre." *Les cahiers du GRIF* 48 (1): 5–11.

United Nations Office at Vienna, Centre for Social Development and Humanitarian Affairs. 1992. *Women in Politics and Decision-Making in the Late Twentieth Century.* Dordrecht: Martinus Nijhoff Publishers. See, in particular, 58–72.

73 At what level of the executive hierarchy are women found?

Not only are governments structured by a horizontal segregation of skills according to gender but they also have an analogous vertical segregation.

What is more, these two axes are closely linked: the prestigious portfolios are found at the top of the executive hierarchy (in fact, they are prestigious because of their lofty position) and are usually (though less and less in recent years, see question 72) entrusted to men.

As table 6 shows (see question 68), few women have reached the pinnacle of executive power as president or prime minister. The paucity of female leadership is not a thing of the past: at time of writing, in summer 2016, just under twenty women were heads of government, three more than when the first French-language edition of this book was published in 2008. In its study on the executive branches of 155 countries, the Centre for Social Development and Humanitarian Affairs of the UN Office at Vienna (1992, 63, 67) noted that the number of female ministers is inversely proportional to the hierarchical level: as a general rule, the more important a ministerial level is in the decision-making process, the less it is feminized, a phenomenon that Putnam (1976, 33) describes as the law of increasing disproportion. In their wide-ranging global studies, Reynolds (1999) and Krook and O'Brien (2012) make the same observation: women are generally confined to the bottom of the executive hierarchy. Borrelli (2010) found that women were appointed disproportionately to less-influential positions in the cabinets of the American presidents Franklin D. Roosevelt, Eisenhower, Ford, Carter, Reagan, and George H.W. Bush. That being said, King and Riddlesperger (2015) note that Barack Obama did better than all of his predecessors by appointing more women to senior level positions in his administration – and I suspect that Donald Trump will not improve on Obama's performance. In their mega-analysis of the composition of governments in the world from 1979 to 2009, Jacob, Scherpereel, and Adams (2014) conclude that international standards with regard to equality of women and men have increased the rate of feminization of positions at the bottom, but not the top, of the ministerial hierarchy.

These observations should not be surprising. First, women are relative newcomers to politics, and the most important portfolios (with economic and international connotations) are entrusted to people with long political experience, a resource that more men than women currently possess. Second, and as a corollary, women often have not accumulated enough legislative experience (particularly on committees) to occupy the positions situated at the top of the executive ladder. Finally, as Paxton and Hughes

(2007, 99–100) point out, sometimes the number (or supply) of women available to assume such positions is simply not sufficient.

However, authors of recent works are hopeful. In the conclusion to their book *Women in Executive Power: A Global Overview*, Tremblay and Bauer (2011) note that as their numbers in cabinets increase, women are holding a broader range of portfolios, including those at the top of the ministerial hierarchy. In addition, aside from a few portfolios whose extreme importance is undeniable (such as foreign affairs and finance), the importance of portfolios changes depending on the situation: defence is less important, and certainly less prestigious, in times of peace than in times of war; healthcare proves very important in death-denying societies obsessed with body performance and healthiness; and public security comes to the fore when governments are on alert to "terrorist threats." These nuances do not, however, constitute a definitive breaking of the law of increasing disproportion.

BIBLIOGRAPHY

Borrelli, MaryAnne. 2010. "The Contemporary Presidency: Gender Desegregation and Gender Integration in the President's Cabinet, 1933-2010." *Presidential Studies Quarterly* 40 (4): 734–49.

Jacob, Suraj, John A. Scherpereel, and Melinda A. Adams. 2014. "Gender Norms and Women's Political Representation: A Global Analysis of Cabinets, 1979–2009." *Governance: An International Journal of Policy and Administration* 27 (2): 321–45.

King, James D. and James W. Riddlesperger. 2015. "Diversity and Presidential Cabinet Appointments." *Social Science Quarterly* 96 (1): 93–103.

Krook, Mona Lena and Diana Z. O'Brien. 2012. "All the President's Men? The Appointment of Female Cabinet Ministers Worldwide." *Journal of Politics* 74 (3): 840–55.

Paxton, Pamela and Melanie M. Hughes. 2007. *Women, Politics, and Power: A Global Perspective*. Los Angeles: Pine Forge Press. See, in particular, 80–100.

Putnam, Robert D. 1976. *The Comparative Study of Political Elites*. Englewood Cliffs, NJ: Prentice-Hall.

Reynolds, Andrew. 1999. "Women in the Legislatures and Executives of the World: Knocking at the Highest Glass Ceiling." *World Politics* 51 (4): 547–72.

Tremblay, Manon and Gretchen Bauer. 2011. "Conclusion." In *Women in Executive Power: A Global Overview*, edited by Gretchen Bauer and Manon Tremblay, 171–90. London: Routledge.

United Nations Office at Vienna, Centre for Social Development and Humanitarian

Affairs. 1992. *Women in Politics and Decision-Making in the Late Twentieth Century*. Dordrecht: Martinus Nijhoff Publishers. See, in particular, 58–72.

74 Is there a connection between the proportion of women in a country's parliament and the proportion of women in its cabinet?

According to Mathiason (2006), there is a clear link between the proportion of women in a country's parliament and the proportion of women in its cabinet. This is also the view of Claveria (2014), Davis (1997, 34–5, 63–4), Krook and O'Brien (2012), Paxton and Hughes (2007, 98–9), and Reynolds (1999). A bilateral correlation performed using data published by the Inter-Parliamentary Union and UN Women on the proportion of female members of parliament and of governments in January 2015 generates a convincing coefficient of 0.55 (at a threshold of significance of 99 per cent). In other words, in January 2015, the proportions of female members of parliament and of cabinets were related. What is more, Studlar and Moncrief (1997, 1999) maintain that the feminization rate of the caucus that forms the government exerts the most significant influence on the proportion of women in cabinet.

That there is a link between the feminization rates in parliaments and in cabinets is not surprising – at least in British-tradition parliamentary regimes, in which the parliament forms the pool of candidates for executive positions. In political regimes in which members of the government cannot come from the legislature but must be recruited from civil society, however, the connection between feminization rates in parliament and in cabinet is more concerning. Tremblay and Bauer (2011) have proposed that even in regimes in which the ministers are selected from outside the legislative arena, the proportion of women in the legislature may form an informal model to be imitated in the cabinet. This hypothesis remains to be verified by empirical research. Another hypothesis is that regimes in which ministers come from outside the legislature may be more influenced by international standards for equality of women and men than are regimes in which female ministers must be selected from within the parliamentary ranks. Indeed, in the latter case, the prime minister may claim that she or he cannot meet international standards because her or his hands are tied by the national political rules, whereas this argument falls flat when the entire female population of the country constitutes (in principle) the pool for picking ministers. This hypothesis also remains to be validated.

BIBLIOGRAPHY

Claveria, Silvia. 2014. "Still a 'Male Business'? Explaining Women's Presence in Executive Office." *West European Politics* 37 (5): 1156–76.

Davis, Rebecca H. 1997. *Women and Power in Parliamentary Democracies: Cabinet Appointments in Western Europe, 1968–1992.* Lincoln: University of Nebraska Press. See, in particular, 29–37.

Inter-Parliamentary Union and UN Women (2015). "Women in Politics: 2015," accessed 20 July 2016, http://www.ipu.org/pdf/publications/wmnmap15_en.pdf.

Krook, Mona Lena and Diana Z. O'Brien. 2012. "All the President's Men? The Appointment of Female Cabinet Ministers Worldwide." *Journal of Politics* 74 (3): 840–55.

Mathiason, John with Loveena Dookhony. 2006. *Women in Governmental Decision-Making in the Early 21st Century: What Has – and Has Not – Been Achieved in the Post-Beijing Period,* accessed 20 July 2016, http://intlmgt.cipa.cornell.edu/sessions/women/Women%20in%20governmental%20decision-making%20publication.pdf.

Paxton, Pamela and Melanie M. Hughes. 2007. *Women, Politics, and Power: A Global Perspective.* Los Angeles: Pine Forge Press. See, in particular, 80–100.

Reynolds, Andrew. 1999. "Women in the Legislatures and Executives of the World: Knocking at the Highest Glass Ceiling." *World Politics* 51 (4): 547–72.

Studlar, Donley T. and Gary F. Moncrief. 1997. "The Recruitment of Women Cabinet Ministers in the Canadian Provinces." *Governance: An International Journal of Policy and Administration* 10 (1): 67–81.

– 1999. "Women's Work? The Distribution and Prestige of Portfolios in the Canadian Provinces." *Governance: An International Journal of Policy and Administration* 12 (4): 379–95.

Tremblay, Manon and Gretchen Bauer. 2011. "Conclusion." In *Women in Executive Power: A Global Overview,* edited by Gretchen Bauer and Manon Tremblay, 171–90. London: Routledge.

75 Is it more important to have women in cabinet or in parliament?

Although the underrepresentation of women in parliaments is regrettable, it is my opinion that keeping them out of the executive branch has even direr consequences. Parliaments are important decision-making bodies whose influence must not be minimized (see question 32), but the real decision-making centre, whether in parliamentary or presidential systems, is the cabinet: it plays the most prominent role in the formulation and application of laws, and it also has means to pressure legislators into adopting those laws. As a consequence, if women are not fully represented in cabinet, they do not have a firm hold on the apparatus essential to the decision-making process in representative democracies. If there are no women in the cabinet, there may be no one to propose a legislative measure on urban security that takes account of how women are integrated into the city. There may be no one to remind the government to include the principle of pay equity when it formulates and reviews labour laws. There may be no one to insist on the importance of evaluating the application of each law in the light of its different effects on women and men (and on different women based on an intersectional approach) and to limit the negative consequences on the former. And there may be no one to emphasize that the application of a policy regarding spousal support sometimes engenders discriminatory effects against women under the tax laws. The results of a recent study by Atchison (2015) back up this reasoning: they show that the presence of female ministers leads to the adoption of public policies encouraging reconciliation between family and work.

Further, it is important that women lead the executive branch as president or prime minister for a number of reasons. First, there is the simple question of equality and justice (see question 40). Second, the appointment of a female president or prime minister may have a ripple effect on the feminization of political life in general. On the symbolic level, a woman's presence as leader of the executive branch demonstrates that it is possible for girls and women to aspire to the highest positions – and shows boys and men that they do not enjoy an inalienable right to occupy those positions (see question 40). Women's presence in a leadership position is even more important when they are members of historically ostracized minorities, such as lesbians (see question 99). One study covering eighty-nine countries has shown that in young democracies, the presence of a woman as head of government is associated with a higher proportion of women in parliament (Tremblay 2007; see also Krook and O'Brien 2012). Davis (1997, 19) similarly found that a female prime minister is more likely to have a feminized cabinet. A concrete example of this is the cabinet formed in July 2016 by British Prime Minister Theresa May, which contained a higher proportion of women (30 per cent) than that of her predecessor, David Cameron (22.7 per cent). What is more, May appointed the first out lesbian, Justine Greening, to the cabinet as education minister. This is in stark contrast to the attitude of the first female prime minister of the United Kingdom. Margaret Thatcher (1979–90) not only argued that her presence as head of state justified naming no (or few) women to cabinet but had the infamous Section 28 of the Local Government Act of 1988 adopted; among its provisions was that "a local authority shall not promote the teaching in any maintained schools of the acceptability of homosexuality as a pretended family relationship." Hillary Rodham Clinton, during her election campaign, promised that if she won the US presidency, she would name as many women as men to her cabinet (Healy 2016). Alas, she did not win, and the team surrounding Donald Trump is notable for its concentration of testosterone – not to mention its whiteness, right-wing extremism, lack of political experience, high proportion of multimillionaires, and so on. That being said, in their analysis of the composition of 206 cabinets in fifteeen countries from 1980 to the mid-2010s, however, O'Brien and her colleagues (2015) did not find that female presidents or prime ministers had such a feminization effect on cabinet members (see also Tremblay and Bauer 2011). Finally, a woman at the head of the executive branch poses a challenge to how the relationships between women and power are conceived: What is a female leader? How should and can she act? What expectations does the population have of her?

The important consequences of exclusion of women from the executive branch must not overshadow the negative effects of their underrepresentation in parliaments. Women should be present both in cabinet and parliament: to the extent that these institutions manage how people live and will live together in society and because women constitute half of the population, it is only justice that they occupy half the positions whose holders write the laws (a responsibility that generally falls to the government), adopt them (the parliament), and apply them (the government via the civil service in the broad sense). From a utilitarian point of view (see question

40), the exclusion of women from parliament and cabinet deprives those who make decisions in government of the full range of resources available through society, notably women's perspectives. What is more, it is possible that women's needs, demands, and interests are not adequately represented in politics, even though they are subjected to the law just as are men.

To sum up, the small number of women within the executive branch of governments is consequential because it means they do not fully participate in the activities of the body at the core of the public decision-making process. This observation should not detract from the fact that their under-representation in parliaments is just as regrettable.

BIBLIOGRAPHY

Atchison, Amy. 2015. "The Impact of Female Cabinet Ministers on a Female-Friendly Labor Environment." *Journal of Women, Politics & Policy* 36 (4): 388–414.

Davis, Rebecca H. 1997. *Women and Power in Parliamentary Democracies: Cabinet Appointments in Western Europe, 1968–1992.* Lincoln: University of Nebraska Press. See, in particular, 11–28.

Escobar-Lemmon, Maria C., Leslie A. Schwindt-Bayer, and Michelle M. Taylor-Robinson. 2014. "Representing Women: Empirical Insights from Legislatures and Cabinets in Latin America." In *Representation: The Case of Women*, edited by Maria C. Escobar-Lemmon and Michelle M. Taylor-Robinson, 205–24. New York: Oxford University Press.

Healy, Patrick. 2016. "'President Hillary Clinton?' She Wants Progress on Immigration and to Drink With G.O.P." *New York Times*, 3 July, accessed 25 July 2016, http://mobile.nytimes.com/2016/07/04/us/politics/hillary-clinton-president.html.

Jalalzai, Farida and Mona Lena Krook. 2010. "Beyond Hillary and Benazir: Women's Political Leadership Worldwide." *International Political Science Review* 31 (1): 5–21.

Krook, Mona Lena and Diana Z. O'Brien. 2012. "All the President's Men? The Appointment of Female Cabinet Ministers Worldwide." *Journal of Politics* 74 (3): 840–55.

O'Brien, Diana Z., Matthew Mendez, Jordan Carr Peterson, and Jihyun Shin. 2015. "Letting Down the Ladder or Shutting the Door: Female Prime Ministers, Party Leaders, and Cabinet Ministers." *Politics & Gender* 11 (4): 689–717.

Tremblay, Manon. 2007. "Democracy, Representation, and Women: A Comparative Analysis." *Democratization* 14 (4): 1–21.

Tremblay, Manon and Gretchen Bauer. 2011. "Conclusion." In *Women in Executive Power: A Global Overview*, edited by Gretchen Bauer and Manon Tremblay, 171–90. London: Routledge.

CHAPTER NINE

Women's Participation in Electoral Politics in Canada

76 Were there "radical" suffragist struggles in Canada similar to those that took place in the United States and Great Britain?

The suffragist struggles in Canada were not as spectacular as were those in the United States and in Great Britain (Cleverdon [1950] 1974, 4), where suffragettes marched in picket lines in front of the White House, chained themselves to the fences of Buckingham Royal Palace, and undertook hunger strikes – and were force-fed under the provisions of the Prisoners (Temporary Discharge for Ill Health) Act of 1913, better known as the Cat and Mouse Act (on this subject, see the excellent films by Sarah Gavron [*Suffragettes*] and Katja von Garnier [*Iron Jawed Angels*]). It is even said that a British suffragette, Emily Davison, threw herself in front of the king's racehorse in the name of her cause, but this interpretation of the incident is not unanimous.

Nevertheless, there were indeed suffragist struggles in Canada (in some provinces the struggle was to regain a right that women had been stripped of in the mid-nineteenth century; see question 77), the richness of which is fully revealed through social movement theory. Two approaches lend themselves to conducting an analysis of the suffragist campaign: resource mobilization and political process.

The resource mobilization approach posits that a social movement can mobilize in the sociopolitical field only if it has resources of various types. These resources may be cultural in nature: knowledge and practical knowhow with regard to mobilization and organization, strategies, and tactics. Socio-organizational resources involve the groups in the movement, which form networks and alliances. Human resources are people prepared to invest in the cause represented by the movement, by being either leaders or simply activists and sympathizers. Material resources refer to financial and physical capital (such as a location for holding meetings or access to a means of spreading the ideas promoted by the movement). Finally, moral resources have to do with the degree of legitimacy that the movement enjoys in public opinion. To this must be added whether a counter-social movement exists – that is, if there is an adversarial group that embodies resistance to the change proposed by a social movement or even tries to reverse it, notably by attacking its legitimacy in public opinion (for example, the social conservative movement is the ultimate adversary for the feminist and the lesbian, gay, bisexual, and trans [LGBT] movements).

An analysis of the suffragist struggles deployed in Canada before women gained the right to vote reveals that the suffragists had access to such resources. Here are some examples taken from the book by Catherine Cleverdon ([1950] 1974), *The Woman Suffrage Movement in Canada*, which is the authority on the subject. In terms of cultural resources, Cleverdon describes a wide range of strategies and tactics used in the struggle for the women's vote. For example, the celebrated American activist Susan B. Anthony and the equally well-known English suffragette Emmeline Pankhurst went to Toronto – the first in 1889 and the second in 1909 (Cleverdon [1950] 1974, 16, 32), and Sylvia Pankhurst went to Saint John in 1912 (189). In 1913, Manitoban suffragists went to the Winnipeg Stampede to fill their petitions with signatures and their coffers with money (57); the following year, they organized a Women's Parliament in which female parliamentarians discussed the appropriateness of giving men the right to vote (59; see also Sharpe and McMahon 2007, 42). One of the missions of the Nova Scotia Equal Franchise League, founded in 1917, was to train people, both female and male, to speak to groups, with the obvious objective of spreading and promoting suffragist ideas. During the 1917 provincial election, New Brunswick suffragist forces sent letters to candidates to solicit their opinion about women getting the vote (191). And this is not to mention a flock of representations made to provincial parliamentarians and governments – during which suffragists submitted petitions and argued that women really wanted to vote – and the many bills that were tabled by parliamentarians allied with the suffragists. Suffragist struggles were also richly endowed in terms of socio-organizational resources: with the exception of Prince Edward Island (198), suffragist organizations were present in all provinces (even in rural areas), and they were usually able to count on support from allies within civil society (women's groups, of course, such as the National Council of Women, the Woman's Christian Temperance Union, and the Women's Institutes, but also unions, such as the Carpenters' and Joiners' Brotherhood of Saint John). With regard to human resources, in every province suffragist struggles drew "their most active recruits in general from that small segment of the feminine population which had a fair degree of economic independence. Outstanding suffragists were most frequently professional and self-employed women, or wives of men with comfortable incomes" (4). The figureheads of suffragism were from the elites: for example, in Québec, Thérèse F. Casgrain, spouse of Pierre Casgrain, member of Parliament (1917–45) and Speaker of the House of Commons (1936–40); in Ontario, Dr Emily Howard Stowe, the first female physician in Canada, and her daughter, Dr Augusta Stowe-Gullen, the first female member of the professional corporation Ontario Medical College for Women, affiliated with the University of Toronto; Dr Eliza Ritchie, first female professor associated with Dalhousie University; and Dr Amelia Yeomans, considered the first female physician in Manitoba. In terms of material resources, Cleverdon mentions examples of fundraising activities (59, 190) and of newspapers promoting suffragist ideas (15). Finally, in terms of moral resources, although the suffragists were able to count on the support of a large number of actors within civil society and the political class and, according to Cleverdon (65n49), on tireless support of public opinion in the Prairie provinces, she also notes that among those most strongly opposed were women who were indifferent to suffrage (3–4). Many other adversaries raised difficulties for the suffragists. The influential Victoria *Daily Times* and Halifax *Morning Chronicle* depicted the struggles of the British suffragettes (84–5, 168) quite unflatteringly. In Ontario, the Conservative premier, James P. Whitney, proved to be a ferocious opponent of women's suffrage. Contrary to a number of Anglophone provinces in which the Protestant clergy supported the suffragist cause (14), in Quebec the Catholic Church scrambled like the devil in holy water to fight female suffrage (see question 79).

Although the suffragists led a determined fight, their own resources alone did not account for their ultimate success; the sociopolitical context also had something to do with it. The political process approach adds this contextual variable through the notion of political opportunity structure, which Staggenborg (2012, 193) defines as "features of the political environment that influence movement emergence and success, including the extent of openness in the polity, shifts in political alignments, divisions among elites, the availability of influential allies, and repression or facilitation by the state." Political opportunity structure thus refers to a group of traits inherent to the political regime itself and also to its interaction with civil society – for instance, the structure of the state (including federalism), elections and the alternation in power of different parties, the parties' ideologies, the availability of allies within both the state and civil society, social movements and their interactions with the state, and an independent legal system. To illustrate this last trait, it was a decision by the Judiciary Committee of the British Privy Council that opened the doors of the Senate to women in 1929 (see question 80).

The political process approach enriches comprehension of suffragist struggles by adding a contextual background of interwoven sociopolitical factors. Here are a few examples. Federalism was instrumentalized by the clerical and political elites in Quebec to refuse women the right to vote: during the debate on women's suffrage in the House of Commons in 1918, Quebec MPs argued that voting, for women, was a question of culture and education, both of which were under provincial jurisdiction as provided in section 92 of the British North America Act. As a consequence, it was up to the provinces to establish the conditions for the federal electoral rolls within their jurisdiction (Tremblay 2010, 54–6). Regional cultures were also evoked to explain suffragist struggles. Cleverdon sees the Prairie provinces as a haven of progressiveness (see question 78), whereas she calls the Maritime provinces a "stronghold of conservatism" and explains, "Nowhere has the traditional conservatism of the Maritime Provinces been more apparent than in the securing of political rights for women" (156). Even liberalism was "unresponsive to modern trends" (173), although it was more open in the Prairie provinces. Finally, economic prosperity had something to do with the flagging of suffragist struggles in the early twentieth century in British Columbia, Manitoba, and the Maritime provinces: "During good times agitation on all scores is likely to be less," Cleverdon observes (54).

In short, suffragist struggles in Canada were not as disruptive as were their counterparts in the United States and Great Britain, but they were nevertheless fertile, and they did result in a positive outcome: women gained the right to vote in legislative elections.

BIBLIOGRAPHY

Cleverdon, Catherine L. (1950) 1974. *The Start of Liberation: The Woman Suffrage Movement in Canada*. Toronto: University of Toronto Press.

Gavron, Sarah, director. 2015. *Suffragette*. Film on suffragist struggles in Great Britain.

Staggenborg, Suzanne. 2012. *Social Movements*, 2nd edition. New York: Oxford University Press.

Tremblay, Manon. 2010. *Quebec Women and Legislative Representation*, translated by Käthe Roth. Vancouver: UBC Press.

Von Garnier, Katja, director. 2004. *Iron Jawed Angels*. Film on suffragist struggles in the United States.

77 In what year did women in Canada obtain the right to vote and to run for office in legislative elections?

Canadian women obtained the right to vote in federal elections in two stages, in 1917 and 1918, putting Canada in the first wave of "female suffragism" (see question 6). In 1917, suffrage was limited to two categories of women: members of the armed forces (under the Military Voters Act) and women with a male relative enlisted in the Canadian or British army (under the Wartime Elections Act; Office of the Chief Electoral Officer of Canada 2007, 63, 66–7). The latter criterion was particularly insulting to women, as it amounted to a vote by proxy: they were granted the right to vote not because they were citizens but because they were mothers, wives, daughters, or sisters of members of the military. (It is also interesting to note that this statute removed the right to vote from conscientious objectors and from people born in "enemy" countries and naturalized after 1902 [Sharpe and McMahon 2007, 44].) The following year, on 24 May 1918, the right to vote in federal legislative elections was extended to more Canadian women. Still excluded were Indigenous women (and men) falling under the Indian Act and those belonging to certain minorities (Chinese, Japanese, and South Asian).

Canadian women also acquired the right run for federal office in two stages. The 1919 Dominion By-Elections Act provides, "Any British Subject, male or female, who is of the full age of twenty-one years, may be a candidate at a Dominion election." The following year, section 38 of the Act Respecting the Election of Members of the House of Commons and the Electoral Franchise (1920) reproduced the terms of the 1919 statute, thus granting women the right to run for office in federal elections.

Canada is a federation, which implies that the federated states (that is, the provinces and territories) also hold legislative elections. As table 7 shows, most Canadian women obtained the rights to vote and to run for office in their provinces between 1916 and 1934. However, even though they could vote in federal elections, Quebec women had to wait until 1940 before being authorized to cast their ballots in provincial elections.

Two comments are in order. The first concerns the wide gap – fifteen years – between women gaining suffrage and obtaining the right to run for office in New Brunswick. Tulloch (1985, 68–9) maintains that after women obtained the right to vote in the province, the suffragist movement dissolved, causing turmoil to which internal tensions in the Women's Enfranchisement Association and a difficult sociolinguistic, economic, and political context contributed. In addition, the question of women's right to run for office was not a terribly attractive campaign plank for political parties. Finally, the Catholic Church may have been partly responsible for the silence of suffragist voices with regard to this issue. Unfortunately, the state of scholarship is such that we cannot yet know for certain. It was only in 1934 that the Women's Institutes finally mobilized to demand completion of the political rights of New Brunswick women in the province (Cleverdon [1950] 1974, 197–8). According to Campbell (2007, 287), the struggles conducted by women to gain their political rights in New Brunswick are evidence of the "very great challenges involved in achieving electoral reforms that are designed to benefit those members of society who are the most vulnerable, who wield the least political, legal, or economic power. It is a reminder of how our definitions of democracy can shift according to expediency as well as ideology, and of how such definitions can be adjusted and readjusted to exclude some groups even as they become more inclusive of others." The second comment concerns Newfoundland: in 1925, women had to be at least twenty-five years old to vote, whereas men could vote when they were twenty-one. This discrimination on the basis of sex/gender and age, which would be abolished only in 1946, was not unique to Newfoundland, as a number of countries imposed two-class systems by sex/gender (see question 4). At the time, Newfoundland was under the jurisdiction of Great Britain, where such discrimination was in effect between 1918 and 1928.

Table 7

The dates when women obtained the rights to vote and to run for office, by province*

Province	Right to vote	Right to run for office
Manitoba	28 January 1916	28 January 1916
Saskatchewan	14 March 1916	14 March 1916
Alberta	19 April 1916	19 April 1916
British Columbia	5 April 1917	5 April 1917
Ontario	12 April 1917	4 April 1919
Nova Scotia	26 April 1918	26 April 1918
Canada	24 May 1918	7 July 1919
New Brunswick	17 April 1919	9 March 1934
Prince Edward Island	3 May 1922	3 May 1922
Newfoundland**	13 April 1925	13 April 1925
Quebec	25 April 1940	25 April 1940

* These dates applied to white women; many women belonging to minorities (for instance, Indigenous women) obtained these rights much later.
** Newfoundland was a "dominion" in 1925 and became a province of Canada in 1949.

It is interesting to note that before the 1867 Confederation women were able to vote in Lower Canada and Upper Canada (which became the United Province of Canada in 1840) and in Prince Edward Island, New Brunswick, and Nova Scotia. It is unlikely that they exercised this right in colonies where common-law tradition prevailed, but between 1791 and 1849, those meeting certain age and property-ownership criteria were allowed to vote in Lower Canada, the constitutional ancestor of Quebec (Cleverdon [1950] 1974, 149, 158, 214–16). Indeed, the Constitutional Act of 1791 provided that "persons" (not men) meeting certain age and property-ownership criteria were "electors." And, in the view of Cleverdon ([1950] 1974, 149, 214–16) and Picard (1993), many women (mainly widows but also single women and married women with a separation as to property, as long as they were taxpayers) exercised this right – until 1849, when the reformist Baldwin-La Fontaine coalition adopted the following legislative measure: "May it be proclaimed and decreed that no woman shall have the right to vote at any election, be it for a county or riding, or for any of the aforesaid towns and cities" (Office of the Chief Electoral Officer of Canada 2007, 64). Prince Edward Island had taken the lead, in 1836, by limiting suffrage to men; New Brunswick followed suit in 1848 and Nova Scotia in 1854 (Cuthbertson 1994, 9, 152–3, 220). Cleverdon ([1950] 1974, 158) hypothesized that the 1848 Seneca Falls Convention (signed in upstate New York), in which American women claimed the right to vote, may have inspired lawmakers in the United Province of Canada, New Brunswick, and Nova Scotia to explicitly exclude women from suffrage for fear that they would actually exercise their right (or, in Quebec, that they would make it an acquired right). What is more, Confederation changed nothing: section 41 of the British North America Act maintained, for federal elections, the conditions of the electoral qualification in force in the founding colonies and explicitly set out that suffrage was limited to men. Confederation was a missed opportunity to broaden the political citizenship of women – as opposed to what happened in Australia, where the advent of the Commonwealth consolidated that citizenship (see question 5), and Finland, where access to national sovereignty in 1906 enshrined the political rights of women (see question 38).

BIBLIOGRAPHY

Campbell, Gail. 2007. "Defining and Redefining Democracy: The History of Electoral Reform in New Brunswick." In *Democratic Reform in New Brunswick*, edited by William Cross, 273–99. Toronto: Canadian Scholars' Press.

Cleverdon, Catherine L. (1950) 1974. *The Start of Liberation: The Woman Suffrage Movement in Canada.* Toronto: University of Toronto Press.

Cuthbertson, Brian. 1994. *Johnny Bluenose at the Polls: Epic Nova Scotian Election Battles 1758–1848.* Halifax: Formac.

Lamoureux, Diane and Jacinthe Michaud. 1988. "Les parlementaires canadiens et le suffrage féminin: un aperçu des débats." *Canadian Journal of Political Science* 21 (2): 319–29.

Office of the Chief Electoral Officer of Canada. 2007. *A History of the Vote in Canada*, 2nd edition, 61–8. Ottawa: Chief Electoral Officer of Canada; accessed 20 June 2016, http://www.elections.ca/res/his/History-Eng_Text.pdf.

Picard, Nathalie. 1993. "Les femmes et le vote au Bas-Canada, 1791–1849." In *Les bâtisseuses de la Cité*, edited by Evelyne Tardy et al., 57–64. Montreal: ACFAS.

Sharpe, Robert J. and Patricia I. McMahon (2007). *The Persons Case: The Origins and Legacy of the Fight for Legal Personhood.* Toronto: University of Toronto Press.

Tremblay, Manon. 2010. *Quebec Women and Legislative Representation*, translated by
   Käthe Roth. Vancouver: UBC Press. See, particularly, 11–60.
Tulloch, Elspeth. 1985. *We, the Undersigned: A Historical Overview of New Brunswick
   Women's Political and Legal Status, 1784–1984*. Moncton: New Brunswick Advisory
   Council on the Status of Women.

78 Did the progressiveness of the Prairie provinces with regard to women's suffrage spread by "contagion"?

To answer this question, one must first decide whether the Prairie provinces
were progressive with regard to women's suffrage. Second, one must see if
a contagion effect can explain the fact that in less than three months the
legislative assemblies of Manitoba, Saskatchewan, and Alberta adopted laws
granting women the right to vote in provincial legislative elections.

There is no doubt that the Prairie provinces had a progressive attitude
regarding women's suffrage. Manitoba, Saskatchewan, and Alberta were the
first provinces to grant women the right to vote in provincial legislative
elections (see question 77). On the other hand, it was in Ontario that the
first demonstrations in favour of the women's vote took place with the
foundation, in 1876, of the Women's Literary Club – a name designed to
camouflage the organization's suffragist mission (Cleverdon [1950] 1974,
20). In the Prairies, the first suffragist demonstrations took place in Manitoba in the early 1890s, more or less at the time as New Zealand women
(Maori and *pakeha*) were obtaining the right to vote in legislative elections
(see question 5). New Zealand was under British guardianship, as was
Canada (and therefore Manitoba); perhaps the former inspired the latter.
The Canadian suffragist elites knew perfectly well what was going on in the
British Empire through the press, correspondence exchanged with their
counterparts in other countries, and their travels and stays abroad. To prepare for their battle, Canadian suffragist forces studied these countries,
where it was possible for women to vote (Cleverdon [1950] 1974, 8, 17).
McLeay (2006) and McAllister (2006) explain the advance of New Zealand
and Australia with regard to women's suffrage by the presence of an egalitarian doxy, essential when everything had to be built from scratch. Cleverdon ([1950] 1974, 46) takes up this reasoning, although she sees the United
States as the main source of inspiration of suffragist struggles in the Prairie

provinces: "[In] the United States … pioneer communities were invariably the first to enfranchise women. On both sides of the border the feeling generally prevailed that women as well as men had opened up the country, had shared the experiences of settling a new land, and were therefore entitled to a voice in making the laws." In a number of American states, women had had the vote for years – for example, in Utah (1870), Oregon (1884), Rhode Island (1887), and Colorado (1893). That being said, in the Maritime provinces, Cleverdon ([1950] 1974, 157, 165, 175) implies, the suffragist influence came from England.

To this egalitarian influence, Cleverdon ([1950] 1974) adds the liberalism and progressivism of the Prairies. She describes Alberta as having "always displayed a liberal attitude towards women" (66). About Manitoba, she writes that granting suffrage to women constituted a decision "typical of Western progressiveness" (49). Similarly, Sharpe and McMahon (2007, 44) argue that Irene Parlby, elected to the Legislative Assembly of Alberta in 1921 and one of the five women involved in the Persons case (see question 80), saw "the relatively easy spread of the female franchise across the Canadian West" as attributable to the fact "that men recognized and respected the courage and hard work of pioneer women." In Cleverdon's view, these attitudes were pervasive in Prairie societies, as the granting of suffrage to women was well supported by the political class and by public opinion and civil society. For example, the Grain Growers' Associations of Manitoba and Saskatchewan and the United Farmers of Alberta endorsed women's suffrage in 1911 (Cleverdon [1950] 1974, 47). It was a context favourable to a contagion effect for suffragist ideas.

The notion of "contagion effect" means that an idea or practice promoted or advanced by actor A is disseminated to and begins to influence the ideas and practices of actor B (see question 39). This notion is used widely to explain how quotas for women in politics have spread like wildfire to one hundred countries since the 1990s (see questions 43 and 44). But can we speak of a contagion effect for suffragist ideas in the Prairie provinces to explain how, in less than three months, Manitoba, Saskatchewan, and Alberta adopted laws granting women the right to vote in provincial elections? I think that several arguments support this interpretation.

A first argument concerns the circulation of ideas. Farmers' associations in Manitoba, Saskatchewan, and Alberta not only endorsed women's suffrage but integrated women into their activities, enabling them to develop the skills needed to debate, organize, establish networks, and, especially, spread their ideas through the *Grain Growers' Guide*, the official newsletter of the three farmers' associations on the Prairies. Cleverdon ([1950] 1974, 15–16) writes, "In the Prairie Provinces the widely circulated farmers' weekly, the *Grain Growers' Guide*, was a loyal and steadfast ally. Had it not been for this journalistic assistance, the road to political emancipation would have been much harder." Suffragist ideas also circulated in the Prairies via dailies sympathetic to the cause, such as the *Manitoba Free Press*, for which many members of an early and energetic suffragist association, the Winnipeg Political Equality League, were journalists (Cleverdon [1950] 1974, 55–6). A second argument involves the circulation of elites. For example, Nellie L. McClung participated in the suffragist struggles in the three Prairie provinces, often making speeches; according to Cleverdon ([1950] 1974, 58), she had an "unusual gift for public speaking." A third argument concerns the networks formed by individuals and groups created in the Prairie provinces. Aside from the farmers' associations, the Woman's Christian Temperance Union was established in all three provinces. Such networks offered fertile soil for exchanging ideas and resources and for spreading "best practices," as we call them today. Finally, it is possible that the emulation and competition inherent to federalism add to the explanation, but this is a hypothesis that remains to be explored.

In short, further research is required to establish whether a contagion effect was at work in the progressivism of the Prairie provinces with regard to women's suffrage. But, at first glance, this idea is very credible.

BIBLIOGRAPHY

Cleverdon, Catherine L. (1950) 1974. *The Start of Liberation: The Woman Suffrage Movement in Canada*. Toronto: University of Toronto Press.

McAllister, Ian. 2006. "Women's Electoral Representation in Australia." In *Representing Women in Parliament: A Comparative Study*, edited by Marian Sawer, Manon Tremblay, and Linda Trimble, 27–46. Abingdon: Routledge.

McLeay, Elizabeth. 2006. "Climbing On: Rules, Values and Women's Representation in the New Zealand Parliament." In *Representing Women in Parliament: A Comparative Study*, edited by Marian Sawer, Manon Tremblay, and Linda Trimble, 67–82. Abingdon: Routledge.

Sharpe, Robert J. and Patricia I. McMahon (2007). *The Persons Case: The Origins and Legacy of the Fight for Legal Personhood*. Toronto: University of Toronto Press.

79 Why did Quebec women obtain the rights to vote and to run in provincial legislative elections so much later than women in other provinces?

Quebec women obtained the right to vote in provincial elections so much later than did other Canadian women for ideological, religious, and political reasons. These factors are closely linked, as the clerical and political elites attended the same schools and frequented the same spaces of socialization, shared a community of ideas, and maintained very close ties that provided them with a platform for jointly assuming the governance of Quebec society. For example, a number of politicians of the time aligned their governance with the social doctrine of the Catholic Church.

Essentially, the suffragist struggles took place between 1922, the year when the Comité provincial du suffrage féminin/Provincial Franchise Committee became active – much later than suffragist mobilizations elsewhere in Canada (see questions 76 to 78) – and 1940, when Quebec women (finally) won the rights to vote and to run for office in provincial elections. In fact, the premiers over the period, Louis-Alexandre Taschereau (1920–36) and Maurice Duplessis (1936–39), were fiercely opposed to female suffrage – and, again, this contrasted with the positions of premiers elsewhere in Canada, such as Alberta premier A.L. Sifton. Premier Taschereau had even declared, "If ever women in Quebec obtain the right to vote, it won't be me who gave it to them" (Casgrain 1971, 77, our translation). Given the considerable power held by the premier under the British parliamentary regime, these men's resistance posed a major obstacle to suffragist demands.

Still on the political level, but this time on the civil society side, the demand for female suffrage was not championed by a social movement, could not count on broad popular support (unlike the situation in the Prairie provinces; see question 78), and might have benefited from high-profile actions led by a small number of suffragist activists. This does not mean, however, that no organization was demanding the rights for women to vote and to run for office in provincial elections. There were, among others, the Alliance canadienne pour le vote des femmes au Québec and the Comité provincial du suffrage féminin/Provincial Franchise Committee, but the influence of these organizations was rather modest; women acquired the right to vote more as a result of backroom negotiations among elites than through vast mobilizations within civil society. The antisuffrage forces gave the impression of being quite well organized and, without a shadow of a doubt, they were influential. For instance, the Church applied pressure to the political class and executed several strategies to hinder suffragists. One of these was the creation of the Comité de propagande contre le suffrage féminin, which, among other things, set out to collect signatures from women as they left church on petitions against women's rights to vote in and to run for provincial election.

In the 1920s and 1930s, Quebec was ideologically conservative, at least when it came to social relations between women and men and gender roles. Unlike in the Prairie provinces, there was no conviction in Quebec that women and men had participated equally in the construction of society and should enjoy equal political rights. The social roles assigned to women and men reflected the division between the private and public spheres: to women went family affairs; to men, state affairs. Essentially, women were defined first and foremost as mothers, a role that de facto excluded their participation in public and political life. On the other hand, men had to assume economic responsibilities (for example, that of providing for the family) and political roles (such as representing their family when they voted). This division of skills by sex – skills that shaped gender (see question 1) – also existed in the other provinces, so how does it contribute to our understanding of why Quebec women were so late in obtaining the rights to vote and to run for office?

In the Quebec context, two factors reinforced the confinement of women to the family: the Catholic religion and French-Canadian nationalism. Catholicism dominated in Quebec, whereas Protestantism was the main religion in the other provinces. A number of studies have shown the negative influence of Catholicism on women's political participation. Cohen (1997) points out that in Quebec the private sphere – that is, the Church and charities – built the welfare state, relegating women to the confined world of the family, whereas in English Canada the construction of the welfare state was accompanied by recognition of the social aspect of maternal roles as a foundation of women's citizenship. French-Canadian nationalism, which honoured the past and traditions, rural life, and state noninterventionism, as well as the French language and the Catholic faith, advocated highly segregated gender roles, entrusting to women and the family the responsibility for protecting and perpetuating the French-Canadian "race." Clearly, any participation by women in social and political life had to be interpreted as a threat to the perpetuity of the French-Canadian community in North America. Interestingly, the Catholic Church's hostility to women's suffrage was not limited to its Quebec chapter but was manifested in other Canadian provinces (Cleverdon [1950] 1974, 62–5). In fact, it simply went against Catholic orthodoxy for women to participate in public life, in any and all political communities.

In short, the conjuncture of ideological, religious, and political forces explains why Quebec women obtained the rights to vote and to run for election to the provincial legislature much later than did Canadian women in other provinces. Since 2012, a monument beside the National Assembly building in Quebec City has honoured the efforts of four women (Thérèse Forget-Casgrain, Marie-Claire Kirkland-Casgrain, Marie Lacoste-Gérin-Lajoie, and Idola Saint-Jean) to gain Quebec women the rights associated with political citizenship: the rights to vote, to run for election, and to represent the population. This monument could be interpreted as the Quebec version of the *Women are Persons!* monument on Parliament Hill that memorializes the Persons case (see question 80).

BIBLIOGRAPHY

Casgrain, Thérèse. 1971. *Une femme chez les hommes.* Montreal: Editions du Jour. See, in particular, 73–143.

Cleverdon, Catherine L. (1950) 1974. *The Start of Liberation: The Woman Suffrage Movement in Canada.* Toronto: University of Toronto Press. See, in particular, 214–64.

Cohen, Yolande. 1997. "Suffrage féminin et démocratie au Canada." In *Encyclopédie politique et historique des femmes,* edited by Christine Fauré, 535–50. Paris: PUF.

Lamoureux, Diane and Jacinthe Michaud. 1988. "Les parlementaires canadiens et le suffrage féminin: un aperçu des débats." *Canadian Journal of Political Science* 21 (2): 319–29.

Trifiro, Luigi. 1978. "Une intervention à Rome dans la lutte pour le suffrage féminin au Québec (1922)." *Revue d'histoire de l'Amérique française* 32 (1): 3–18.

Trofimenkoff, Susan Mann. 1977. "Henri Bourassa et la question des femmes." In *Les femmes dans la société québécoise. Aspects historiques,* edited by Marie Lavigne and Yolande Pinard, 109–24. Montreal: Boréal.

80 What is the Persons case?

The term refers to the fight led by five Albertan women during the 1920s, especially late in the decade, to get women appointed to the Senate. Sharpe and McMahon (2007, 60–5) situate the trigger for the Persons case at the time that Emily Murphy, an Albertan suffragist, was appointed the position of police magistrate to sit on the newly founded Woman's Court in Edmonton. The appointment occurred in June 1916, only a few months after Albertan women had gained the right to vote in provincial elections, buttressing the thesis that the Prairie provinces were in the lead with regard to women's rights (see question 78). However, when a defence attorney took umbrage at a ruling made by Murphy, he argued that she was not a person under the terms of the British North America Act and therefore simply could not be a judge. Murphy later recalled, "On my initial appearance as a Police Magistrate in and for Alberta … my jurisdiction was sharply challenged by counsel for the defence … It was then argued in almost every case upon which I sat that women were not eligible to hold this office" (quoted in Sharpe and McMahon 2007, 60). The same doubt compromised the career of her colleague Alice Jamieson, magistrate at the Woman's Court in Calgary, and in June 1917 her competence to perform her job was challenged because of her sex. The case went to the Alberta Supreme Court Appellate Division, where, in the Cyr ruling, a progressive judge, Charles Allan Stuart, stated, "In this province and at this time in our presently existing conditions there is at common law no legal disqualification for holding public office in the government of the country arising from any distinction of sex" (quoted in Sharpe and McMahon 2007, 64). Although the question was settled for Alberta, it was not necessarily settled elsewhere.

In 1919, the Federated Women's Institutes of Canada, then led by Judge Murphy, adopted a resolution requesting that Prime Minister Borden appoint a woman to the Senate. A number of other women's groups adopted similar resolutions. In 1921, the Montreal Women's Club asked Prime Minister Meighen to appoint Judge Murphy to the Senate when a seat opened up. Although Meighen refused, during the 1921 election campaign he committed to striving to secure the admission of women to the Senate if he was reelected. His successor, William Lyon Mackenzie King, was subjected to similar pressures, as Judge Murphy directly proposed that he appoint her (Cleverdon [1950] 1974, 144; Sharpe and McMahon 2007, 88–96, 189). King proved to be open to the idea of women's admission to the Senate; he stated that he was prepared, if necessary, to seek an amendment to the British North America Act for that purpose, although his many equivocations threw legitimate doubt on his real determination to act in this area (Sharpe and McMahon 2007, 88–96).

It seems, in any case, that these good intentions were just a smokescreen for the indifference and inaction of the political class: by 1927 nothing had yet been done to make it possible for women to be appointed to the Senate. After years of political lobbying, Judge Murphy decided to move the battle to the courts. The Supreme Court Act authorized the Governor General in Council (that is, the Cabinet) to submit to the Supreme Court of Canada questions of law or of fact concerning interpretation of the Constitution or the constitutionality or interpretation of all federal and provincial statutes (Sharpe and McMahon 2007, 105–6). Following the advice of her brother, Justice William Ferguson, Murphy attempted to convince the federal government to submit to the Supreme Court of Canada the question of women's eligibility to sit in the Senate. With the support of Nellie Mc-Clung (1873–1951, author and journalist, suffragist and activist in the temperance movement, representative in the Legislative Assembly of Alberta from 1921 to 1925), Irene Parlby (1868–1965, suffragist, representative in the Legislative Assembly of Alberta and minister from 1921 to 1935), Louise McKinney (1868–1931, also an activist in the temperance movement, representative in the Legislative Assembly of Alberta from 1917 to 1921) and Henrietta Muir Edwards (1849–1931, jurist and suffragist, founder in Montreal in 1875 of what became the Young Women's Christian Association and convenor of laws of the National Council of Women of Canada), Murphy submitted, via the federal Cabinet, the following request for interpretation: "Does the word 'Persons' in section 24 of the *British North America Act, 1867*, include female persons?" (Sharpe and McMahon 2007, 115). Section 24 provides, "The Governor General shall from Time to Time, in the Queen's Name, by Instrument under the Great Seal of Canada, summon qualified Persons to the Senate." This ambiguity was not at all exceptional: it had made it possible for certain women in Lower Canada to vote from 1791 to 1849, because the word "person" used in the Constitutional Act (1791) did not deliberately exclude them (see question 77). Interestingly, only two provinces manifested interest in the question: Alberta supported the appointment of women to the Senate and Quebec opposed it – a position it had to take in order to avoid having women become legislative councillors even though they could not be provincial representatives or even voters. Indeed, section 73 of the British North America Act, 1867, provided, "The Qualifications of the Legislative Councillors of Quebec shall be the same as those of the Senators for Quebec." As Sharpe and McMahon (2007, 119) spelled it out, "If Quebec wanted to keep women out of its provincial upper house, it also had to make sure women were not allowed into the Senate in Ottawa."

One year later, in April 1928, the verdict came in: "Understood to mean 'Are women eligible for appointment to the Senate of Canada,' the question is answered in the negative" (Reference re the Meaning of the Word 'Persons' in Section 24 of the British North America Act, [1928] S.C.R. 276 at 304). The five (male) justices of the Supreme Court of Canada opined, among other things, that the British North America Act had to be interpreted according to the intention of the 1867 legislature and that it had not been its intention to open the doors of the Senate to women or it would have said so explicitly. This formal and conservative interpretation of the British North America Act ignored the very convincing argument by those who supported the appointment of women to the Senate. The Interpretation Act of 1850 (also known as Lord Brougham's Act), a statute of the British Parliament used to interpret Canadian statutes, provided that the male gender designated women and men, unless otherwise specified (Cleverdon [1950] 1974, 148; Sharpe and McMahon 2007, 66). In fact, this was the spirit in which sections of the British North America Act had been interpreted in the past, including section 11, concerning the appointment of "persons" to the Queen's Privy Council for Canada, and sections 41 and 84, concerning "persons" authorized to vote and be elected in legislative elections, which had had the consequence that women had voted in elections and some had been elected and even served as ministers (Mary Ellen Smith in British Columbia and Irene Parlby in Alberta, see question 86). So, why did the word "person" in section 24 of the British North America Act have to be interpreted restrictively – that is, be limited to men? For that matter, was it not a basic principle of interpretation of laws that multiple occurrences of a word in a single law should be understood uniformly (Sharpe and McMahon 2007, 66, 120)?

At the time, opinions issued by the Supreme Court in response to a reference could be appealed to the Judicial Committee of the British Privy

Council, which was the highest constitutional court. An appeal of the Supreme Court decision was therefore filed with the Committee, which, in October 1929, reversed the negative verdict of the Supreme Court: "Their Lordships are of opinion that the word 'persons' in sec. 24 does include women, and that women are eligible to be summoned to and become members of the Senate of Canada" (*Edwards v. Attorney General for Canada*, [1930] A.C. 124 at 127). Noting that "the exclusion of women from all public offices is a relic of days more barbarous than ours" (*Edwards v. Attorney General for Canada*, [1930] A.C. 124 at 128), the justices, under the leadership of the progressive Lord Chancellor John Sankey, concluded that the nature of the word "persons" used in section 24 of the British North America Act was inclusive: "Their Lordships have come to the conclusion that the word 'persons' in s. 24 includes members of both the male and female sex, and that, therefore, the question propounded by the Governor General should be answered in the affirmative, and that women are eligible to be summoned to and become members of the Senate of Canada" (*Edwards v. Attorney General for Canada*, [1930] A.C. 124 at 143).

Other than treating their colleagues on the Supreme Court of Canada with barely disguised disdain and continuing the longstanding tensions between the British and Canadian legal communities (Sharpe and McMahon 2007, 142–53), their Lordships were stating a fundamental principle, the living tree approach to constitutional interpretation: "The British North America Act planted in Canada a living tree capable of growth and expansion within its natural limits" (*Edwards v. Attorney General for Canada*, [1930] A.C. 124 at 136). By using an approach of evolving interpretation, it was possible to adapt old texts to new societal contexts. It no doubt had not been the intention of the legislature in 1867 for women to sit in the Senate, but times change. Today the living tree approach is still used in Canada, particularly with regard to interpretation of the Canadian Charter of Rights and Freedoms – for example, the Supreme Court forcefully invoked the doctrine in its reference regarding same-sex marriage in 2004. Sharpe and McMahon (2007, 206) even went so far as to conclude, "The legacy of the *Persons* case – the ideal of universal personhood and the living tree approach to constitutional interpretation – embodies the very purpose of the *Charter of Rights and Freedoms*."

Research remains to be conducted on the more general context surrounding this decision. The preceding year, in 1928, the British legislature had levelled at twenty-one years the age required for women and men to vote (since 1918, women had had to be thirty years old to vote, whereas men could vote at age twenty-one). Above all, with the publication of Radclyffe Hall's book *The Well of Loneliness*, in 1928, not only was "the lesbian" created (just as Oscar Wilde's trial in the late nineteenth century had created the "homosexual") but public debates about gender conventions were expanded (Doan 2001). It is possible that the decision to open the doors of the Canadian Senate to women fell within the broader dynamic of decompartmentalization of gender roles.

Despite her sustained efforts and barely hidden ambitions, Emily Murphy was not appointed to the Senate. The first female Canadian senator was Cairine Reay Mackay Wilson, appointed in February 1930 by Prime Minister King.

The versos of Canadian fifty-dollar notes in the *Canadian Journey* series (issued in 2004) portrayed the Famous Five in the background (with Quebec suffragist Thérèse Casgrain in a medallion portrait). The fifty-dollar notes in the *Frontiers* series (2012) turned the page on these women's struggles, as Stephen Harper's Conservative government decided to replace the icons of feminism with the icebreaker MGCC *Amundsen*. Nevertheless, the official memory of the Persons case is not yet completely erased: aside from a page in the new biometric Canadian passport portraying Nellie McClung (the only woman represented in a passport adorned with images evoking Canadian history and identity), a magnificent bronze installed on Parliament Hill in Ottawa recalls Canadian women's struggle for full citizenship.

BIBLIOGRAPHY

Cleverdon, Catherine L. (1950) 1974. *The Start of Liberation: The Woman Suffrage Movement in Canada*. Toronto: University of Toronto Press. See, in particular, 141–55.

Doan, Laura. 2001. *Fashioning Sapphism: The Origins of a Modern English Lesbian Culture*. New York: Columbia University Press.

Edwards v. Attorney General for Canada, (1930) A.C. 124.

Iacovetta, Franca. 1989. "'A Respectable Feminist': The Political Career of Senator Cairine Wilson, 1921–1962." In *Beyond the Vote: Canadian Women and Politics*, edited by Linda Kealey and Joan Sangster, 63–85. Toronto: University of Toronto Press.

Library and Archives Canada, "Famous Five," accessed 5 August 2017, http://epe.lac-bac.gc.ca/100/206/301/lac-bac/famous_five-ef/www.lac-bac.gc.ca/famous5/index-e.html.

Reference re Same-Sex Marriage (2004) 3 S.C.R. 698.

Reference re the Meaning of the Word 'Persons' in Section 24 of the British North America Act, (1928) S.C.R. 276.

Sharpe, Robert J. and Patricia I. McMahon. 2007. *The Persons Case: The Origins and Legacy of the Fight for Legal Personhood*. Toronto: University of Toronto Press.

81 How do women position themselves in terms of electoral options and political debates?

In Canada, as elsewhere in the world, both today and in the past, there is no "women's vote," with women forming an electoral and political bloc (see question 12). Nevertheless, a gender gap exists within the Canadian electorate (see questions 2 and 10); in the view of Gidengil and her colleagues (2003, 2013), gender generates cleavages that analyses of Canadian politics cannot ignore. For instance, with regard to electoral choices, women and men tend to choose different parties: since the 1993 elections, women have manifested a preference for the left (identified notably with the New Democratic Party) and men for the right (identified with the Conservative Party of Canada). In the 2015 election, this cleavage was still evident; the preelection polls showed that both women and men supported the New Democratic Party and the Liberal Party of Canada, but a gap persisted in support for the Conservative Party (McInturff 2015). This modern expression of the gender gap, in which women vote further to the left than do men, is opposite to the traditional version, in which women leaned right and men left (Erickson and O'Neill 2002). For Quebec, Gidengil and Harell (2013) have also brought to light a new gender gap that apparently was manifested for the first time during the 2012 provincial election: women were significantly more inclined than were men to vote for the Parti Québécois; men preferred the Coalition Avenir Québec. In short, the electoral preferences of Canadian women (and Canadian men) fluctuate over time and, especially, with variables such as age, education and income, civil status, place of residence (large city, town, or rural area), religion, and sexual preference (a variable analyzed more recently; Perrella et al. 2012).

Canadian women and men also diverge when it comes to support for various social issues. For instance, women are more inclined than are men to support the welfare state and its wealth-redistribution policies, whereas they are less enthusiastic about neoliberal discourse regarding taxation and free enterprise, deployment of military forces, and recourse to draconian measures to contain crime and violence. More than men, women support arms and gun control, the opening of civil marriage to lesbian and gay couples, and feminism and its struggles. And yet, they consider themselves to understand politics less than do men (Gidengil et al. 2008).

Gidengil and her colleagues (2003) distinguish two main types of explanations for the fact that Canadian women – like women in other Western countries – have opinions further to the left. In structural and situational explanations, the sources of women's and men's different political positions are seen to be their different societal experiences. For example, women are said to be further to the left because, more than men, their quality of life depends on state redistribution policies; in addition, more of them are employed in sectors that benefit from these policies. Sociopsychological explanations dwell more on the socialization process and the gender regime: women are seen as less individualistic and more turned toward others than are men. Although neither of these explanations seems to be fully satisfactory in elucidating the distinct electoral and political positions of Canadian women and men, each no doubt gives a partial explanation.

BIBLIOGRAPHY

Erickson, Lynda and Brenda O'Neill. 2002. "The Gender Gap and the Changing Woman Voter in Canada." *International Political Science Review* 23 (4): 373–92.

Gidengil, Elisabeth, André Blais, Richard Nadeau, and Neil Nevitte. 2003. "Women to the Left? Gender Differences in Political Beliefs and Policy Preferences." In *Women and Electoral Politics in Canada*, edited by Manon Tremblay and Linda Trimble, 140–59. Don Mills: Oxford University Press.

Gidengil, Elisabeth, Joanna Everitt, André Blais, Patrick Fournier, and Neil Nevitte. 2013. "Explaining the Modern Gender Gap." In *Mind the Gaps: Canadian Perspectives on Gender and Politics*, edited by Roberta Lexier and Tamara A. Small, 48–63. Halifax: Fernwood.

Gidengil, Elisabeth and Allison Harell. 2013. "L'appui des Québécoises aux partis politiques provinciaux." In *Les Québécois aux urnes: les partis, les médias et les citoyens en campagne*, edited by Éric Bélanger, Frédérick Bastien, and François Gélineau, 209–22. Quebec City: Presses de l'Université Laval.

Gidengil, Elisabeth, Janine Giles, and Melanee Thomas. 2008. "The Gender Gap in Self-Perceived Understanding of Politics in Canada and the United States." *Politics & Gender* 4 (4): 535–61.

Gidengil, Elisabeth, Neil Nevitte, André Blais, Joanna Everitt, and Patrick Fournier. 2012. *Dominance and Decline: Making Sense of Recent Canadian Elections*. Toronto: University of Toronto Press. See, in particular, 22–3, 30–2.

McInturff, Kate. 2015. "Filling In the Blanks: What Do the Polls Say about Women Voters?" *Behind the Numbers we did the Math*, accessed 8 July 2016, http://behindthenumbers.ca/2015/09/18/filling-in-the-blanks-what-do-the-polls-say-about-women-voters/.

Perrella, Andrea M.L., Steven D. Brown, and Barry J. Kay. 2012. "Voting Behaviour among the Gay, Lesbian, Bisexual and Transgendered Electorate." *Canadian Journal of Political Science* 45 (1): 89–117.

82 Do Indigenous and non-Indigenous women in Canada vote similarly?

Harell and Panagos (2013), who have published one of the few scholarly studies on the subject in Canada, put forth two hypotheses to shed some light on this issue. The first is the hypothesis of a gender gap (see questions 2, 10, and 81): because the gender regime shapes women and men to diverge, or even to oppose each other, according to a hierarchical order, Indigenous women and men (like their non-Indigenous counterparts) adopt divergent electoral behaviours. The second hypothesis is that Indigenous women and men share a history and an identity similarly modelled by colonialism that leads them to vote similarly and distinguishes their electoral behaviours from those of non-Indigenous women and men. However, far from ignoring the gender regime, colonialism transposed it, modelling Indigenous women and men in distinct ways and inscribing them within unequal relationships; in other words, colonialism (re)produced the non-Indigenous gender regime, imposing upon Indigenous women and men genders foreign to their culture – non-Indigenous gender roles (Cannon 1998).

Although neither the gender gap hypothesis nor the colonialism hypothesis can entirely explain the electoral behaviour of Indigenous women, each contributes – the second more than the first, according to Harell and Panagos (2013). Indigenous women and men differ in various ways. For example, in proportion, more Indigenous women than Indigenous men vote for the New Democratic Party (NDP). Women's preference for the NDP does not change whether they are Indigenous or non-Indigenous, buttressing the idea that the gender regime is a structural variable for electoral behaviour, beyond influences such as ethnocultural community, education, region, language spoken, and sexual preference. That being said, Harell and Panagos (2013) maintain that Indigenous women and men vote similarly more often than not, feeding the colonialism hypothesis. First, although more than 80 per cent of the non-Indigenous population say that they vote in federal and provincial elections, only 48 per cent of Indigenous women and men say that they do. This abstention could be interpreted as a form of resistance to a regime that, both in the past and today, orchestrates colonialist policies responsible for their confinement to reserves. Second, although more Indigenous women than men vote for the NDP, Indigenous people on the whole support the party to a much greater extent than do non-Indigenous Canadians. The NDP may attract votes from Indigenous people because it promotes a higher level of wealth redistribution and is more open to First Nations demands. That being said, in coming years we will have to see if the Indigenous preference for the NDP changes in response to the new willingness of the Liberal Party of Canada, under the leadership of Justin Trudeau, to listen to First Nations claims.

To sum up, the gender gap hypothesis reminds us that gender is a basic variable that cannot be ignored or dismissed in analyses of electoral behaviour. It is not a given, however, that women form a political community on the basis of their gender (see questions 11, 12, 17, and 60). Indeed, the colonialism hypothesis reminds us of the appropriateness of an intersectional approach to analyzing women's electoral (and, more generally, political) behaviours. Women's experiences are modelled by their gender, of course, but in combination with a myriad of other identity markers that are sources of both oppression and privilege.

BIBLIOGRAPHY

Cannon, Martin. 1998. "The Regulation of First Nations Sexuality." *Canadian Journal of Native Studies* 18 (1): 1–18.

Groundwork for Change, accessed 29 June 2016, http://www.groundworkforchange. org/.

Hancock, Ange-Marie. 2014. "Intersectional Representation or Representing Intersectionality? Reshaping Empirical Analysis of Intersectionality." In *Representation: The Case of Women*, edited by Maria C. Escobar-Lemmon and Michelle M. Taylor-Robinson, 41–57. New York: Oxford University Press.

Harell, Allison and Dimitrios Panagos. 2013. "Locating the Aboriginal Gender Gap: The Political Attitudes and Participation of Aboriginal Women in Canada." *Politics & Gender* 9 (4): 414–38.

Indigenous Studies Portal, accessed 28 June 2016, http://iportal.usask.ca/.

Native Women's Association of Canada, accessed 28 June 2016, https://nwac.ca/.

Voyageur, Cora. 2011. "Out in the Open: Elected Female Leadership in Canada's First Nations Community." *Canadian Review of Sociology* 48 (1): 67–85.

83 Where do women fit in Canada's political parties?

The position – and especially, the proportion – of women in political parties is a well-guarded secret; when numbers are revealed, their reliability is suspect. One reason is that no political party wants to expose to the public that it has not satisfied certain target social groups or, worse, that it is unpopular among certain segments of the electorate. This is even truer in majority voting systems such as the one used in Canada, in which parties promote programs that seek to appeal to broad segments of society, whereas in proportional voting systems parties may be more specialized without fearing that they will be excluded from parliamentary representation (see question 21).

In one of the first books published on women in federal political parties in English Canada, Bashevkin (1985) concludes that Putnam's (1976, 33) law of increasing disproportion, formulated a number of years before, is well founded: the higher a political position, the fewer the women found in it. Although Bashevkin's book is about the situation in the early 1980s, the basis for the law of increasing disproportion is still valid today, although there are indications that its heuristic potential has subsided somewhat.

As proof, we may simply look at a few of the most important roles within parties: leader, minister, parliamentarian, and candidate. According to Bashevkin (1985, 56, 58), in the early 1980s, women occupied 0 per cent and about 4 per cent, 6 per cent, and 8 per cent, respectively, of these roles. However, since the 1990s, a number of women have been premier or prime minister (for the international scene, see question 68): Rita Johnston (1991, premier of British Columbia), Nellie Cournoyea (1991–95, premier of the Northwest Territories), Kim Campbell (1993, prime minister of Canada), Catherine Callbeck (1993–96, premier of Prince Edward Island), Pat Duncan (2000–02, premier of the Yukon), Eva Aariak (2008–13, premier of Nunavut), Kathy Dunderdale (2010–14, premier of Newfoundland and Labrador), Alison Redford (2011–14, premier of Alberta), Christy Clark (2011–17, premier of British Columbia), Pauline Marois (2012–14, premier of Quebec), Kathleen Wynne (2013–18, premier of Ontario), and Rachel Notley (since 2014, premier of Alberta). Following the 2015 federal election, the proportion of women in the cabinet was almost double that in the House of Commons: 50 per cent versus 26 per cent. Moreover, as table 11 (see question 89) shows, in December 2016, a clear majority of provinces and territories had a higher proportion of women in their cabinets than in their legislative assemblies. Whereas the law of increasing disproportion predicts lower proportions of women among ministers than among elected representatives, Tremblay and Andrews (2010) have reported the inverse: 286 women were appointed ministers within a federal or provincial cabinet in Canada between March 1921 and December 2007; far from being absent, they were proportionally more numerous in cabinets on the whole than within parliaments as a whole, and even than within the caucus of the party forming the government – the recruitment pool for a ministerial career. Finally, in the 2015 federal election, there were 29.9 per cent (536/1,792) female candidates – much higher than the 8 per cent observed by Bashevkin in the early 1980s.

So, essentially, although the law of increasing disproportion may still be useful in analyzing the presence of women in political parties in Canada, it no longer applies as broadly.

BIBLIOGRAPHY

Bashevkin, Sylvia B. 1985. *Toeing the Lines: Women and Party Politics in English-Canada.* Toronto: University of Toronto Press. See, in particular, 65–92.

Elections Canada, "Report on the 42nd General Election of October 19, 2015," accessed 24 June 2016, http://www.elections.ca/content.aspx?section=res&dir=rep/off/sta_2015&document=p2&lang=e.

Putnam, Robert D. 1976. *The Comparative Study of Political Elites.* Englewood Cliffs, NJ: Prentice-Hall.

Tremblay, Manon with Sarah Andrews. 2010. "Les femmes nommées ministres au Canada pendant la période 1921–2007: la loi de la disparité progressive est-elle dépassée?" *Recherches féministes* 23 (1): 143–63.

84 Which women have led a political party represented in the House of Commons or a provincial or territorial legislative assembly?

Four women have led a political party represented in the House of Commons: Audrey McLaughlin (New Democratic Party, from 1989 to 1995), Alexa McDonough (New Democratic Party, from 1995 to 2003), Kim Campbell (Progressive Conservative Party, from June to December 1993), and Elizabeth May (Green Party, since 2006). During Campbell's term at the head of the Progressive Conservative party, she was also prime minister of Canada.

Table 8 lists the women who have led a "major" provincial or territorial party. Although it seems self-evident, the notion of "major" is somewhat subjective. Of course, it refers to the great partisan traditions in Canada: the conservative, liberal, nationalist, and social-democratic parties. However, these parties have variable electoral bases and legislative representation depending on the province or territory and the conjuncture. For example, the Progressive Conservative Party is firmly rooted in Alberta but the Liberal Party has held no great appeal to the electorate in that province, and it is similar for the New Democratic Party in Quebec in provincial elections. Also, although she has been leader of the Communist Party of Alberta since 1992 and is regularly a candidate in provincial elections, Naomi Rankin does not appear in the table because her political party does not have a solid electoral base. On the other hand, some parties whose name does not include the term "conservative, "liberal," "nationalist," or "social democratic" are firmly situated within these ideological currents and eminently significant to the politics of a province or territory; this is the case for the Coalition Avenir Québec, the Parti Québécois, and Québec solidaire; the Saskatchewan Party; the Wildrose Alliance in Alberta; and the Yukon Party. In short, the list presented in table 8 is not exhaustive, and its composition involves a certain amount of analytic subjectivity. It also excludes interim mandates.

Table 8

Female leaders of a major political party represented in a provincial or territorial legislative assembly, Canada, 1978–2016

Province or Territory	Name	Party	Period of time
Alberta	Pam Barrett	New Democrats	1996–2000
Alberta	Nancy MacBeth	Liberal	1998–2001
Alberta	Rachel Notley*	New Democrats	2014 to present
Alberta	Alison Redford*	Progressive Conservative	2012–14
Alberta	Danielle Smith	Wildrose Alliance	2009–14
British Columbia	Christy Clark*	Liberal	2011–17
British Columbia	Carole James	New Democrats	2003–11
British Columbia	Rita Johnston*	Social Credit	1991–92
British Columbia	Grace McCarthy	Social Credit	1993–94
British Columbia	Shirley McLoughlin	Liberal	1981–84
Manitoba	Rana Bokhari	Liberal	2013–16
Manitoba	Sharon Carstairs	Liberal	1984–93
Manitoba	Ginny Hasselfield	Liberal	1996–98
Manitoba	Judy Klassen	Liberal	2016–17
New Brunswick	Barbara Baird-Filliper	Progressive Conservative	1989–91
New Brunswick	Allison Brewer	New Democrats	2005–06
New Brunswick	Elizabeth Weir	New Democrats	1988–2005
Newfoundland and Labrador	Kathy Dunderdale*	Progressive Conservative	2010–14
Newfoundland and Labrador	Yvonne Jones	Liberal	2007–11
Newfoundland and Labrador	Lorraine Michael	New Democrats	2006–15
Newfoundland and Labrador	Lynn Verge	Progressive Conservative	1995–96
Nova Scotia	Helen MacDonald	New Democrats	2000–01
Nova Scotia	Alexa McDonough	New Democrats	1981–94
Ontario	Andrea Horwath	New Democrats	2009 to present
Ontario	Lyn McLeod	Liberal	1992–96
Ontario	Kathleen Wynne*	Liberal	2013–18
Prince Edward Island	Catherine Callbeck*	Liberal	1993–96
Prince Edward Island	Olive Crane	Progressive Conservative	2010–13

Table 8

Continued

Province or Territory	Name	Party	Period of time
Prince Edward Island	Pat Mella	Progressive Conservative	1990–96
Quebec	Françoise David**	Québec solidaire	2007–17
Quebec	Manon Massé	Québec solidaire	2017 to present
Quebec	Pauline Marois*	Parti québécois	2007–14
Saskatchewan	Lynda Haverstock	Liberal	1989–95
Yukon	Pat Duncan*	Liberal	1998–2005
Yukon	Elizabeth Hanson	New Democrats	2009 to present
Yukon	Hilda Watson	Progressive Conservative	1978–79

Source: Trimble, Arscott, and Tremblay (2013, 37, 56, 116, 193, 234); "Female Canadian political party leaders,"(accessed 24 June 2016, https://en.wikipedia.org/wiki/Category:Female_Canadian_political_party_leaders.
* Was also premier.
** Québec solidaire does not have a leader; instead it has "spokespersons."

What can we learn from this table? First, women have been leaders of a significant party on the provincial political scene in every province. Nunavut and the Northwest Territories (which have had female premiers; see question 93) are absent from this table simply because the rules of the political game in those territories exclude parties (this is not true for the Yukon). Second, a number of women have led parties on the right-hand side of their province's political spectrum: Redford and Smith in Alberta; Clark, Johnson, and McCarthy in British Columbia; Baird-Filliper in New Brunswick; Dunderdale and Verge in Newfoundland and Labrador; Crane and Mella in Prince Edward Island; and Watson in the Yukon. This mitigates the idea that right-wing parties are hostile toward women and vice-versa. Third, a majority of the thirty-five leaders identified remained at the head of their political parties for the length of one parliamentary term (four years); only fourteen led their party for five years or more. Deeper analysis would be necessary before drawing conclusions, but, at first glance, women seem to spend a relatively brief time leading their parties. Could it be, as suggested by Bashevkin (2009) and O'Brien (2015), that women accede to leadership when their parties are less competitive on the political chessboard? Yet, and fourth, nine female party leaders out of thirty-five have been premiers, a rate of access of 25.7 per cent. There are two ways to look at this figure. One is that this percentage is not very different from the average feminization rate of the House of Commons and the provincial and territorial legislative assemblies between 2011 and 2016, which is 27.3 per cent (see question 89). The other is that of the just under 300 premiers and prime ministers that Canada has had since Confederation, only twelve (adding Eva Aariak in Nunavut, Kim Campbell in the federal government, and Nellie Cournoyea of the Northwest Territories to the nine premiers mentioned above) were women, for a feminization rate of less than 4 per cent (12/293). In other words, female premiers and prime ministers are pretty rare.

BIBLIOGRAPHY

Bashevkin, Sylvia. 2009. "'Stage' versus 'Actor' Barriers to Women's Federal Party Leadership." In *Opening Doors Wider: Women's Political Engagement in Canada*, edited by Sylvia Bashevkin, 108–26. Vancouver: UBC Press.

Female Canadian political party leaders, accessed 24 June 2016, https://en.wikipedia.org/wiki/Category:Female_Canadian_political_party_leaders.

O'Brien, Diana Z. 2015. "Rising to the Top: Gender, Political Performance, and Party Leadership in Parliamentary Democracies." *American Journal of Political Science* 59 (4): 1022–39.

Trimble, Linda, Jane Arscott, and Manon Tremblay, eds. 2013. *Stalled: The Representation of Women in Canadian Governments*. Vancouver: UBC Press.

85 Do women run in ridings that are lost in advance?

The results of research on this question are a bit contradictory. On the one hand, analyses conducted by Pelletier and Tremblay (1992) in Quebec reveal that in general, women do not run in ridings that are lost in advance. On the other hand, the findings of Thomas and Bodet (2013) suggest that female candidates are sometimes sacrificial lambs. The conclusions of these studies may diverge due to their different methodologies, including how the competitiveness of the election is measured, and the different temporal and spatial contexts. Yet, in some respects, these conclusions correspond.

Over the seven general elections that took place in Quebec between 1976 and 2003, there were 317 female Liberal and Parti Québécois candidates (one woman was a candidate several times) and 1,344 male candidates. In general, the success rate for women was 45 per cent and that for men was 51 per cent. The success rates varied depending on the nature of the candidacy. For instance, 84 per cent of incumbent female representatives were reelected, compared to 75 per cent of incumbent male representatives; 59 per cent of women who ran in a riding freed up by the departure of a representative of their own party won their riding, as opposed to 54 per cent of men in the same position. However, only 17 per cent of female candidates running against an incumbent representative were elected, compared to 27 per cent of male candidates in that position. In short, it seems that women seeking to be elected to the National Assembly for the first time by winning against an incumbent representative were less successful than their male counterparts in the same unfortunate position and than were other female candidates.

To increase feminization in legislative assemblies in Canada, the proportion of female representatives must be maintained, of course, but new faces must also be brought in. Neophyte female candidates have the best chances of election if they run in a riding with an outgoing male representative (it must be a man, as a woman who replaces a woman only keeps the feminization rate constant) of their party, whose party affiliation they retain – known as an inherited candidacy. Yet, not all inherited candidacies present equal potential for victory; this potential is modulated by a number of factors, including the margin of victory in the preceding election. In comparison to this aspect, and looking once again at Quebec, a subgroup of female inheriting candidates were effectively disadvantaged during the seven general elections between 1976 and 2003: those who lost ran in ridings that their party had won in the previous election by an average margin of 7 per cent (as opposed to a margin of 15 per cent for male inheriting candidates who lost). It is very different for winning female inheriting candidates: these women ran in ridings that their party had won in the previous election by an average margin of 22 per cent (compared to a margin of 25 per cent for male candidates). In short, in all of the electoral battles analyzed, defeated inheriting candidates were the only group in which the gap between women and men was statistically significant – specifically, to the disadvantage of women.

Considering that inherited candidacies offer the best chance of winning a first mandate, and considering the regrettable underrepresentation of women in politics in Canada, the parties should make it a priority to reserve these promising ridings for women. In the 2007 Quebec general election, the Liberal Party and the Parti Québécois used divergent strategies: of the eight ridings left vacant by a retiring Liberal MNA, half had women candidates, whereas no female Parti Québécois candidate inherited any of the seven ridings freed up by the departure of a representative from that party. The defeat of female PQ candidates was simply a repetition of the 1981 scenario: fewer women than men running in ridings with good potential in terms of electoral victory (Pelletier and Tremblay 1992).

In the view of Thomas and Bodet (2013), women's disadvantage is less haphazard and more generalized. Analyzing the results of federal elections from 2004 to 2011, they write, "When we examine the relationship between candidate gender and district competitiveness … we find evidence to support the sacrificial lamb hypothesis … A majority (62%) of women but only a plurality (47%) of men run in another party's stronghold. Men are more likely than women to be candidates in competitive and safe seats" (160) – the Bloc Québécois being an exception to this trend. When local riding associations choose who will run for the party, women seem to find it difficult to convince these elites to select them (see question 18). Cheng and Tavits (2011) also observed that local executives are reluctant to select a woman as a candidate, with few exceptions: local riding associations led by a woman are more likely to select a female candidate.

To sum up, studies indicate that there is still discrimination against women who wish to run for political office, notably that they face electoral conditions less favourable than those faced by men. It is not possible to prove that the parties *systematically* confine women to ridings lost in advance but they certainly do not roll out the red carpet for them.

BIBLIOGRAPHY

Cheng, Christine and Margit Tavits. 2011. "Informal Influences in Selecting Female Political Candidates." *Political Research Quarterly* 64 (2): 460–71.

Pelletier, Réjean and Manon Tremblay. 1992. "Les femmes sont-elles candidates dans des circonscriptions perdues d'avance? De l'examen d'une croyance." *Revue canadienne de science politique* 25 (2): 249–67.

Thomas, Melanee and Marc André Bodet. 2013. "Sacrificial Lambs, Women Candidates, and District Competitiveness in Canada." *Electoral Studies* 32 (1): 153–66.

Tremblay, Manon. 2008. "Des femmes candidates dans des circonscriptions compétitives: le cas du Québec." *Revue suisse de science politique* 14 (4): 691–714.

86 Who were the "first" female candidates, representatives, and ministers in the federal, provincial, and territorial governments in Canada?

This question could be answered with a wide variety of "firsts," depending on the criteria used: region, race/ethnicity, language spoken, religion, sexual preference, and physical capacity, among others. I will therefore limit myself to three political roles: first female candidate, first female representative, and first female minister. I am aware that this approach favours women who are members of the majority and in a privileged position, while disadvantaging women belonging to minorities of all sorts for the contrary reason. The authors in the edited volume *Stalled: The Representation of Women in Canadian Governments* (Trimble, Arscott, and Tremblay 2013) present a fairly complete portrait of "female firsts" in Canadian politics in the light of a rich palette of identifiers.

Two observations emerge. The first is that there is a gap of almost three decades, on average, between the year women gained the right to run in elections and the year a first woman was appointed to a cabinet. In some cases, the gap is much smaller. In Nunavut, women were candidates in the first election held, in 1999, and a woman acceded to cabinet the same year; this is explained, however, by the fact that the election took place in the near past. In British Columbia, the progression took only three years; it took four in Alberta, ten in Quebec, and eleven in the Yukon. But in other cases it took much longer: sixty-five years in Nova Scotia and Saskatchewan, fifty-three in Ontario, and forty-six in Manitoba (despite the fact that it was the first province in which women won the right to vote in provincial elections; see question 77), thirty-five in New Brunswick, and twenty-one in Prince Edward Island. What is more, no stable model emerges. It is not possible to say that the progression from candidacy through election to appointment to cabinet took less time in the Prairie provinces (and British Columbia) because that part of the country was more advanced with regard to women's suffrage but

Table 9

The first female candidates, representatives, and ministers in federal, provincial, and territorial politics

Jurisdiction	First woman …	Name (Party)	Year
Alberta	to run for office	Louise McKinney (Non-Partisan League) Roberta MacAdams (Soldiers' Representative)	1917
	to be elected	Louise McKinney (Non-Partisan League) Roberta MacAdams (Soldiers' Representative)	1917
	appointed to cabinet	Irene Parlby (UFA)	1921
British Columbia	to run for office	Mary Ellen Smith (Ind.)	1918
	to be elected	Mary Ellen Smith, (Ind.)	1918
	appointed to cabinet	Mary Ellen Smith (Lib.)	1921
Federal	to run for office	Rose Mary Louise Henderson (Lab.) Elizabeth Bethune Kiely (Lib.) Agnes Macphail (Progressive) Harriet Dunlop Prenter (Lab.) Harriet S. Dick (Ind.; Winnipeg Centre)	1921
	to be elected	Agnes Macphail (Progressive)	1921
	appointed to cabinet	Ellen Fairclough (PC)	1957
Manitoba	to run for office	Harriet Dick (Ind.) Alice Holling (Ind.) A. Pritchard (Lab.) Edith Rogers (Lib.) Genevieve Lipsett Skinner (C)	1920
	to be elected	Edith Rogers (Lib.)	1920
	appointed to cabinet	Thelma Forbes (PC)	1966
New Brunswick	to run for office	Dr. Frances Fish (C)	1935
	to be elected	Brenda Robertson (PC)	1967
	appointed to cabinet	Brenda Robertson (PC)	1970

Table 9

Continued

Jurisdiction	First woman …	Name (Party)	Year
Newfoundland and Labrador	to run for office	Grace Sparkes (PC)	1949
	to be elected	Hazel McIsaac (Lib.)*	1975
	appointed to cabinet	Hazel Newhook (PC)	1979
Northwest Territories	to run for office	Lena Pederson	1967
	to be elected	Lena Pederson	1970
	appointed to cabinet	Nellie Cournoyea	1984
Nova Scotia	to run for office	Grace McLeod Rogers (C) Bertha A. Donaldson (Lab.)	1920
	to be elected	Gladys Porter (PC)	1960
	appointed to cabinet	Maxine Cochran (PC)	1985
Nunavut	to run for office	Eleven women (see question 96)	1999
	to be elected	Manitok Thompson	1999
	appointed to cabinet	Manitok Thompson	1999
Ontario	to run for office	Henrietta Bundy (Lib.) Justerna Sears (Ind.)	1919
	to be elected	Agnes Macphail (CCF) Rae Luckock (CCF)	1943
	appointed to cabinet	Margaret Birch (PC)	1972
Prince Edward Island	to run for office	Hilda Ramsay (CCF)	1951
	to be elected	Jean Canfield (Lib.)	1970
	appointed to cabinet	Jean Canfield (Lib.)	1972
Quebec	to run for office	Gisèle Bergeron (CCF) Marie-Thérèse Forget-Casgrain (CCF) Ange Paradis (Ind.) Jeannette Pratte-Walsh (OP)	1952
	to be elected	Marie-Claire Kirkland-Casgrain (Lib.)	1961
	appointed to cabinet	Marie-Claire Kirkland-Casgrain (Lib.)	1962
Saskatchewan	to run for office	Zoa Haight (Non-Partisan League)	1917
	to be elected	Sarah Ramsland (Lib.)	1919
	appointed to cabinet	Joan Duncan (PC)	1982
Senate	appointed	Cairine Reay Mackay Wilson	1930

Jurisdiction	First woman …	Name (Party)	Year
Yukon	to run for office	Jean Gordon	1967
	to be elected	Jean Gordon	1967
	appointed to cabinet	Meg McCall	1978

C: Conservative; CCF: Co-operative Commonwealth Federation; Ind.: Independent; Lab.: Labour; Lib.: Liberal; OP: Ouvrier Progressiste; PC: Progressive Conservative; UFA: United Farmers of Alberta.
* In 1929, before Newfoundland joined Canada, a woman was elected to the House of Assembly – Lady Helena E. Squires. I want to thank Käthe Roth for drawing my attention to this fact.
Source: Trimble, Arscott, and Tremblay (2013, 37, 56, 76, 94, 116, 136, 155, 174, 193, 215, 234, 254, 274).

more time in the "conservative" Maritime provinces (see question 78). In fact, in both the Prairies and the Maritimes, the process took time – some thirty years. Although the Prairie provinces led the race to women's suffrage (see question 78), when it came to soliciting female candidates and occupying cabinet positions Alberta (and British Columbia) kept its nose in front, but Manitoba and, especially, Saskatchewan fell behind. The hostility of Quebec political elites to seeing women voting in provincial elections is well known (see question 79), but it took only a little more than a decade from the first female candidate to the first woman in the cabinet – in comparison to the six and a half decades in Nova Scotia and Saskatchewan.

The second observation is that on average, the gap between selection of the first female candidate and election of the first female representative is shorter than the time between election of the first female representative and appointment of the first female minister: eleven years versus seventeen. This is interesting because election concerns the population whereas appointment is the prerogative of the prime minister or premier (see questions 18 and 66). Is it possible that leaders are less enthusiastic about having women participate in governance than are the people about being represented by them?

BIBLIOGRAPHY

Trimble, Linda, Jane Arscott, and Manon Tremblay, eds. 2013. *Stalled: The Representation of Women in Canadian Governments*. Vancouver: UBC Press.

87 How has women's representation in the House of Commons and in provincial and territorial legislative assemblies changed since the 1980s?

In general, women's presence in provincial and territorial legislative assemblies grew from the early 1980s to 2016. However, from time to time, this advance has been halted or even rolled back. It is this discontinuous evolution about which Trimble, Tremblay, and Arscott (2013) wrote in the conclusion to their book *Stalled: The Representation of Women in Canadian Governments*. The authors devised three models to describe the evolution of the proportion of women in the House of Commons and in the provincial and territorial legislative assemblies.

The first model is "overall progression": over the long term, there is a relatively constant and sustained increase in the proportion of female representatives. In other words, each election results in an influx of a greater number of female representatives than there were when the election was called. However, this general trajectory does not mean that one election will not reverse the general trend; it is the exception that makes the rule. During the period from 1980 to 2012, four provinces (British Columbia, Manitoba, Nova Scotia, and Ontario), the Yukon, and the House of Commons followed this model. The results of elections that occurred since 2013 have maintained the trend, except in the House of Commons and Manitoba. Since 2011, Manitoba seems to have been on a downward slide: the proportion of female representatives dropped from 31.6 per cent in 2007 to 28.1 per cent in 2011 and to 22.8 per cent in 2016. The proportion of federal representatives grew from 2008 (22.4 per cent) to 2011 (24.7 per cent), essentially due to the performance of the New Democratic Party in Quebec, but only inched upward following the 2015 election (26.0 per cent). It could also be said that the federal legislature follows the "plateau" model. Since the mid-1990s, the proportion of women in the House of Commons has remained essentially stagnant: it stood at 21 per cent from 1997 to 2008, after which it gained one percentage point, to 22 per cent. Following a modest advance of 2.3 per cent from 2008 to 2011, feminization of the House of Commons grew by only 1.3 per cent in 2015. This does not give great hope for the future. A reform of the voting system may change the game – although past proposals have not always sought to respond to the problem of underrepresentation of women in politics (see question 96).

The second model is "lost peak": a peak is reached in the proportion of female representatives, followed by a clear drop. For the period from 1980 to 2012, five provinces (Alberta, New Brunswick, Newfoundland and Labrador, Prince Edward Island, and Saskatchewan) and Nunavut followed this model. All elections after 2012 resulted in an increased proportion of female representatives. Will this upward trend continue in the years to come so that these five provinces and Nunavut follow the "overall progression" model? This situation will have to be monitored.

The last model is the above-mentioned "plateau" model: the proportion of female representatives is more or less stagnant over a relatively long period. The Northwest Territories, Quebec, and the Senate followed this model from 1980 to 2012; Quebec diverged thereafter but only to move to the "lost peak" model: the 2012 election resulted in a high point in the feminization rate in the National Assembly, but after the 2014 election this proportion dropped by 5 per cent, from 32.8 per cent to 27.2 per cent.

In short, although in general the proportion of women in the House of Commons and the provincial and territorial legislative assemblies is increasing, this advance is not at all linear: it has standstills and even backward steps. The idea that, over time, women will occupy half of the seats in parliaments (see question 31) must therefore be taken with a grain of salt. It may happen, but it is likely not yet within sight.

BIBLIOGRAPHY

Trimble, Linda, Manon Tremblay, and Jane Arscott. 2013. "Conclusion: A Few More Women." In *Stalled: The Representation of Women in Canadian Governments*, edited by Linda Trimble, Jane Arscott, and Manon Tremblay, 290–314. Vancouver: UBC Press.

88 In Canada, how can we compare representation of women in the House of Commons and in the Senate?

One basic observation is that since the 1980s, the proportion of female senators has been higher than that of female members of Parliament. Not only was the feminization rate in the Senate between 1980 and 2016 higher than that in the House of Commons (26.9 per cent versus 18.7 per cent) but in each of the eleven parliaments formed during this period there were higher proportions of women in the Senate than in the House of Commons. The gap between the feminization rates in the two houses of the Canadian Parliament began to grow in 1997, no doubt due to choices made by the prime minister. During the decade of his leadership of the federal government, from 1993 to 2003, Prime Minister Chrétien appointed a large number of women to the Senate (a procedure related to access to the Cabinet; see question 66), as well as designating female candidates for federal legislative elections. However, this advance of the Senate over the House of Commons is recent; before the late 1990s, the proportion of women in the Senate was only a few percentage points higher than that in the House of Commons. Table 10 shows that the proportion of female members grew more rapidly in the Senate than in the House of Commons: in the mid-1990s, the Senate reached the milestone of one fifth of women among its members, and by the turn of the millennium it had reached critical mass, whereas the progression of women in the House of Commons seemed to have hit the glass ceiling of 25 per cent in 2016 (on the notions of "critical mass" and "glass ceiling," see question 39).

Why have women had greater access to the Senate than to the House of Commons? For a prime minister, appointing women to the Senate involves little political cost but potentially much benefit. Although, in principle, the Senate has the same legislative powers as the House of Commons (although the Senate cannot initiate a finance bill), in fact it is a second chamber without real power (except under specific circumstances). There is little risk in appointing women to the Senate – except that of reinforcing the concept that the less power a political institution has, the more it is feminized (see question 32). Conversely, appointing women to the Senate may generate political dividends for the prime minister. The composition of the Senate is the prime minister's prerogative; not only does it give her or him a way to respond to a low feminization rate in her or his party's parliamentary caucus (without calling into question the systemic factors responsible for this situation) but it tends to imply that she or he is concerned with seeing more women in politics. This may lead to electoral gains down the road.

BIBLIOGRAPHY

Mullen, Stephanie with Manon Tremblay and Linda Trimble. 2013. "'Way Past That Era Now?' Women in the Canadian Senate." In *Stalled: The Representation of Women in Canadian Governments*, edited by Linda Trimble, Jane Arscott, and Manon Tremblay, 273–89. Vancouver: UBC Press.

Table 10

Percentage of women in the House of Commons and the Senate, Canada, 1980–2016

Parliament	House of Commons (N)	Senate (N)
32nd (1980–84)	5.0 (14/282)	11.0 (14/127)
33rd (1984–88)	9.6 (27/282)	13.4 (16/119)
34th (1988–93)	13.2 (39/295)	15.1 (21/139)
35th (1994–97)	18.0 (53/295)	21.6 (27/125)
36th (1997–2000)	20.6 (62/301)	28.7 (39/136)
37th (2001–04)	20.6 (62/301)	34.7 (42/121)
38th (2004–05)	21.1 (65/308)	35.1 (40/114)
39th (2006–08)	20.8 (64/308)	35.3 (36/102)
40th (2008–11)	22.4 (69/308)	33.6 (42/125)
41st (2011–15)	25.6 (79/308)	35.8 (44/123)
42nd (2015–16)	26.0 (88/338)	38.9 (35/90)*
Average (1980–2016)	18.7 (622/3,326)	26.9 (356/1,321)

* As of 28 June 2016.
Sources: Mullen (2013), 276; Parliament of Canada, "Senators," accessed 28 June 2016, http://www.lop.parl.gc.ca/ParlInfo/lists/senators.aspx?Parliament=b67c82bf-0106-42e5-9be1-46ecb5feaf60&Name=&Party=&Province=&Gender=&Current=False&Prime Minister=&TermEnd=&Ministry=&DivisionName=&Picture=False&Language=E; Young (2013), 256.

Parliament of Canada, "Senators," accessed 28 June 2016, http://www.lop.parl.gc.ca/ParlInfo/lists/senators.aspx?Parliament=b67c82bf-0106-42e5-9be1-46ecb5feaf60&Name=&Party=&Province=&Gender=&Current=False&PrimeMinister=&TermEnd=&Ministry=&DivisionName=&Picture=False&Language=E.

Young, Lisa. 2013. "Slow to Change. Women in the House of Commons." In *Stalled: The Representation of Women in Canadian Governments*, edited by Linda Trimble, Jane Arscott, and Manon Tremblay, 253–72. Vancouver: UBC Press.

89 What positions do women hold in Canadian cabinets and parliaments?

In the mid-2010s, a clear majority of jurisdictions in the Canadian federation (six provinces, three territories, and the federal level) had higher proportions of female ministers than of female elected representatives (see

Table 11

Percentage of female ministers and elected representatives by jurisdiction and year of election

Jurisdiction	Year of election	Ministers* (N)	Representatives (N)
Alberta	2015	52.6 (10/19)	33.3 (29/87)
British Columbia	2017	47.8 (11/23)	39.1 (34/87)
Manitoba	2016	30.8 (4/13)	22.8 (13/57)
New Brunswick	2014	15.4 (2/13)	16.3 (8/49)
Newfoundland and Labrador	2015	23.1 (3/13)	25.0 (10/40)
Northwest Territories	2015	14.3 (1/7)	10.5 (2/19)
Nova Scotia	2017	29.4 (5/17)	33.3 (17/51)
Nunavut	2013	12.5 (1/8)	9.1 (2/22)
Ontario	2014	40.0 (12/30)	34.6 (37/107)
Prince Edward Island	2015	20.0 (2/10)	18.5 (5/27)
Quebec	2014	39.3 (11/28)	27.2 (34/125)
Saskatchewan	2016	22.2 (4/18)	26.2 (16/61)
Yukon	2016	42.9 (3/7)	36.8 (7/19)
Canada (House of Commons)	2015	50.0 (15/30)	26.0 (88/338)
AVERAGE		35.6 (84/236)	27.7 (302/1,088)

* Including premier and prime ministers, as of 2 December 2017.
Sources: See bibliography, question 89.

table 11). What is more, in only three jurisdictions (British Columbia, Newfoundland and Labrador, and Prince Edward Island) were the feminization rates in the cabinet and the legislative assembly neck and neck – a gap of less than 2 per cent between them. That being said, table 11 generates at least two observations with regard to the place that women occupy in cabinets and parliaments in Canada.

The first observation mitigates Putnam's (1976, 33) law of increasing disproportion according to which the more important the political role the less likely a woman is to occupy it (see question 73). In British-tradition parliamentary regimes, cabinet members have much more power than do backbenchers. Yet, many cabinets have a feminization rate above that of the respective provincial or territorial legislatures; this is also true in the federal government. In his study of appointments to the federal cabinet between 1935 and 2008, Kerby (2009) concluded that women had excellent chances of acceding to cabinets – better than men's chances.

The second observation is that women's access to the higher strata of state power depends on the leader's desire (see question 66), of course, but this desire (or demand) is also dependent on the supply of "minister-available" backbenchers – that is, the proportion of women within the parliamentary caucus of the party forming the government. In this respect, Studlar and Moncrief (1997) have shown that for Canada the feminization rate in the parliamentary caucus of the party forming the government exerted a greater influence on the proportion of women in Cabinet than did the overall proportion (all parties combined) of members of Parliament. As a consequence, if the party that formed the government had few women within its parliamentary wing, the prime minister had fewer options for appointing a large number to cabinet. However, as Justin Trudeau's first cabinet showed, it is not impossible; with a caucus that was 27 per cent feminized, Trudeau was able to form a parity cabinet. But this is an exception, unfortunately, not the rule. As his parliamentary caucus was 46 per cent (19/41) women, it was much easier for British Columbia premier John Horgan to put together a parity cabinet following the 2017 provincial election.

The feminization rate of the parliament in general (and of the ministerial caucus in particular) is one of the informal reference points for forming the cabinet in general and for appointing women in particular. Research remains to be done to better understand the political calculations that the formation of a cabinet requires, notably with regard to the appointment of female ministers (see question 66).

BIBLIOGRAPHY

Alberta Government, "Premier of Alberta, Cabinet," accessed 23 June 2016, http://www.alberta.ca/premier-cabinet.cfm.

Annesley, Claire. 2015. "Rule of Ministerial Recruitment." *Politics & Gender* 11 (4): 618–42.

Assemblée législative de la Nouvelle-Écosse, "Cabinet," accessed 2 December 2017, http://nslegislature.ca/index.php/fr/people/cabinet/.

British Columbia, "Executive Council of the B.C. Government," accessed 2 December 2017, http://www2.gov.bc.ca/gov/content/governments/organizational-structure/cabinet/cabinet-ministers.

Claveria, Silvia. 2014. "Still a 'Male Business'? Explaining Women's Presence in Executive Office." *West European Politics* 37 (5): 1156–76.

Government of Northwest Territories, "Cabinet," accessed 23 June 2016, http://www.gov.nt.ca/premier/cabinet.

Government of Saskatchewan, "Cabinet," accessed 23 June 2016, https://www.saskatchewan.ca/government/government-structure/cabinet.

Government of Yukon, "Premier's Team," accessed 31 December 2016, http://www.yukonpremier.ca/premiersteam.html.

Kerby, Matthew. 2009. "Worth the Wait: Determinants of Ministerial Appointment in Canada, 1935–2008." *Canadian Journal of Political Science* 42 (3): 593–611.

Legislative Assembly of Manitoba, "Cabinet Ministers," accessed 23 June 2016, http://www.gov.mb.ca/legislature/members/cabinet_ministers.html.

New/Nouveau Brunswick, "Membres du Conseil exécutif du Nouveau-Brunswick," accessed 23 June 2016, http://www2.gnb.ca/content/gnb/fr/contacts/minister_list.html.

Newfoundland Labrador, "Cabinet Ministers," accessed 23 June 2016, http://www.exec.gov.nl.ca/exec/cabinet/ministers/.

Nunavut, "Department of Executive and Intergovernmental Affairs, Cabinet," accessed 23 June 2016, http://www.gov.nu.ca/fr/eia/information/le-cabinet.

Ontario, "Newsroom – Cabinet," accessed 23 June 2016, https://news.ontario.ca/cabinet/en.

Parliament of Canada, "Current ministry, cabinet," accessed 23 June 2016, http://www.parl.gc.ca/Parliamentarians/en/ministries?page=1.

– "Women in the provincial and territorial legislatures: Historical list," accessed 23 June 2016, http://www.lop.parl.gc.ca/ParlInfo/compilations/ProvinceTerritory/Women.aspx?Language=E.

Prince Edward Island, "Executive Council Office," accessed 23 June 2016, http://www.gov.pe.ca/eco/index.php3?number=1030751&lang=E.

Putnam, Robert D. 1976. *The Comparative Study of Political Elites.* Englewood Cliffs, NJ: Prentice-Hall. See, in particular, 33.

Québec, "Premier ministre. Membres du Conseil des ministers," accessed 23 June 2016, http://www.premier.gouv.qc.ca/equipe/conseil-des-ministres.asp.

Studlar, Donley T. and Gary F. Moncrief. 1997. "The Recruitment of Women Cabinet Ministers in the Canadian Provinces." *Governance: An International Journal of Policy and Administration* 10 (1): 67–81.

90 What positions do women fill in Canadian cabinets?

Two approaches may be used to answer this question. One could be called "vertical," in that it examines where women are situated in the ministerial hierarchy, and the finding is that women are concentrated at the bottom of the pyramid that constitutes the cabinet. The other is "horizontal," in that it considers which ministerial responsibilities women handle in cabinets. The finding in this approach is that women have responsibilities that fit traditional gender roles: family and childcare, social services, and the status of women, among others. Far from being mutually exclusive, these two approaches reinforce each other: men sit at the top of the ministerial hierarchy, managing the most important portfolios (such as finance, international relations, and defence), whereas women work as the foot soldiers of the cabinet, taking on the "pink portfolios." Even though it is a parity cabinet, Trudeau's cabinet conforms with these approaches to a certain extent: female ministers are at the bottom of the ministerial hierarchy, and many of their portfolios fit within the gender regime – although some counter it (see questions 1 and 91).

Recent research on female ministers in Canada adds nuance to both approaches. These studies indicate that women are not systematically confined to the bottom of the ministerial hierarchy; once admitted to cabinet they take on top-priority portfolios. In fact, the careers of female and male ministers do not differ in terms of the importance of the portfolios entrusted to them – at least in Quebec (Tremblay et al. 2015). On the other hand, the vast majority of women are still assigned portfolios with missions that are socioeconomic (such as municipal and regional affairs, employment, housing, recreation and sports, tourism) and sociocultural (such as citizenship and immigration, communications, family, childhood, and the elderly). In other words, although today women are in roles that were traditionally beyond their reach (those associated with the public decision-making process), they do not pose a great threat to the gender regime (see question 1).

That being said, two details must be added. First, it is not possible to assert that the responsibilities considered appropriate for women are of lesser importance. For example, in Canada, health – a portfolio that transposes into the public space the responsibility and care for others traditionally performed by women in the family – falls essentially under the public sector (in terms of regulations and service provision, for example). This portfolio is associated with one of the biggest budget items in the provinces; above all, it has been the focal point of one of the most sensitive political and electoral issues in the last three decades. As a consequence, maintaining that the health portfolio is of lesser importance is simply not credible. It is possible that such portfolios are less prestigious – but who defines "prestige," and what criteria are used? Second, in Canada the vast majority of ministerial roles are deployed on the provincial and territorial levels because there are thirteen provincial and territorial cabinets but only one federal cabinet. In fact, under the power-sharing agreement between the federal government and the provinces set out in the Constitution of Canada, a wide variety of socioeconomic and sociocultural responsibilities fall to the provinces and territories. As a consequence, it is very possible that responsibility for such portfolios will fall to both women and men in provincial cabinets.

In short, even though the gender regime and its attendant inequalities always colour experiences within cabinets in Canada, it cannot be said that women's ministerial careers are less remarkable than those of men.

BIBLIOGRAPHY

Tremblay, Manon with Sarah Andrews. 2010. "Les femmes nommées ministres au Canada pendant la période 1921–2007: la loi de la disparité progressive est-elle dépassée?" *Recherches féministes* 23 (1): 143–63.

Tremblay, Manon and Daniel Stockemer. 2013. "Women's Ministerial Careers in Cabinet, 1921–2010: A Look at Socio-demographic Traits and Career Experiences." *Canadian Public Administration* 56 (4): 523–41.

Tremblay, Manon, Daniel Stockemer, Réjean Pelletier, and Matthew Kerby. 2015. "Les carrières ministérielles au Québec: Existe-t-il des différences entre les femmes et les hommes." *Canadian Journal of Political Science* 48 (1): 51–78.

91 How should we interpret Prime Minister Justin Trudeau's parity cabinet?

Following the 2015 federal election, Prime Minister Trudeau appointed a parity cabinet – a cabinet composed of an equal number of women and men. How should this gesture be interpreted? Before going further, it is important to mention that this decision, although progressive, was not the first of its type in Canada; following the Quebec provincial elections of 2007 and 2008, Premier Jean Charest had done the same thing. Nevertheless, Trudeau was the first to do so on the federal scene. Whether his decision will have a contagion effect within the Canadian federation remains to be seen, although the ministerial team formed by the premier of the Yukon following the November 2016 election was a parity one: three female and three male ministers. The same is true of the cabinet formed by British Columbia premier John Horgan following the 2017 provincial election.

If, as Annesley and Franceschet (2015) maintain, the presence of women in cabinet is now a well-established norm, parity is not. We may interpret Trudeau's decision several ways. A first would be that he wanted to mark a clear break with the previous Conservative government of Stephen Harper. In his years in power, from 2006 to 2015, Harper was criticized more than once for his position regarding women and its consequences: the few women among Conservative candidates and within the Conservative caucus, the less-important portfolios given to female ministers, neoliberal policies whose application certainly did not contribute to the equality of women and men, his sympathies with the social conservative movement (including REAL Women Canada), and his old-fashioned attitudes toward women. Harper also had a barely veiled hostility toward other minority groups, including LGBT people.

Aside from marking a clear break with the Conservative government, Trudeau wanted to build up the image of his party – that is, to reaffirm that the Liberal Party of Canada is the party of the Canadian Charter of Rights and Freedoms, which, among other things, guarantees the right to equality for women and men (sections 15 and 28). One way for Trudeau to state that this principle was fundamental to him was to position it at the core of his governance by surrounding himself with a team composed of an equal number of women and men. This choice of a parity cabinet was even more political because it flouted the low feminization rate of the Liberal caucus in the House of Commons – the pool for ministerial recruitment – which was 27.3 per cent (fifty women out of 183 members). By forming a parity cabinet, Trudeau was stating that even if legislative representation was not at parity, executive governance, the result of his own choice, would be.

Of course, both interpretations fall within a broader political dynamic, the positioning of the Canadian party system following the 2015 election. The election of Andrew Scheer to the leadership of the Conservative Party sends a message that the orientation of the party established under Stephen Harper will be maintained. In addition, the electoral consequences of Jagmeet Singh's recent election as leader of the New Democratic Party remain to be seen. In this context, it is clear that a Liberal Party at the centre of the political spectrum remains the natural second choice both of Conservative voters with progressive leanings and of voters still uncertain about Singh's leadership.

A third interpretation of Trudeau's parity cabinet is more critical in tone: although it has an equal number of women and men, this initiative has not completely escaped the *diktats* of the gender regime. Women's participation in cabinets can be viewed from two angles: the vertical approach considers the location of women within the ministerial hierarchy; the horizontal approach is concerned with the distribution of portfolios (see questions 72, 73, and 90). A look at the composition of Trudeau's cabinet by order of precedence reveals a vertical cleavage by gender: women are lower in the hierarchy and men are higher. The distribution of portfolios responds in part to the gender regime: men receive the sovereign portfolios (foreign relations, defence, finance), and women have responsibility for cultural and socioeconomic areas (employment and labour development, justice, health, heritage). That being said, an analysis of the cabinet through the horizontal approach generates less-convincing observations than does the vertical approach. A number of the portfolios going to women confirm the gender regime, it is true, but some counter it (procurement, science) and others are more neutral (environment, justice), and a man, Jean-Yves Duclos, heads the Department of Family, Children and Social Development, a jurisdiction traditionally under the aegis of women. On the other hand, it is clear that women are at the bottom of the ministerial ladder and men are at the top.

This is made even clearer when one examines the composition of the cabinet committees (see table 12) in which parity is put to a tough test. It is true that five committees (Ad Hoc Committee on Defence Procurement; Environment, Climate Change and Energy; Inclusive Growth, Opportunities and Innovation; Parliamentary Affairs; Treasury Board) have a relatively balanced membership by gender – half and half for the Cabinet Committee on Parliamentary Affairs and Treasury Board, and around 40 per cent–60 per cent for the three other committees, with women in the minority. That being said, only one of these committees (Inclusive Growth, Opportunities

Table 12

Composition of Prime Minister Justin Trudeau's cabinet committees
by gender, July 2016

Cabinet Committee	*Chair*	*Vice-Chair*	*Members*	
			Women	*Men*
Agenda, Results and Communications	M	–	4	7
Treasury Board*	M	M	2	2
Parliamentary Affairs	M	W	3	3
Inclusive Growth, Opportunities and Innovation	W	M	6	7
Diversity and Inclusion	M	W	7	2
Canada in the World and Public Security	M	W	3	5
Sub-Committee on Canada–United States Relations	W	M	3	7
Intelligence and Emergency Management	M	W	2	4
Open and Transparent Government	W	W	7	3
Environment, Climate Change and Energy	M	W	3	4
Ad Hoc Committee on Defence Procurement	M	M	2	3

W: woman; M: man
*Four out of the five alternate members are male.

and Innovation) is chaired by a woman, and two (Ad Hoc Committee on Defence Procurement; Treasury Board) have men as both chair and vice-chair. In four committees, women represent less than 40 per cent of the membership – including the very important priorities committee, renamed Agenda, Results and Communications. On the other hand, women are in the majority (seven out of nine members) on the Cabinet Committee on Diversity and Inclusion and the Cabinet Committee on Open and Transparent Government (70 per cent of membership), both of which have mandates that correspond to virtues traditionally associated with women – a concern for others and honesty. Although women serve as vice-chairs of these committees, a man chairs the Cabinet Committee on Diversity and Inclusion (even though, as mentioned above, most of the committee's members are women).

In short, Trudeau's cabinet may have parity, and we should celebrate this fact, but the committees in which the debates are held and from which decisions are recommended to the cabinet as a whole do not.

BIBLIOGRAPHY

Annesley, Claire and Susan Franceschet. 2015. "Gender and the Executive Branch." *Politics & Gender* 11 (4): 613–17.

Assemblée nationale du Québec, "Nombre de ministres dans les cabinets et la représentation féminine depuis 1962," 29 accessed June 2016, http://www.assnat.qc.ca/fr/patrimoine/ministrescabinets.html.

"Cabinet Committee Mandate and Membership," accessed 2 July 2016, http://pm.gc.ca/sites/pm/files/docs/Cab_committee-comite.pdf.

92 Are there more women proportionally in municipal politics than in parliamentary politics in Canada?

Some authors posit that in Canada, municipal politics is more accessible to women than is parliamentary politics (the House of Commons and the provincial and territorial legislative assemblies). Several reasons are given to support this hypothesis. First, it is easier for female politicians (especially mothers) to find a balance between political ambitions and family responsibilities in municipal politics because it takes place where they reside. Second, it is more straightforward for women to be elected to city hall because there is less competition in municipal than in federal and provincial politics, and they avoid many of the difficulties faced by women who aspire to be parliamentarians (such as costly election campaigns and sexist political parties; see questions 18 and 23). Finally, municipal politics attract more women because the areas covered (such as culture, families, and social affairs) are a better match for their socialization, fields of interest, and skills.

Table 13 shows the proportions (rounded off) of female mayors, municipal councillors, and legislative representatives for each province and territory in Canada between 2011 and 2016. These data seriously undermine the idea that municipal politics is more accessible to women than is parliamentary politics – at least, as measured by these statistics. Tolley (2011) and Tremblay and Mévellec (2013) reach a similar conclusion. As the table shows, in Alberta, British Columbia, Manitoba, Nova Scotia, Ontario, and Saskatchewan, the proportion of legislators in the legislative assembly is higher than is the proportion of female mayors and councillors in the provinces. This is also true for the federal level: the feminization rate in the House of Commons is higher than are the proportions of female mayors and municipal councillors in Canada as a whole. However, New Brunswick, Nunavut, and Prince Edward Island show the opposite trend, and Newfoundland and Labrador, Quebec, and the Yukon are in the middle position. In the Northwest Territories, the proportions of female elected representatives and mayors are essentially equal.

Why is municipal politics not more permeable to women than is parliamentary politics? There are almost no studies addressing this question, but two hypotheses may be advanced. The first is that municipal politics is not without obstacles for women and may be more competitive than it seems, especially in large cities. Indeed, being elected as a councillor or mayor in a large city such as Montreal, Toronto, or Vancouver requires much time (making it difficult to reconcile family and politics for those who must negotiate this balance) and money. It is even possible that campaigning in a large and diverse city such as Toronto poses more challenges than does campaigning in a small, relatively homogeneous riding in Prince Edward Island, but this remains to be proved. Nevertheless, being a councillor in a large city is appealing because it imparts a certain prestige, a range of social benefits, and attractive pay. The second hypothesis has to do with the absence of parties in municipal politics (with the exception of a few cities, such as Montreal, Quebec City, and Vancouver). Although many researchers conclude that political parties pose an obstacle to women who run for election (see questions 18 and 23), it is also possible that parties favour their election. Indeed, parties today must have women among their candidates, and so they are forced to select and support them so that they can be elected. This way – indirectly, by selecting women as candidates – parties contribute to the political and electoral socialization of female citizens by encouraging them to become interested in "local public affairs," to vote,

Table 13

Percentage of female mayors, municipal councillors, and elected representatives by jurisdiction, 2013–17

Jurisdiction	Female mayors (2015)	Female municipal councillors (2015)	Female legislative representatives (year)
Alberta	23	28	33 (2015)
British Columbia	28	36	39 (2017)
Manitoba	10	18	23 (2016)
New Brunswick	21	32	16 (2014)
Newfoundland and Labrador	21	37	25 (2015)
Northwest Territories	10	–	11 (2015)
Nova Scotia	13	26	33 (2017)
Nunavut	20	–	9 (2013)
Ontario	17	27	35 (2014)
Prince Edward Island	28	31	19 (2015)
Quebec	17	32	27 (2014)
Saskatchewan	13	18	26 (2016)
Yukon	25	40	37 (2016)
Canada	18	25	26 (2015)

Sources: For proportions of female mayors and councillors, see Federation of Canadian Municipalities, "2015 – Municipal Statistics: Elected Officials Gender Statistics," accessed 30 June 2016, https://fcm.ca/Documents/reports/Women/2015-05-01_FCM%20_gender_stats_EN.pdf; for proportions of female legislative representatives, see Parliament of Canada, "Women in the Provincial and Territorial Legislatures: Historical List," accessed 30 June 2016, http://www.lop.parl.gc.ca/ParlInfo/compilations/ProvinceTerritory/Women.aspx?Language=E.

and (for some) to follow in the footsteps of inspiring female politicians by becoming active and filling positions in a political party or even by running for office. Put simply, by selecting women as candidates, parties stimulate the supply-and-demand cycle of women in politics (see question 18).

In short, the proportions of female municipal councillors, representatives, and mayors across Canada do not offer much evidence that municipal politics is more accessible to women. At least two hypotheses offer explanations for this observation. One is that municipal politics may be more competitive than it seems. The other is that although political parties raise obstacles to the election of women, they may also contribute to their election – depending on the situation.

BIBLIOGRAPHY

Federation of Canadian Municipalities, "2015 – Municipal Statistics. Elected Officials Gender Statistics," accessed 30 June 2016, https://fcm.ca/Documents/reports/Women/2015-05-01_FCM%20_gender_stats_EN.pdf.

Parliament of Canada, "Women in the Provincial and Territorial Legislatures: Historical list," accessed 30 June 2016, http://www.lop.parl.gc.ca/ParlInfo/compilations/Province Territory/Women.aspx?Language=E.

Tolley, Erin. 2011. "Do Women 'Do Better' in Municipal Politics? Electoral Representation Across Three Levels of Government." *Canadian Journal of Political Science* 44 (3): 573–94.

Tremblay, Manon and Anne Mévellec. 2013. "Truly More Accessible to Women than the Legislature? Women in Municipal Politics." In *Stalled: The Representation of Women in Canadian Governments*, edited by Linda Trimble, Jane Arscott, and Manon Tremblay, 19–35. Vancouver: UBC Press.

93 What is the representation of Indigenous women in political structures in Canada?

This question is of great interest, as Indigenous women face conditions that are, in many ways, worse than those experienced by non-Indigenous women: shorter life expectancy, low-quality and overcrowded housing, insufficient education, low income and high unemployment, devastating conjugal violence, and more, in addition to living under the detrimental Indian Act. Starting from the principle that winning an election requires social capital built through a favourable conjuncture (see question 20), do the prejudicial living conditions of Indigenous women mean that none (or few) of them get elected?

To answer this question, it is important to distinguish between Indigenous and non-Indigenous political structures. A handful of First Nations, Métis, and Inuit women have been elected to the House of Commons of

Canada or to one of the provincial or territorial legislative assemblies. Eight have sat in the House of Commons: Ethel Dorothy Blondin-Andrew (Dene, Liberal Party of Canada, 1988–2006), Nancy Karetak-Lindell (Inuit, LPC, 1997–2008), Tina Keeper (Cree, LPC, 2006–08), Leone Aglukkaq (Inuit, Conservative Party of Canada [CPC], 2008–15), Shelly Glover (Métis, CPC, 2008–15), Yvonne Jones (Inuit, LPC, since 2013), Georgina Jolibois (Dene, New Democratic Party, since 2015), and Jody Wilson-Raybould (Kwakwaka'wakw, LPC, since 2015). Blondin-Andrew, Aglukkaq, Glover, and Wilson-Raybould have also been ministers (or secretaries of state). Three have been appointed to the Senate: Thelma Chalifoux (Métis, LPC, 1997–2004), Lillian Eva Dyck (Gordon First Nation, independent NDP then LPC, since 2005), and Sandra Lovelace Nicholas (Tobique, LPC, since 2005). First Nations, Métis, and Inuit women have been elected to the legislative assemblies of the three Canadian territories and also to some provinces: Alberta (Pearl Calahasen, Métis, Conservative Party, 1989–2015); Manitoba (Amanda Lathlin, Cree, NDP, since 2015); Saskatchewan (Joan Beatty, Cree, NDP, 2003–08; Jennifer Campeau, Yellow Quill, Saskatchewan Party, 2011–17; Lisa Lambert, Métis, Saskatchewan Party, since 2016) (Trimble, Arscott, and Tremblay 2013: 37, 215, 234). Inuit women have been premiers in Nunavut (Eva Aariak, 2008–13) and the Northwest Territories (Nellie Cournoyea, whose mother was Inuit, 1991–95). In short, the presence of First Nations, Métis, and Inuit women in non-Indigenous political institutions remains largely symbolic.

Representation of women in Indigenous political structures is barely better than that of their non-Indigenous counterparts in federal, provincial, and territorial legislative institutions. As table 14 shows, as of 1 July 2015, in First Nations band councils, 17.2 per cent of band chiefs and 30.5 per cent of councillors were women. Everywhere except New Brunswick and Prince Edward Island, the proportion of women among chiefs is lower than is the feminization rate in the respective provincial or territorial legislative assembly (see table 11). However, in the vast majority of cases, the proportion of female councillors was higher than or equal to that of the respective provincial or territorial female members of the legislature. This generalized exclusion of women from political representation indicates that, whether or not they are Indigenous, those who wish to be elected to political office in Canada encounter similar obstacles (see the questions in chapter 4) – although Indigenous women also face specific difficulties

Table 14

Percentage and number of female chiefs and councillors elected in First Nations band councils in Canada, by jurisdiction, 1 July 2015

Jurisdiction	Chiefs (N)	Councillors (N)
Alberta	2.3 (1/44)	20.8 (47/226)
British Columbia	21.9 (40/183)	38.6 (292/756)
Manitoba	11.6 (5/43)	23.8 (44/185)
New Brunswick	26.7 (4/15)	33.0 (33/100)
Newfoundland and Labrador	0.0 (0/4)	40.9 (9/22)
Northwest Territories	9.1 (1/11)	43.6 (24/55)
Nova Scotia	30.8 (4/13)	27.4 (26/95)
Nunavut*	–	–
Ontario	21.7 (25/115)	30.4 (189/622)
Prince Edward Island	50.0 (1/2)	20.0 (1/5)
Quebec	8.6 (3/35)	40.2 (68/169)
Saskatchewan	9.1 (6/66)	14.3 (56/392)
Yukon	28.6 (4/14)	53.1 (26/49)
Canada	17.2 (94/545)	30.5 (815/2 676)

Source: Indigenous and Northern Affairs Canada, "Regional Breakdown by Gender of Chiefs and Councillors, July 1, 2015," accessed August 10, 2016, https://www.aadnc-aandc.gc.ca/eng/1314985445480/1314985485565.
* There are no First Nations people in Nunavut.

arising from the racism and colonialism embedded in Canadian society, as Voyageur (2011) explains.

Broken down by jurisdiction, the figures in table 14 lead to two observations. The first is that the proportions vary widely among provinces and territories; for chiefs, they range between 0 and 31 per cent (with parity in Prince Edward Island, although there are only two chiefs in the province); for councillors, between 14 per cent and 53 per cent. These variations indicate that regional cultures may exert an influence on women's access to band councils (see question 19). The other observation is that there is no correspondence between percentages of female chiefs and of female councillors in a province or territory: there is a gap of at least 10 per cent in most jurisdictions, with female chiefs almost always at the low end of the range. Such gaps indicate that First Nations women are not exempt from the law of increasing disproportion according to which the higher a position is in the hierarchy of power, the more difficult it is for women to access it (see questions 83 and 89).

BIBLIOGRAPHY

Indigenous and Northern Affairs Canada, "Regional Breakdown by Gender of Chiefs and Councillors, 1 July 2015," accessed 10 August 2016, https://www.aadnc-aandc.gc.ca/eng/1314985445480/1314985485565.

O'Donnell, Vivian and Susan Wallace. 2011. "First Nations, Métis and Inuit Women." In Canada (Statistics Canada, Social and Aboriginal Statistics Division), *Women in Canada: A Gender-based Statistical Report*. Ottawa. Minister of Industry, no. 89–503–X.

Parliament of Canada, "House of Commons, Biographical information, Inuit, Métis or First Nation Origin," accessed 1 July 2016, http://www.lop.parl.gc.ca/ParlInfo/Compilations/Parliament/Aboriginal.aspx?Menu=HOC-Bio&Role=MP.

– "Senate, Biographical information, Inuit, Métis or First Nation Origin," accessed 1 July 2016, http://www.lop.parl.gc.ca/ParlInfo/Compilations/Parliament/Aboriginal.aspx?Role=Senators&Language=E.

Trimble, Linda, Jane Arscott, and Manon Tremblay, eds. 2013. *Stalled: The Representation of Women in Canadian Governments*. Vancouver: UBC Press.

Voyageur, Cora. 2011. "Out in the Open: Elected Female Leadership in Canada's First Nations Community." *Canadian Review of Sociology* 48 (1): 67–85.

White, Graham. 2013. "In the Presence of Northern Aboriginal Women? Women in Territorial Politics." In *Stalled: The Representation of Women in Canadian Governments*, ed. Linda Trimble, Jane Arscott, and Manon Tremblay, 233–52. Vancouver: UBC Press.

94 Who are the Indigenous women elected to political office in Canada?

According to Voyageur (2011), the typical female Indigenous leader is middle aged and well educated, born in the community that she leads, and belongs to a family involved in politics. The age and education criteria are similar for Indigenous and non-Indigenous women: both form elites compared to their counterparts in the population (see question 57). However, it is possible that because of the difficult living conditions facing the First Nations in Canada, the elitism of Indigenous elected women is more pronounced than is that of non-Indigenous female politicians; this is a hypothesis to be explored. On the other hand, place of birth and belonging to a political family provide a clearer line of demarcation between Indigenous and non-Indigenous women.

A female Indigenous politician who was born and has grown up in the community that she leads is well known to the electorate, as is her family, and has had her leadership capacities publicly assessed since her early career. Given that Indigenous communities are relatively small and closed environments, it is possible that having spent one's entire life in a particular community is a requirement weighing more heavily on the political ambitions of Indigenous than non-Indigenous women. For the same reason, it is possible that belonging to a political family as a springboard to election is a more important requirement in Indigenous than non-Indigenous environments; Brodie (1985, 25–42) and Mévellec and Tremblay (2016, 51–60) have shown that a number of female mayors and municipal councillors come from politically engaged families. Both of these hypotheses remain to be validated. That being said, whether or not she is Indigenous, if a woman has grown up in a political family that fact will have a significantly positive impact in terms of political socialization: having people with great confidence in what they can achieve as models, seeing doors open (rather than close) when one's family name is mentioned, having access to networks, knowing the ropes and having a loyal following, learning to navigate in troubled waters and drown enemies in them, and developing negotiating skills and strengths are just some of the benefits of growing up in a political family.

In sum, Indigenous or not, female politicians belong to the elite.

BIBLIOGRAPHY

Brodie, Janine. 1985. *Women and Politics in Canada*. Toronto: McGraw-Hill Ryerson.

Mévellec, Anne and Manon Tremblay. 2016. *Genre et professionnalisation de la politique municipale. Un portrait des élues et élus du Québec*. Quebec City: Presses de l'Université du Québec. See, in particular, 51–60.

Voyageur, Cora. 2011. "Out in the Open: Elected Female Leadership in Canada's First Nations Community." *Canadian Review of Sociology* 48 (1): 67–85.

95 Should Canada change its voting system to increase the number of female representatives?

This question is even more important given that during the 2015 election campaign, one of the planks in Justin Trudeau's platform was to review the voting system used to elect members of Parliament. Could this electoral reform offer women the hope of redressing their underrepresentation in politics (Tremblay 2016)?

First, it is important to note that if the objective is to increase the number of women in the House of Commons, electoral reform is not necessarily the appropriate solution; as Darcy, Welch, and Clark (1994, 147) observe, "Changing election systems is not necessarily a quick or reliable way to elect more women." This does not entirely excuse the voting system from responsibility for the underrepresentation of women in politics. As Rule (1994, 16) explains,

> Electoral systems explain almost 30 percent of the varying proportions of women in democracies' national legislatures. "Woman-friendly"- electoral systems are very significant but insufficient for explaining women's successes. Sixty percent is generally due to political, socioeconomic, and cultural factors, while 10 percent is unexplained. However, favorable societal conditions will not substitute for unfavourable electoral systems relative to women reaching their optimum representation in parliament.

In short, trading a majority single-constituency voting system for a list-proportional or mixed-proportional list system does not guarantee that more women will sit in parliament (see questions 20 to 23). In Farrell's (2001, 167) view, "It is not the electoral system which is at fault [for the underrepresentation of women in politics] so much as the party selection committees." Of course, political parties organize the selection of their candidates according to the rules of the electoral game – including the voting system. For instance, if they are able to designate a number of candidates per electoral district rather than a single candidate, it is legitimate to believe they will be more inclined to present a team that is diversified in terms of sex, age, cultural and ethnic origin, sexual preference, and other traits (see questions 20, 21, and 23). It remains to be proved that the electorate wishes to have such a diversified candidate list. A recent study by Matland and Lilliefeldt (2014) shows that what is often presented as an "ideal electoral list" does not exist. Rather, the parties compose their lists according to the expectations of their electoral base: left-wing parties will have more women on their lists because their electorate wants that, whereas right-wing parties will have fewer. Unless it offers a list that meets expectations, a political party's electoral base may well impose its own law – especially under a preferential voting system.

In short, adopting a new voting system does not guarantee that the number of female elected representatives will increase. The proposals advanced for this purpose in the provinces have all come up short (see question 96). Instead, political parties must be reformed.

BIBLIOGRAPHY

Darcy, R., Susan Welch, and Janet Clark. 1994. *Women, Elections, & Representation*, 2nd ed. Lincoln: University of Nebraska Press. See, in particular, 138–71.

Farrell, David M. 2001. *Electoral Systems: A Comparative Introduction*. Houndmills: Palgrave. See, in particular, 165–8.

Matland, Richard E., and Emilie Lilliefeldt. 2014. "The Effect of Preferential Voting on Women's Representation." In *Representation: The Case of Women*, edited by Maria C. Escobar-Lemmon and Michelle M. Taylor-Robinson, 79–102. New York: Oxford University Press.

Rule, Wilma. 1994. "Parliaments of, by, and for the People: Except for Women?" In *Electoral Systems in Comparative Perspective: Their Impact on Women and Minorities*, edited by Wilma Rule and Joseph F. Zimmerman, 15–30. Westport: Greenwood Press.

Tremblay, Manon. 2016. "La réforme électorale: une lueur d'espoir pour les femmes?" *Policy Options politiques*, accessed 3 July 2016, http://policyoptions.irpp.org/fr/magazines/juin-2016/la-reforme-electorale-une-lueur-despoir-pour-les-femmes/.

96 What place has women's representation had in plans for electoral reform formulated by several Canadian provinces and Nunavut?

At the turn of the twenty-first century, several provinces instituted public forums to reflect on the appropriateness of reforming the voting system used to elect members of their legislative assemblies. Hearings were also conducted in Nunavut in the mid-1990s, when the constitutional and institutional parameters of the future territory were being decided. Recently, Justin Trudeau's government struck a legislative committee on electoral reform.

Two Atlantic provinces, New Brunswick and Prince Edward Island, also held hearings. The Prince Edward Island government began its reflection process in January 2003. In its final report, the Commission on Prince Edward Island's Electoral Future promoted a descriptive conception of political representation of women (see question 60) by recommending "that the make-up of the party lists reflect the population of the province" (Prince Edward Island 2005, 18). Aside from positioning women as one minority among others even though they form half the population, the question remains of how parties can be encouraged to compile lists that reflect the demographic fabric, given that quotas are difficult to envisage as a realistic solution in Canada (see question 97).

In New Brunswick, the Commission on Legislative Democracy (CLD) was formed in December 2003. Composed of an equal number of women and men (three commissioners and cochairs of each sex/gender), the CLD held a wide-ranging series of public hearings from May to October 2004 on the theme "Women and Democracy." The commission made three recommendations "with the goal of increasing the representation of women in New Brunswick's Legislative Assembly to 35 per cent by the year 2015" (Commission on Legislative Democracy 2004, 27). The first recommendation was to increase the annual allocation by one dollar for each vote obtained by parties that presented at least 35 per cent female candidates in the most recent provincial election. The second recommendation, also financial in nature, suggested that groups working to increase the presence of women in politics receive funding. And the third recommendation was to require parties to report every two years on what they had done to open their doors to women. It is interesting to consider the 35 per cent threshold: why did a proportion of about one third suffice for women's legislative representation, when women form more than half of the population? It is possible that the CLD subscribed to the notion of critical mass (see question 39).

In British Columbia, the legislative assembly launched a plan to create the Citizens' Assembly on Electoral Reform (BCCAER) in 2002. Three values were to guide the BCCAER's reflections: 1) proportionality of votes to seats – that is, that the representation of each political party in the legislative assembly should be proportional to the support it receives from the electorate; 2) local representation – the link between the representative and her or his constituents; 3) an enhanced choice for voters – that is, each voter can make a nuanced electoral choice thanks to a multitude of electoral options. In other words, despite its parity membership, the BCCAER did not make a larger proportion of women in the legislature a pivotal value in its reformist reflections. Lang (2007) maintains that not only did the eighty female members of the BCCAER not acknowledge that they might have a mandate to promote the representation of women but many members, both female and male, did not even see it as an issue worth discussing.

In central Canada, Ontario and Quebec instituted public forums on the voting system used to elect members of their legislative assemblies. Nine values inspired the reformist consultations conducted by the Ontario Citizens' Assembly on Electoral Reform (OCAER): 1) legitimacy – that is, the population's trust in their elected members in Queen's Park (where the Ontario Legislative Assembly is housed); 2) fair, or descriptive, representation under which the Ontario Legislative Assembly should constitute a scale model of the province's population; 3) enhanced choice for the electorate; 4) effective parties; 5) a stable and effective government; 6) a functional parliament; 7) a higher rate of political and electoral participation; 8) accountability of members of the Legislative Assembly; 9) simplicity and practicality of the voting system. Even though it had parity membership, and even though fair (descriptive) representation was one of the guiding values of its reflections, the OCAER made no recommendation that would encourage the election of women to the provincial legislature.

It is worth repeating, for emphasis, that parity membership in citizens' assemblies in Ontario and British Columbia did not result in recommendations for women's representation in the respective legislative assemblies to be increased. This is troubling, as it seriously calls into question the pivotal idea that a critical mass of women in decision-making positions would result in public policies more favourable to the female population (see question 60). It seems that this was not the case in these two situations.

Quebec also engaged in a reflection concerning its voting system in 2001; the resulting forums have been described by Tremblay (2010). For our purposes, we may simply note that in December 2004, Jean Charest's Liberal government presented a bill to replace the province's election act. One objective stated in the bill was to "encourage the attainment of fair representation of women [and ethno-cultural minorities] in the National Assembly" (Quebec 2004, 6, our translation). The inclusion of women's representation as a core objective of the Quebec bill was likely related to the ongoing work of the Quebec women's movement directed at reforming representative institutions. The Quebec Liberal Party's (QLP) proposed model set out two strategies to increase the number of female candidates and, eventually, the number of female members of the National Assembly: first, to enhance both the annual allocation for parties as a function of the proportion of its female candidates in the previous election; second, to increase the reimbursement due to female candidates. (The Quebec government may have taken inspiration from a similar proposal made in the early 1990s on the federal level by the Royal Commission on Election Reform and Party Financing.) In 2007, in his evaluation of the compensatory mixed voting system envisaged at the time by the Quebec government, the Directeur général des élections du Québec supported two strategies that were much more powerful than financial incentives to increase the number of women in the National Assembly of Quebec: alternation of female and male candidates on party lists and the obligation to place a female candidate at the top of 50 per cent of the lists (Directeur général des élections du Québec, 2007, 17).

Nunavut went even further. In December 1995, the Nunavut Planning Commission proposed to the federal government that it create binominal parity ridings – ridings with two representatives, obligatorily one woman and one man. In each of Nunavut's eleven ridings, voters would cast two votes, one for a female and the other for a male candidate. The female candidate declared elected (therefore a member of the assembly) and the male candidate declared elected (also therefore a member of the assembly) for a single riding would be those who obtained the most votes from among the candidates of their respective sex/gender in that riding (a mechanism similar to the blocked vote). If it had been adopted (it was rejected by 57 per cent of voters in a referendum in May 1997; see Tremblay and Steele 2006), the Nunavut Legislative Assembly would have had an equal number of women and men, under a system that amounted to a quota in the form of seats reserved half for women and half for men (see question 44). In May 2013, France adopted such a mechanism (called *binôme paritaire*) for elections to departmental councils, with the result that after the March 2015 election these bodies had half female councillors and half male councillors.

However, women held only 10 per cent of the presidencies of departmental councils because of the absence of legal constraints regarding these political positions (see question 49).

Finally, to follow up on the campaign promise "that 2015 will be the last federal election conducted under the first-past-the-post voting system" (Liberal Party of Canada 2015), in June 2016 Justin Trudeau's Liberal government formed the Special Committee on Electoral Reform the mandate of which was "to identify and conduct a study of viable alternate voting systems to replace the first-past-the-post system, as well as to examine mandatory voting and online voting, and to assess the extent to which the options identified could advance the following principles for electoral reform: 1) Effectiveness and legitimacy … 2) Engagement … 3) Accessibility and inclusiveness … 4) Integrity … 5) Local representation …" (Special Committee on Electoral Reform 2016a). The mandate of the Special Committee on Electoral Reform did not refer specifically to political representation of women. However, it did refer to it indirectly via the principle of engagement: "That the proposed measure would … offer opportunities for inclusion of underrepresented groups in the political process." One might not know whether to laugh or cry at this offer. In December 2016, the Special Committee on Electoral Reform released its report, *Strengthening Democracy in Canada: Principles, Process and Public Engagement for Electoral Reform*. The underrepresentation of women in Canadian politics is certainly discussed but only as a component of the underrepresentation of other groups that do not have the demographic weight of women (such as Indigenous people). This is a dubious approach given that women account for half of the population of Canada, and Indigenous people less than 5 per cent (in 2011, according to Statistics Canada). That being said, recommendation 8 deals specifically with women: "To create a financial incentive … for political parties to run more women candidates and move towards parity in their nominations" (Special Committee on Electoral Reform 2016b: 126). This recommendation is disappointing at best. First, the idea of funding political parties so that they will open their doors to women is far from original. As mentioned above, this measure was proposed in the early 1990s by the Royal Commission on Electoral Reform and Party Financing and was taken up by provincial governments (including those in New Brunswick and Quebec). Second, this recommendation concerns women who are candidates and not elected. Yet, as was observed in question 85, female candidates do not necessarily have the same chance of winning as do male candidates. Finally, because it targets female candidates rather than female elected representatives, the most cynical will see a financing plan enabling parties to fill their coffers without any obligation to feminize their parliamentary caucuses: it is not unreasonable to ask why it is deemed necessary to resort to financial incentives to feminize politics.

To sum up, the scenarios for electoral reform proposed in a few provinces and in the federal government have generally regarded the objective of increasing the proportion of female parliamentarians as relatively unimportant. In fact, this goal has never inspired electoral reform proposals outlined in Canada, as it has been at the bottom of the list of priorities in reformist scenarios – although there are differences depending on the legislative space under consideration.

BIBLIOGRAPHY

Commission on Legislative Democracy. 2004. *Final Report and Recommendations*. Fredericton: Commission on Legislative Democracy, accessed 3 July 2016, http://www.elec tionsnb.ca/content/dam/enb/pdf/cld/CLDFinalReport-e.pdf.

Directeur général des élections du Québec. 2007. *Les modalités d'un mode de scrutin mixte compensatoire. Le rapport du Directeur général des élections. Résumé*. Quebec City: DGÉQ, accessed 3 July 2016, http://www.electionsquebec.qc.ca/documents/pdf/ Resume.pdf.

France (Premier ministre, Haut Conseil à l'Égalité entre les femmes et les hommes). 2015. *Parité en politique: entre progrès et stagnations. Évaluation de la mise en œuvre des lois dites de parité dans le cadre des élections de 2014: municipales et communautaires, européennes, sénatoriales*. Paris: Haut Conseil à l'Égalité entre les femmes et les hommes, accessed 4 July 2016, http://www.haut-conseil-egalite.gouv.fr/IMG/pdf/hce_ rapport-parite_2015-02-26-par-015-bdef.pdf.

Lang, Amy. 2007. "But Is It for Real? The British Columbia Citizens' Assembly as a Model of State-Sponsored Citizen Empowerment." *Politics & Society* 35 (1): 35–69.

Liberal Party of Canada. 2015. *Electoral Reform*, accessed 31 December 2016, https://www. liberal.ca/realchange/electoral-reform/.

Prince Edward Island. 2005. *Commission on Prince Edward Island's Electoral Future. Final Report*. Charlottetown: Commission on Prince Edward Island's Electoral Future, accessed 3 July 2016, http://www.gov.pe.ca/photos/original/elec_elecrfrm05.pdf.

Québec (Réforme des institutions démocratiques). 2004. *Avant-projet de loi remplaçant la Loi électorale, Document explicative*. [Quebec City]: Gouvernement du Québec, accessed 3 July 2016, http://www.institutions-democratiques.gouv.qc.ca/publications/resume_avant_projet_loi.pdf.

Special Committee on Electoral Reform. 2016a. "About. Mandate," accessed 31 December 2016http://www.parl.gc.ca/Committees/en/ERRE/About.

– 2016b. "Strengthening Democracy in Canada. Principles, Process and Public Engagement for Electoral Reform." Report of the Special Committee on Electoral Reform, [Ottawa], House of Commons, accessed 31 December 2016, http://www.parl.gc.ca/content/hoc/Committee/421/ERRE/Reports/RP8655791/errerp03/errerp03-e.pdf.

Tremblay, Manon. 2010. "Bilan des reformes électorales au Canada: Quelle place pour les femmes?" *Revue canadienne de science politique* 43 (1): 25–47.

Tremblay, Manon and Jackie F. Steele. 2006. "Paradise Lost? Gender Parity and the Nunavut Experience." In *Representing Women in Parliament: A Comparative Study*, edited by Marian Sawer, Manon Tremblay, and Linda Trimble, 221–35. Abingdon: Routledge.

97 Is it realistic to think that Canada would use legislative quotas to increase the presence of women in politics?

Before starting this discussion, it is important to remember that there are different types of electoral quotas, including legislative quotas prescribed by law, whether in a constitution or an electoral statute.

It is not realistic to think of integrating quotas into the Canadian Constitution. For that to happen, either the Constitution would have to be amended to clearly mention electoral quotas (similar to how section 22 of the Constitution Act of 1982 mentions clearly and explicitly the quotas for regional representation in the Senate) or paragraphs 3 (democratic rights of citizens), 15 (equality rights), and 28 (rights guaranteed equally to both sexes) of the Canadian Charter of Rights and Freedoms would have to be interpreted as being compatible with quotas for representation of women and men in legislative elections. The first scenario is barely within the realm of possibility and the second raises the spectre of protracted legal battles. For example, considering the persistent underrepresentation of women in politics, how should section 3 of the Charter be interpreted in light of the notion of "effective representation"? Might it be in the sense of a descriptive conception of political representation (see question 60)? The Charter applies only to government actions and actors (and not to the private sector), it is true, but could it be argued that because political parties receive public financing they are public entities and, as a consequence, the state can require that they present an equal number of female and male candidates in elections? At first glance, changing the electoral statute (federal or at the provincial level) to insert electoral quotas on the basis of gender seems a less difficult and more promising route to take, but it probably minimizes ideological, political and institutional, and social opportunity structures. For example, what party forms the government? What gains can the government party draw from such a measure and what costs might it incur? Which social actors promote quotas and which object to them, and what are their relative strengths on the political chessboard? Where does public opinion stand on the question?

I will mention four other arguments that militate against Canada's adoption of legislative quotas to increase the presence of women in politics. First, the political class is not favourable to it and public opinion is divided. When it comes to public opinion, Everitt and Gidengil (2013) have analyzed the responses to questions asked in Canadian electoral studies in 2000, 2004, 2006, and 2008 about the idea of forcing political parties to present an equal number of female and male candidates, or a minimal proportion of female candidates. Although more women than men supported such an obligation, overall support was in the minority (41 per cent of female respondents and 34 per cent of male respondents). However, a poll conducted in May 2016 by SOM (a Quebec-based survey firm) for the Conseil du statut de la femme du Québec reached a different conclusion: 64 per cent of the 1,000 respondents stated they were in complete agreement or in agreement with the idea of "forcing political parties to run between 40 percent and 60 percent female candidates in order to bring the National Assembly closer to parity" (SOM 2016, our translation). In Canada, as elsewhere in the world, quotas need political parties' full and complete commitment to be effective. Tremblay (2010) revealed a lack of enthusiasm by the political class (composed of mainly majority males) for these mechanisms: 42.9 per cent of female candidates and 21.8 per cent of male candidates who ran in a Quebec riding (and participated in the study) in the 1997 federal election supported the idea that parties should have quotas to balance their female and male candidacies; these proportions were 60 per cent and 32.1 per cent, respectively, in the 2000 election (Tremblay 2010, 134). Of course, these data are a bit outdated, but have things changed since? Perhaps not in the Quebec Liberal Party: although, at a special general council of his party, held in June 2017, Premier Couillard stated that he wanted to have 40 per cent women among the Liberal candidates for the 2018 election, the youth committee of the QLP (which has very few female members) rejected a resolution at its annual congress in August 2017 to establish a "parity zone" that would have led to a minimum of 40 per cent female Liberal candidates for the 2018 election (Richer 2016).

Second, the women's movement is very cautious with regard to quotas. For example, Equal Voice wants more women to be elected in Canada through "promoting electoral and other changes that would increase the numbers of women in politics" but does not mention quotas. In Quebec, the Groupe Femmes, Politique et Démocratie (GFPD) is very active in the quest to attain parity representation of women and men in sites of influence and power, and its position regarding quotas is mixed. For example, in its position paper *Agir pour une démocratie paritaire!*, presented to the Quebec government's Secrétariat à la condition féminine in December 2015, the GFPD stated that adoption of compulsory measures (8) and quotas (9) was essential – but on a temporary basis (15). It is possible that certain spokespeople for the women's movement view quotas with fear or see them as suffering from a lack of legitimacy. In a document titled *Canadian Provincial Policies and Programs for Women and Leadership*, Guppy (2012, 24) discusses electoral quotas with caution. After calling quotas "debatable" and a "last-resort method," she suggests that they be used "as a test basis for an election or two," but to withdraw them "if there is progress and the gender quota has been successful in encouraging women to become involved in politics." Thus, quotas may be used as a "push start," but as the number of women in politics increases they must be replaced by other measures. Bhavnani (2009) has shown that even after they are withdrawn, quotas may help to increase political representation by women through the institutional heritage that they pass along.

Third, although it does not make adoption of electoral quotas for women impossible, the majority first-past-the-post voting system certainly makes it more complex. A quota initiative would require that the candidate selection process, the exclusive domain of local riding associations, be reviewed within political parties. In Canada, this process is very decentralized, and the adoption of candidacy quotas on the regional or national scale would require more centralization. Such concentration of power might be perceived as impinging on the sacrosanct freedom of activists and the laws of free political competition dear to liberal individualism. Given these positions, some voices might point out that the majority voting system offers alternatives to quotas for raising the feminization rate in the House of Commons and legislative assemblies, such as training and networking (see questions 49 and 98).

Fourth, the argument could be advanced that women's representation in Canadian politics is not so disastrously low that quotas need to be adopted. Indeed, with 26 per cent of members of Parliament, the House of Commons is above the global average (which, in June 2016, was at 22.8 per cent for single and lower chambers) and the United States (19.4 per cent in June 2016), a country with which Canada is often compared for historical and geographical reasons, and equal with France (26.2 per cent). That being said, a few political parties in Canada have voluntarily endorsed parity or a quota policy – but without using the word. For example, section 5.2 of the statutes of Québec solidaire provides that parity between women and men applies to the party's structures and "to the choice of candidates for a general election" (Québec solidaire 2012, 4, our translation). During its congress in Edmonton in 2016, the NDP adopted the following resolution designed to encourage more diversified representation of genders (including women) in Canadian federal politics: "Increase funding, through a ballot box premium, for political parties with at least 50 percent of candidates who identify as a gender other than male; increase funding, through a second ballot box premium, of political parties that elect a deputation of at least 40 percent of people who identify as a gender other than male" (New Democratic Party 2016). In February 2016, NDP MP Kennedy Stewart tabled Bill C-237, An Act to Amend the Canada Elections Act (Gender Equity), which proposed to amend "the *Canada Elections Act* to reduce the reimbursement each registered party receives for its election expenses if there is more than a 10 per cent difference in the number of male and female candidates on the party's list of candidates for a general election" (Canada 2016).

In short, it would be surprising if Canada adopted legislative quotas to increase the presence of women in politics, even though some parties have voluntarily embarked on the path to balanced representation of women and men in politics.

BIBLIOGRAPHY

Bhavnani, Rikhil. 2009. "Do Electoral Quotas Work after They Are Withdrawn? Evidence from a Natural Experiment in India." *American Political Science Review* 103 (1): 23–35.

Canada (2016), *An Act to amend the Canada Elections Act (gender equity) (Bill C-237)*, accessed 8 July 2016, http://www.parl.gc.ca/HousePublications/Publication.aspx?Language=F&Mode=1&DocId=8125430.

Equal Voice, "EV Mission," accessed 12 August 2016, https://www.equalvoice.ca/mission.cfm.

Everitt, Joanna and Elisabeth Gidengil. 2013 "Public Attitudes Towards Women's Political Representation." In *Mind the Gaps: Canadian Perspectives on Gender and Politics*, edited by Roberta Lexier and Tamara A. Small, 34–47. Halifax: Fernwood.

Groupe Femmes, Politique et Démocratie (GFPD). 2015. *Agir pour une démocratie paritaire!Mémoire présenté au Secrétariat à la condition féminine dans le cadre de la consultation sur la question de l'égalité entre les femmes et les hommes*, accessed 9 July 2016, http://www.gfpd.ca/files/documents/dm/33/m-moire.pdf.

Guppy, Lynn. 2012. *Canadian Provincial Policies and Programs for Women in Leadership*. St. John's: Memorial University, Harris Centre, accessed 4 July 2016, https://www.mun.ca/harriscentre/reports/arf/2011/11-SPHCSRF-Final-Guppy.pdf

New Democratic Party. 2016. "Resolutions passed at Convention 2016," accessed 8 July 2016, http://xfer.ndp.ca/2016/documents/EDM2016-Resolutions-BIL-APP_v1.pdf

Québec solidaire. 2012. *Statuts. Tel qu'adoptés par le Congrès le 28 avril 2012*. Montreal: Québec solidaire.

Richer, Jocelyne. 2016. "Campagnes électorales: les jeunes libéraux rejettent la parité hommes-femmes." *Le Devoir*, 14 August 2016, accessed 14 August 2016, http://www.ledevoir.com/politique/quebec/477719/les-jeunes-liberaux-rejettent-la-parite-hommes-femmes.

SOM. 2016. *Sondage au sujet de la parité à l'Assemblée nationale*, accessed 17 August 2016, https://www.csf.gouv.qc.ca/wp-content/uploads/som_mars.pdf.

Tremblay, Manon. 2010. *Quebec Women and Legislative Representation*, translated by Käthe Roth. Vancouver: UBC Press. See, in particular, 132–41.

98 What strategies has the women's movement in Canada used to encourage women to make the jump into politics?

Historically, the women's movement in Canada, like its British and French counterparts but unlike those in Scandinavia, has chosen not to get involved with the question of participation in political institutions. This choice explains, in part, the underrepresentation of women in democratic institutions today. However, the women's movement is not ideologically homogeneous, and some groups (most of them in the liberal current) have, for a long time, sought to increase the number of female politicians. Nor is the movement linguistically homogeneous, and its efforts have been deployed differently, for the most part, in English Canada and in Quebec.

In English Canada, Equal Voice, founded in 2001, is a "national, bilingual, multi-partisan organization dedicated to electing more women to all levels of political office in Canada." It has ten chapters across Canada (in Alberta, British Columbia, Ontario, Saskatchewan, and the Atlantic provinces). The organization has a very active program, offering a variety of events, programs, public-awareness campaigns, and various initiatives to encourage women to take on mandates of political representation. In this sense, it fits within a tradition of reformist activism aiming to increase the number of women in politics; it does not, however, question the operational economy of representative institutions, which no doubt has something to do with their low feminization rate. An earlier group was Women for Political Action (WPA), founded in 1972 with the objective of increasing the proportion of women in political institutions in Canada. In the 1972 federal election, two WPA members ran for election as independent candidates. WPA subsequently adjusted its strategy to encourage existing parties to take on more women rather than acting as a party on its own. Assuming this role was the Feminist Party of Canada (FPC), established in 1979 to pursue the objective of increasing women's representation on the federal political scene by encouraging electoral participation in harmony with feminist ideals. The FPC ceased activity in 1982. The Committee for '94 came into being two years later. Its objective was to reach parity of representation between women and men in the House of Commons by 1994 (no need to mention that this goal wasn't met). Until 1996, when it was dissolved, the group organized various activities to encourage the election of women in federal politics, including conferences and a program of parliamentary internships so that women could become familiar with political structures. In 1986, Canadian Women for Political Representation was founded. This Ottawa-based group had the mission of encouraging women to take part in various forms of political engagement. It ceased activity in 1989.

The Quebec counterpart of Equal Voice is Groupe Femmes, Politique et Démocratie. Founded in 1999, it is not associated with any particular political party. Its mandate is to promote and support women's commitment to political and democratic participation through awareness raising and education. The goal is to educate the public about the need to increase the presence of women in democratic institutions and to train and support women who are seeking election. GFPD has deployed a number of initiatives, including production of awareness-raising tools such as publications, videocassettes, and DVDs. It has organized colloquiums and congresses and, above all, it has offered – and still offers – a wide range of educational activities. In 2016, it offered more than thirty courses covering topics as diversified as communications and rhetoric, political culture, ethics, feminism, and governance.

In parallel with these initiatives, some governments have instituted programs and provided funding. For example, the Nova Scotia government, via the Nova Scotia Advisory Council on the Status of Women, started running the Nova Scotia Campaign School for Women in 2004; its objective is to provide "women with experience and information about the nomination process, putting together a campaign team, campaign finance regulations, working with the media, political ethics and public speaking" (Carbert 2011, 79). In Quebec, the À égalité pour décider program, created in 1999, encourages women to take leadership by offering financial support to local, regional, and national not-for-profit groups for projects designed to increase the presence of women in decision-making positions at all levels. The projects funded by the program, which has an annual budget of $1 million, are proposed by women's groups. Similar initiatives have been taken elsewhere in Canada (Guppy 2012), and the Federation of Canadian Municipalities is actively working to increase the number of women in municipal politics.

In short, the women's movement in Canada has deployed a number of strategies to encourage women to make the leap into the political arena. However, the real effect of these initiatives on the feminization of political assemblies remains uncertain. Far from throwing into question the rules of the political game, which no doubt bear some responsibility for the absence of women from political spaces, these initiatives seek to improve the performance of aspiring female politicians through training, financial support, and networking, thereby confirming and strengthening the existing environment. In other words, in this view the problem is not politics but women, and the solution is not to review the rules of the political game but to give women tools to become more skilful warriors in the electoral battle.

BIBLIOGRAPHY

Carbert, Louise. 2011. "Making it Happen in Practice: Organized Efforts to Recruit Rural Women for Local Government Leadership." In *Women and Representation in Local Government: International Case Studies*, edited by Barbara Pini and Paula McDonald, 76–94. Abingdon: Routledge.

Equal Voice, "EV Mission," accessed 4 July 2016, https://www.equalvoice.ca/mission.cfm.

Federation of Canadian Municipalities, "Women in Local Government, accessed 4 July 2016, https://www.fcm.ca/home.htm.

Guppy, Lynn. 2012. *Canadian Provincial Policies and Programs for Women in Leadership.* St John's: Memorial University, Harris Centre, accessed 4 July 2016, https://www.mun.ca/harriscentre/reports/arf/2011/11-SPHCSRF-Final-Guppy.pdf.

Québec, "Secrétariat à la condition féminine, À égalité pour decider," accessed 4 July 2016, http://www.scf.gouv.qc.ca/?id=32.

Zaborszky, Dorothy. 1987. "Feminist Politics: The Feminist Party of Canada." *Women's Studies International Forum* 10 (6): 613–21.

99 How important is it that the premier of Ontario is openly lesbian?

In winning the race for leadership of the Liberal Party of Ontario in February 2013, Kathleen Wynne not only became the first female leader of that party and the first female premier of Ontario but also the first person in Canada – and, in fact, in the Commonwealth – identified with LGBT communities, and open about her sexuality, to be a premier. In 2015, an openly gay man, Wade MacLauchlan, became premier of Prince Edward Island. Only a handful of out LGBT people have been heads of government worldwide: Jóhanna Sigurðardóttir, prime minister of Iceland from 2009 to May

2013 and the first LGBT leader of government to come out of the closet; Elio Di Rupo, prime minister of Belgium, from 2011 to 2014; Xavier Bettel, prime minister of Luxembourg since 2013; and Leo Varadkar, prime minister of Ireland (Taoiseach) since 2017.

Having a premier who is an open lesbian is important in terms of political representation, especially descriptive representation. Only a handful of lesbians have been elected to legislatures in Canada: Sheri Benson (House of Commons, Saskatchewan), Joanne Bernard (Nova Scotia Legislature), Estefania Cortes-Vargas (Legislative Assembly of Alberta), Libby Davies (House of Commons, British Columbia), Cheri DiNovo (Legislative Assembly of Ontario), Mable Elmore (Legislative Assembly of British Columbia), Julia Green (Legislative Assembly of the Northwest Territories), Jennifer Howard (Legislative Assembly of Manitoba), Agnès Maltais (Assemblée nationale du Québec), Manon Massé (Assemblée nationale du Québec), Jenn McGinn (Legislative Assembly of British Columbia), Jennifer Rice (Legislative Assembly of British Columbia), and Gerry Rogers (House of Assembly, Newfoundland and Labrador). Nancy Ruth was appointed to the Senate. What is more, fewer lesbians than gays sit in the federal, provincial, and territorial legislatures, mirroring the general underrepresentation of women in politics. By rising to the pinnacle of provincial power, Wynne highlights both the rarity of lesbians in legislative politics in Canada and the exceptional nature of her accomplishment.

Wynne's visibility as an open lesbian is also important in terms of symbolic representation: it constitutes a model on several fronts. First, by her presence at the peak of state power, Wynne shows that it is no longer possible to ignore the existence of LGBT individuals and communities, to pretend that they don't exist, or to acknowledge their existence only through denigration. She affirms not only that LGBT people and communities participate in the diversity of the Canadian social fabric and are stakeholders in the Canadian multicultural identity, but that they may take on the highest responsibilities in government. Second, by her visibility, Wynne may change the public's perceptions and opinions toward sexual minorities. Because she is not that different from other women, she undermines the worst prejudices about lesbians. Studies show that prejudices that certain straight people have toward sexual minorities weaken when they see and spend time with them. Of course, because of who she is, Wynne projects a certain image of an LGBT person – that of a homonormalized lesbian. (This is a different debate.) Finally, Wynne may be a model for young lesbians (and gays) who have a difficult time with their nonheteronormative sexuality, are aware of the sometimes barely veiled social ostracism reserved for LGBT people, and wonder about their place in heteronormative society. Wynne crystallizes the message that it is possible to be lesbian (or gay) and a politician and also to overcome resistance, and even hate, from lesbophobes (and gayphobes). Put simply, Wynne bears a message of hope for people of all ages who have lived through state-propagated lesbophobia.

The effects of Wynne's visibility as an open lesbian are less clear in terms of substantive representation. Certainly, studies have shown that the presence of LGBT people in politics is conveyed by a representation of LGBT interests (Haider-Markel 2010; Herrick 2009; Reynolds 2013). However, since closeted LGBT politicians may also substantively represent LGBT people and communities, it is not clear what and how the "outness" of LGBT politicians brings substantive representation of LGBT people and communities. Could it be, for example, that the presence of open LGBT people in politics sends the message to LGBT people that the government is open to hearing them and that they can call upon it to try to influence the public decision-making process in their favour? This is a question that, for the moment, remains unanswered.

BIBLIOGRAPHY

Haider-Markel, Donald P. 2010. *Out and Running: Gay and Lesbian Candidates, Elections, and Policy Representation*. Washington: Georgetown University Press.

Herrick, Rebekah. 2009. "The Effects of Sexual Orientation on State Legislators' Behavior and Priorities." *Journal of Homosexuality* 56 (8): 1117–33.

Reynolds, Andrew. 2013. "Representation and Rights: The Impact of LGBT Legislators in Comparative Perspective." *American Political Science Review* 107 (2): 259–74.

100 Will we see increasing numbers of female premiers and prime ministers in Canada in the near future?

Any response to this question can only be hypothetical, as politics is a soap opera with highly unpredictable plot twists. There is no reason to think that over time women will come to occupy half the seats in parliaments (see question 31), and this is also true for the position of premier or prime minister. Between February and November 2013, six women were premiers of a province or territory: Eva Aariak, in Nunavut (from 19 November 2008 to 19 November 2013), Christy Clark in British Columbia (from 14 March 2011 to 18 July 2017), Kathy Dunderdale in Newfoundland and Labrador (from 3 December 2010 to 24 January 2014), Pauline Marois in Quebec (from 19 September 2012 to 23 April 2014), Alison Redford in Alberta (from 7 October 2011 to 23 March 2014), and Kathleen Wynne in Ontario (from 11 February 2013 to 29 June 2018). As this manuscript was being finalized, in December 2017, there were only two: Wynne and Rachel Notley (Alberta, since 2014).

The position of prime minister of Canada will belong to a man for a few years yet. The Trudeau government was elected in late 2015 and will remain in power until 2019. The Conservative Party of Canada and the New Democratic Party of Canada have just elected new leaders – two males: Andrew Scheer for the Conservatives and Jagmeet Singh for the New Democrats. There is every reason to believe that Kim Campbell will, for a long time to come, retain her title as the only woman to make it into the old boys' club of Canadian prime ministers.

Index

The letter "t" or "f" following a page number indicates, respectively, a table or a figure.